Culture & Beyond
MYANMAR

Meiji Soe

Culture & Beyond
MYANMAR

By Meiji Soe

Cover Price	:	6,000 Kyats
Circulation	:	2,000 copies
Published by	:	Sarpay Beikman (03911) Printing and Publishing Enterprise
Printed by	:	U Kyaw Htay Min, Aung Thein Thann Press (00435) No. 138, Bogyoke Aung San Road, Pazuntaung Tsp, Yangon.
First Edition	:	September, 2013
Second Edition	:	September, 2014
Third Edition	:	October, 2017
Cover Painting	:	Sayagyi U Lunn Gywe
Cover & Layout	:	Khin Zaw, AKO The Frontier Myanmar
Photo & Drawing	:	Kyaw Phyu San, Thura Nyein Chan, Ye Lwin Oo, Ko Lay Win, Zaw Lay, Meiji Soe
Typography & Cover Text	:	Calibri, Arial, SwitzerlandNarrow, MTM Metrix 1 New Palatino Linotype, Helvetica Medium
Distributor	:	Meiji Soe Publishing House. Ph: 09 975322952, E-mail: mayjisoe@gmail.com

Meiji Soe   CIP-306

Culture & Beyond - Myanmar
284 pages, 14.6 cm x 22.25 cm
(1) Culture & Beyond - Myanmar
   978-99971-0-036-8

To My Silent Trainer

Let me be a little softer to bear the blemish of the people;
Let me be a little harder to be patient with the life's vicissitudes;
Let me be a little stronger to wipe away the fears and tears of others;
Let me be a little wiser to forgive faults and to value virtue more.

Lord, who is dwelling in this body?
Please put the seed of kindness in this inner heart.
I will adore it.
And help me pull out the ego weeds.
I am just a small particle in this expansive universe,
And thy yoke will disappear like morning dew.
Realizing this short existence,
Lord, may I know 'the truth',
May I practise 'the better',
Finally, may I attain 'my level best'.

When the time to say 'adieu' to this so-called 'life' arrives,
Let me leave this colourful world quietly and
Let me take refuge in Your secure lap.
Lord, now I understand,
Without Your Love, there will be no safe corner in this world.

Other publication by the same author:

Amnesty-Winning Poems During Myanmar Monarchy

PREFACE FOR THIRD EDITION

Dear readers,

Everything which I wanted to say about this book has already been mentioned in the preface to the first edition. So, I simply do not have much to add to this edition except some more information such as 'Notice! for eaters of cat and dog', 'You should not do stitching the clothing while wearing it', and 'Do not tie a rope between the house and a tree', etc...

The first edition came out in 2013, the second in 2014, and now, this third edition in 2017. Without the encouragement of my dear readers, this edition would never have been possible.

Again, I am deeply thankful to my dear readers, my family members, as well as supporters and colleagues.

With kind thoughts,

Meiji Soe

PREFACE

This is my very first book. Writing spirit started to cling to me since while I was in my University days. A will to write did not wane although I continued to walk on my Life journey either at work or at home. Finally, I promised myself to fulfil what is pending in my inner mind.

The little book in your hand consists of two parts; one is 'Culture' and the other is 'Beliefs and Superstitions'. You may notice that some topics can be regarded as culture as well as beliefs. The second part is more personal than informative writing because I simply want to share my highlighted memories, personal experiences and knowledge what I was told in my life, before all those things are fading away from my memory; plus a glimpse of the culture of a beautiful and conservative country called 'Myanmar', formerly known as 'Burma'.

Although this book comes out from the deep emotion of sharing my knowledge to others (local and abroad), without the invitation of Sarpay Beikman to local inspired writers to submit their unpublished manuscripts in English language, this book will never be accomplished.

For me, to write a book is like a collection of uncountable small single sands which becomes a hard rock. If the readers find any weakness in this book, it is not the fault of the country or its people or any association or any individual. I am the only one who has to take the blame.

Three Gems, my parents, all my teachers are always in my mind. Special thank is due to my beloved family who inspired me to write this book. I would like to express my heartfelt thanks to all the beings - seen and unseen and every single character - inside or outside this book which supported me to make 'Culture & Beyond' possible. Last but definitely not the least, my thanks go to Ashin Khemacara and uncle Milton who helped me as mentors in writing this book.

Meiji Soe
January, 2012

Part (I)
MYANMA CULTURE

Where is Myanmar?

Myanmar (formerly known as Burma) (မြန်မာ) is bordered by China, India, Bangladesh, Laos, Thailand and the Indian Ocean. The population is about 60 million. 'Myan' means 'fast' and 'Mar' means 'strong' in the Myanmar language. It is also known as 'the golden land' for its plentiful pagodas and rich cultural traditions. Myanmar is blessed with natural resources and has won the International attention for the wealth of natural resources which remain intact.

Myanmar belongs to ASEAN and is the second largest country in South East Asia with a total area of 678,500 sq kilometres making it the 40th largest country in the world. Myanmar is composed of seven States and seven Regions. There are eight main races in Myanmar: Kachin, Kayah, Kayin, Chin, Bamar, Mon, Rakhine and Shan. In addition, each race has its own distinct language.

Four Main Rivers	:	Ayeyarwady (the longest river in Myanmar), Chindwin, Thanlwin and Sittaung
Capital City	:	Nay Pyi Taw
Seven States	:	Kachin, Kayah, Kayin, Chin, Mon, Rakhine and Shan
Seven Regions	:	Yangon, Mandalay, Tanintharyi, Magway, Ayeyarwady, Sagaing and Bago
Language	:	Myanmar
Main Religion	:	Buddhism
Main food	:	Rice and Curry
Currency	:	Kyat
Main Business	:	Agriculture
Main Resources	:	Teak, Gems, Black oil
Climate	:	Three seasons; Summer (March to May), Rainy (June to October) and Winter (November to February)

Seasonal Fruits

Avocado	-	October to April
Banana	-	All the year round
Durian	-	May to September
Jackfruit	-	March to June
Mango	-	April to July
Mangosteen	-	May to September
Orange	-	October to February
Papaya	-	All the year round
Pomelo	-	All the year round
Pineapple	-	June to September
Watermelon	-	November to April

Public holidays

(In Western Calendar)

Independence Day	- January 4
Union Day	- February 12
Peasant's day	- March 2
Armed Forces Day	- March 27
May Day	- May 1
Martyr's Day	- July 19
Christmas Day	- December 25

(In Myanmar Calendar)

Full Moon Day of Tabaung	- In March
New Year Holidays	- 5 days (13 - 17 April)
Full Moon Day of Kasone	- In May
Full Moon Day of Waso	- In July (First Day of Buddhist Lent)
Full Moon Day of Thadingyut	- 3 days in October (End of Buddhist Lent)
Full Moon Day of Tazaungmone	- 2 days in November
National Day	- In November or December (10th waning day of Tazaungmone)

Seven States and Seven Regions

Myanma Eight Major National Races

Kachin

Rakhine

Shan

Bamar

Kayah

Kayin

Mon

Chin

Tourism

If your heart longs for romantic, simple and natural sightseeing, you are invited to pay a visit to Myanmar, a land full of hidden beauty and warm smiles. Myanmar has one of the lowest tourist crime rates in the world, so travellers can feel safe as they journey to cultural sightseeing, unspoiled beaches, old stupas, snow-capped mountains and jungle wilderness. Myanmar will slowly enchant you to come again.
Every state and region has its own highlights and the following are some outstanding areas for foreign visitors:

No	State/Region	Capital	Population (million)	Area (sq mile)	How to get there?	Places of Interest
1	Kachin State	Myitkyina	Over 1.2	34379	By plane, train, car	1. Mt. Khakaborazi, highest peak in SEA (5882 m) 2. Indawgyi Lake and Shwe Minzu Pagoda 3. The source of Ayeyarwady River (Myit Sone), where the two sister rivers (Maykha and Malikha) meet. 4. Puta-O
2.	Kayah State	Loikaw	Over 0.25	4530	By plane, train, car	1. Taunggwe Zedi 2. Lawpita Waterfall 3. Seven Step Pond and Htee Pwint Pond (Demoso)

No.	State	Capital	Area	Population	How to reach	Attractions
3.	Kayin State	Hpa- An	Over 1.4	11731	By plane, car	1. Mt. Zwegabin (Symbol of peace) 2. Saddan Cave and Bayint Nyi Cave 3. Thandaung Hill Resort
4.	Chin State	Hakha	Over 0.47	13907	By car	1. Mt. Victoria (3109 m), Highest in Chin Bum (the Best Bird-watching Site) 2. Heart-shaped lake named 'Reed Lake'
5.	Mon State	Mawlamyine	Over 2.46	4748	By plane, cruise, train, car	1. Kyaikhtiyo (the Golden Rock) Pagoda 2. Kyaikkami Yele Pagoda 3. Set-sei Beach Resort 4. Thanbyuzayat War Memorial 5. Thamyinya – famous for 'Thamyinya sayadaw' (vegetarian saint) who passed away in 2005.

No	State/Region	Capital	Population (million)	Area (sq mile)	How to get there?	Places of Interest
6.	Rakhine State	Sittwe	Over 2.7	14200	By plane, cruise, car	1. Mrauk-U (the ancient Kingdom of Arakan) 2. Ngapali Beach Resort (35min flight, 14 hours drive) 3. Kanthaya Beach 4. Sittwe Seaside Resort
7.	Shan State	Taunggyi	Over 4.7	60155	By plane, train, car	1. Inlay Lake, sea among the hazy Shan mountains. (900 metres above sea-level 22km long and 10km across) 2. Padalin Cave of the stone age culture 3. Magnificent Goke-hteik Bridge 4. Hsipaw Bawgyo Pagoda 5. Mwetaw-Kuckku Pagoda 6. Kalaw Hill Station 7. Pindaya Cave, Htan-san Cave
8.	Ayeyarwady Region	Pathein	Over 6.6	13567	By cruise, train, car	1. Chaung Thar Beach Resort 2. Ngwe Saung Beach Resort 3. Inyegyi Pond 4. Shwe-mok-htaw Pagoda 5. Large production area of rice

No.	Region		Rating		Transport	Attractions
9.	Bago Region	Bago	Over 5	15214	By train, car	1. Shwe Tharlyaung (Reclining Buddha Statue) 2. Sein Tharlyaung Pagoda 3. Shwe Mawdaw Pagoda 4. Kyaikpun Pagoda 5. Kan-baw-za-thadi Palace 6. Monyingyi Bird Sanctuary 7. Sein Ye Forest Camp
10.	Magway Region	Magway	Over 4.4	17305	By cruise, train, car	1. Mya Thalon Pagoda 2. Shwe Settaw Pagoda 3. Pon-daung and Pon-nya Region (for fossils)
11.	Mandalay Region	1) Nay Pyi Taw (New Capital) 2) Mandalay	Over 6.4	14295	By plane, cruise, train, car	1. National Landmark Garden 2. Zoological Garden 3. Water Fountain Garden 4. Mandalay Palace 5. Maha Muni Pagoda 6. Mandalay Hill 7. U Bein Bridge 8. Mt. Popa 9. Bagan Archaeological Sites (Ancient Myanmar Kingdom) 10. Pyin Oo Lwin (Maymyo)

No	State\Region	Capital	Population (million)	Area (sq mile)	How to get there?	Places of Interest
12.	Sagaing Region	Sagaing	Over 5.3	36534	By cruise, train, car	1. Innwa Bridge (the oldest bridge across the Ayeyarwady River) 2. Mingun Bell (the largest ringing bell in the world) 3. Nyaung-gan archaeological site (Bronze age culture influence) 4. Twin-daung lake (natural spirulae)
13.	Tanintharyi Region	Dawei	Over 1.3	16736	By plane, cruise, train, car	1. Myeik Archipelago 2. Maung-ma-gan Beach 3. Mali Island Wildlife Sanctuary 4. Andaman Club (Thahtay Kyun)
14.	Yangon Region	Yangon	Over 5.4	3972	By plane, cruise, train, car	1. Shwe Dagon Pagoda 2. Sule Pagoda 3. Botahtaung Pagoda 4. Kabaraye Pagoda 5. Thanlyin-Kyauktan Yele Pagoda 6. Kyauk Taw Gyi Pagoda 7. Hlawga Wildlife Park 8. National Museum 9. Bogyoke Aung San Market

According to statistics from the Ministry of Hotel and Tourism, there are more than 3 million visitors in 2014, 4.68 million in 2015 and 2.9 million in 2016. The percentage showing tourist countries of origins are as follows:

No.	Country	In Percentage (%)
	ASIA	67.94
1.	Thailand	19.13
2.	China	14.45
3.	Japan	7.92
4.	Korea	5.06
5.	Singapore	3.94
6.	Vietnam	3.84
7.	Malaysia	3.45
8.	India	3.03
9.	Taiwan	2.84
10.	Philippine	1.30
11.	Others	2.98
	WEST EUROPE	18.70
1.	France	4.11
2.	U.K	4.01
3.	Germany	3.07
4.	Italy	1.41
5.	Netherlands	1.10
6.	Switzerland	1.10
7.	Spain	1.00
8.	Belgium	0.61
9.	Austria	0.38
10.	Others	1.91
	NORTH AMERICA	7.19
1.	America	6.01
2.	Canada	1.18
	OCEAN	3.08
1.	Australia	2.67
2.	New Zealand	0.40
3.	Others	0.01
	EAST EUROPE	1.37
1.	Russia	0.43
2.	Others	0.94
	OTHERS AMERICAS	0.86
	MIDDLE EAST	0.56
	AFRICA	0.30
	TOTAL	100

Places of Interest for Visitors

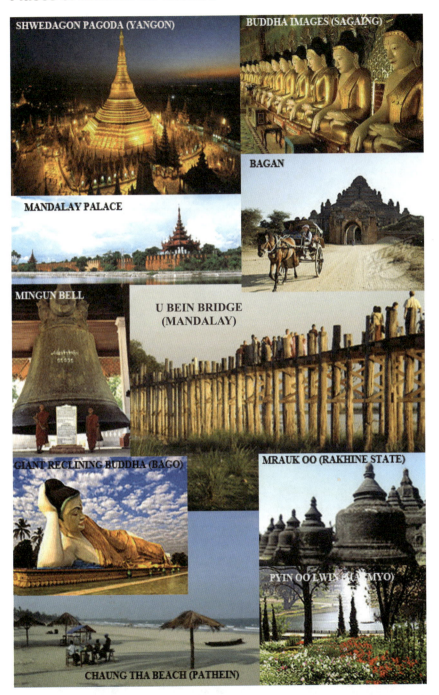

SHWEDAGON PAGODA (YANGON)

BUDDHA IMAGES (SAGAING)

BAGAN

MANDALAY PALACE

MINGUN BELL

U BEIN BRIDGE (MANDALAY)

GIANT RECLINING BUDDHA (BAGO)

MRAUK OO (RAKHINE STATE)

PYIN OO LWIN (MAYMYO)

CHAUNG THA BEACH (PATHEIN)

Places of Interest for Visitors

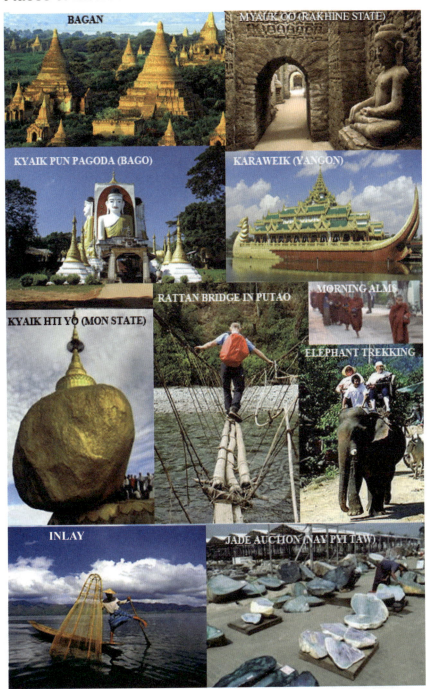

BAGAN

MYAUK OO (RAKHINE STATE)

KYAIK PUN PAGODA (BAGO)

KARAWEIK (YANGON)

RATTAN BRIDGE IN PUTAO

MORNING ALMS

KYAIK HTI YO (MON STATE)

ELEPHANT TREKKING

INLAY

JADE AUCTION (NAY PYI TAW)

Shwedagon Pagoda and Some Mythical Images

Shwedagon Pagoda in Yangon, Myanmar

There is a saying 'A visit to Myanmar is incomplete without a visit to Shwedagon.' Shwedagon pagoda is one of the wonders of the world and it never fails to enchant visitors. It is believed to be the earliest pagoda of the Gautama Buddha Era and is said to have been built on Theinguttara Hill around 400 BC. The perimeter of the base of the pagoda is 1,420 feet and it reaches a height of 326 feet above the platform. It is comprised of not only a single stupa but also a complex of many stupas. The base is surrounded by 64 small stupas with four larger ones facing each of the cardinal directions. There are four entrances to the pagoda and the staircases are lined with shops selling flowers, candles, incense sticks, local-made toys, souvenirs, handicrafts, religious accessories, and lacquer wares, which attract both young and old. When you walk around the pagoda platform, you will see that people are offering water, flowers, candles, and incense sticks at their birthday corners. The best time to go to Shwedagon Pagodas is sunset, when the gilded stupa is bathed in the fading rays of the sun and takes on a magical glow.

A short history of Shwedagon Pagoda

Two thousand six hundred years ago, several weeks after the Buddha attained Enlightenment, two merchant brothers, Tapussa and Bhallika from Okkalapa (an ancient city near Yangon), arrived in India where the Buddha was residing. Both of them were very delighted to hear the Buddha's perfect preaching and offered rice cakes and honey to Him. Some sources said that they were the first two people who paid respects to Buddha and that the first snacks that Buddha took after his enlightenment were Myanmar rice cakes and honey. They brought eight sacred hairs (four hairs for each) of Buddha, from India, across the ocean. On their way to Myanmar, the two brothers were relieved of two hairs by the King of Ajetta. Two more were stolen by the King of the Nagas, who had transformed himself into a human being and boarded the ship at night. So, by the end of their journey, they had only four hairs left. But when they arrived at Okkalapa and opened the casket they had carried the hairs in, the two brothers miraculously found eight original hairs.

On arrival in Myanmar, a great festival was celebrated by the king for several days in honour of the sacred hairs. At first, the king of Okkalapa and two merchant brothers could not find Theinguttara Hill, which was where the Buddha had asked them to enshrine his hairs. The Buddha had explained that the relics of three previous Buddhas were previously enshrined there. So, Thagyarmin (the King of celestial beings) came down to earth and assisted in finding the place. He had to invoke the aid of the 4 spirits: Sule, Amyitha, Yawhani, and Dakkhina. When he discovered the site, it was just a lake and he created the hill within one night. So legend tells us that Shwedagon is made with the help of heavenly beings and it is beyond human efforts alone. In short, not only the participation of the whole city, but also heavenly beings, came into action to fulfil the Pagoda's completion. After the pagoda was finished, the earth shook in celebration. The year which Shwedagon pagoda had been erected was the same with the year which Lord Buddha attained Enlightenment. Shwedagon pagoda is 2600 years old in 2012.

Nowadays, you can see King of Okkalapa's statue at the north-west corner of the platform and the statue of the king's parents, Thagyarmin and Mae Lamu, standing at the south west corner.

When you go to Shwedagon pagoda, you will see several mythical images including elephants, Nagas (Dragon), Galon (Garuda), Hintha (Brahminy duck), Kainnari and Kainnara (A couple of Mythical birds with human head and body), lions, serpents, ogres, Zawgyi (alchemist) and so on. The followings are some of the outstanding mythical images at Shwedagon pagoda:

Manussiha (Lion Man)

One day, while I was working at the office, two of us (Ma Lwin Mar and I) were assigned to send some Singaporean visitors to Shwedagon pagoda, as the staff of the Protocol department was occupied by another assignment at the time. When we arrived at Shwedagon pagoda, both of us tried to explain as best as we could. We walked around the pagoda from the right side, as usual. At first, they asked only simple questions. Unexpectedly,

Manussiha

I was asked by one of them, "What is that outstanding creature?" indicating the 'Manussiha' (မနုဿီဟ). That statue sits at the Tuesday corner of the pagoda. The visitor could not control his curiosity and, to his eyes, it might seem very strange. It is a fabulous creature, with a man's head and the lion's bodies, squatting on forked haunches and looks very similar to the 'Sphinx' in Egypt. The visitor's question was very simple but, the problem was, I didn't know the history of it. I know it only as a mythical being from history. I replied his question simply, "It is a mythical being from history called 'Manussiha'." Luckily, he did not ask me again. I knew that the visitor wanted to know more about it and I, myself, was not satisfied with my answer to him. So one day I asked my uncle who was working in a travel agency about it.

He explained to me. "Manussiha is a very mighty, fabulous creature with a man's head and the lion's hindquarters, always seen squatting on forked haunches. 'Manussa' means human and 'Siha (Thiha)' means lion in the Pali language. It means that this mythical being possesses a man's wisdom and a lion's bravery and strength. 'Manussiha' has a story, too.

Over two thousand years ago in the capital of 'Suvannabhumi', near 'Thaton', there was a crisis that whenever a baby was born, an ogress would arise from sea to eat the baby. The whole country was in a helpless situation. At that time two Buddhist monks, 'Sona' and 'Uttara', arrived at the capital. These two were the persons who first brought Buddhism to Suvannabhumi. Soon after their arrival, the queen delivered a baby and she asked the monks for help. The two monks prayed and created three thousand 'Manussiha' with the help of the other holy beings. As usual, a group of ogresses entered the capital to eat the royal baby. When they saw the wonderful creatures, 'Manussiha', which were much stronger than they were, they ran away. That's the reason why, when a baby is born, people do not say "too fat" or "too heavy", because the ogress might hear and come to give trouble to the baby. Sometimes you may see a small Manussiha pendant hangs around the baby's neck.

I was quite satisfied with his explanation and was as happy as a student who had just passed her exam.

Wishing Stone

You may find a smooth round stone in front of some Buddha statues or stupas, near the worshipping place of those pagodas. What

Wishing Stone

is that stone for? It is not an ordinary stone. We sit in front of that stone and make a vow. For example, we make a vow like "If I will pass the exam, may the stone be as light as a feather; if I will fail the exam, may the stone be as heavy as a mountain", and then slowly lift the stone. We believe that we get the answer if we have strong faith. If you want to be sure of the stone's answer, you can pray in reverse and lift again, "If I will pass the exam, may the stone be as heavy as a mountain; if I will fail the exam, may this stone be as light as a feather".

Wish fulfilling square

If you go to Shweda-gon pagoda from north entrance by lift and walk the main platform around the pagoda, you may see people sitting and praying within a square. That place is called the wish fulfilling

People Praying from Wish Fulfilling Square

square. People strongly believe that it is more effective if you pray from that place and your wishes with good intention will be fulfilled sooner or later. That place is also called 'victory land' (Aung Myay).

Why are two big lions sitting in front of the pagoda?

When we go to the pagodas in Myanmar, we can see two big lions sitting in front of the pagoda entrance. Why? Most of the people think that the two giants are put there as guards to the pagoda, but that is not the whole truth. There is a hidden story behind these two lions. Shall we unfold the history about it?

Once upon a time, a princess and her followers visited a forest. At that time, she was pregnant. Unfortunately, they bumped into a lion there. Once they saw the lion, the faithful followers quickly ran away and could not protect the princess anymore. But the princess could not run due to her

Two Big Lions at Pagoda Entrance

mature pregnancy. Instead of eating the princess, the lion brought her into a cave because he felt great sympathy for her. The lion took care of the princess until the baby was born by protecting her from danger and bringing her food everyday. It was a baby boy, and the lion loved the boy as if he were his own child. He had to find enough food for two human beings now. Sometimes love is very mysterious. The lion did not allow them to go back to the palace as he already had a great attachment to the princess and the boy. (Some sources say that that lion was originally the lover of the princess.)

Time went on and the boy reached the age of reason. One day, the boy asked the mother, with great curiosity,

"Mother, why are we here? Why is my father a lion instead of a human being?"

His mother explained the whole story. "My dear, you are not an ordinary boy. Your grandpa is a King, the ruler of this country, but nobody knows that we are here..."

The boy was very excited with the mother's explanation and said, "Don't worry mother, we will not be like this for our whole life. I am strong enough already.   We will run away while the lion goes out to find food."

Mother and son quickly ran away once they got a chance. When the lion came back, he realized what had happened and quickly chased after them. When the lion saw them, they had just crossed a river. The lion pleaded (by roaring) with them to come back to him. The boy shouted, "Please do not follow us or I will shoot you!". When the boy shot his arrows, they changed into bananas and coconuts in front of the lion, and could not hurt the lion. As the lion's love for the boy was so deep, the arrows could not penetrate the power of his love. The lion roared and roared and the boy kept on shooting at the lion. All of the arrows changed into fruits like offerings (Ka-dawt-pwe - ကန့်တော့ပွဲ).

But once, a single thought entered into the lion's mind. "Oh, this boy is very ungrateful and all my love and affection for him is in vain now". With that thought, an arrow hit the lion's head and was killed.

They reached the palace and the king was overjoyed at the

unexpected return of his long-lost daughter and his grandson. After the King passed away, the grandson ascended the throne, but the story is not finished yet. Later, the new King suffered from a terrible migraine and could not be cured. All the royal physicians gave up. So the King's wise men sought a solution to this problem. They found out that this incurable disease was due to the sin of killing the lion. There was no remedy to cure the migraine except the lion's forgiveness. So the king asked, "How can I ask forgiveness from the lion? He is dead already." The wise men advised the king to make a lion statue, put it in a shrine, and pray for forgiveness. The king accepted that advice and paid obeisance to the lion statue every day and night. He also decided to build big lion statues in front of the pagodas to remind him of the gratitude he owed to the lion.

The tradition of erecting the lion statues at pagoda entrances began from that time.

The meaning of 'Water dropping' (yay set cha) after donations

Wathone Daray Natmin

A great donation is not complete without 'yay set cha' (ရေစက်ချအမျှဝေခြင်း), the donor pouring water from a cup, drop by drop, after the monk's sermon to a group of people. We usually see it in Myanmar Buddhist donation ceremonies. It is very meaningful. Buddhists believe that nothing can be carried to the next life except their good deeds. Donation (dana) is one of the main things which can raise them up to higher existence. The people repeat after the monk: "The merit that we have done today will be shared to all the beings which could be seen or unseen by reciting, "A Hmya, A Hmya, A Hmya" and all the beings can gain our merit by reciting gladly, "Sadhu, Sadhu, Sadhu (well-done)". The donors continue, "If we forget this merit, the friendly witnessing nats will bear testimony by wringing the water out of their streaming hair".

After death, when they sit in the heavenly interview for the next existence, these water drops are the testimony for their donations, as man may be forgetful of all of the donations accumulated in his whole lifetime. At that time, 'Wathone Daray Nat Min' (chief god of the Earth's guardians) will appear and he will approve your donations by squeezing the water out of his long hairs without leaving a single drop. The water in his hair is that which he collected at all your 'yey set cha' water libations for donations. (Please see the picture on page 25). You can see this statue in some pagodas. So it is advisable not to forget to 'Yey set cha' after any of your outstanding donations.

In Lord Buddha's history, just before He attained the enlightenment and while He was meditating under the Bo tree, 'Mara', the evil one, marched with a great army which was full of fierce animals and devils to deter from attaining the Buddhahood. At that time, Lord Buddha calmly made an asseveration to Wathone Daray Nat Min and all His 'Yay-set cha' water from the previous lives flowed uncontrollably like a river and Mara and his followers were drowned and collapsed.

The Bells

"Today I just made the merit in this pagoda by worshipping, putting some alms into the donation box, lighting the candles and incense sticks, offering the flowers and water. O, Wathone Daray Natmin (chief of the earth guardian), please hear my striking the bell like I strike the earth and I am pleased to share this merit to other people and everyone who hears the sound of my striking the bell, please say 'Sadhu' to gain the same merit with me."

This is a prayer of a hermit which I heard at Shwedagon pagoda when I

Big Bell and the Kids

passed near a bell. Lay people seldom pray like that hermit, although they may pray in their mind. It is quite similar to the water dropping (yay-set-cha) in donation ceremonies. But, at pagodas, we can share our mert by striking the bells and the donor's merit will be multiplied, too. People usually strike the bell with a wooden stick, lying near it, three times, five times, or more as they wish, and some young people strike the bell according to the number of their age. Children enjoy striking the bells for their fine and loud echoing tone but the adults usually strike the bell with the noble intention of sharing merit to others, and at the same time, as a notice to holy beings for their merit. Bells are abundant in pagodas in many sizes. The biggest bell in Shwedagon Pagoda can be found at the north-east corner of pagoda platform.It was presented by King Tharrawaddy in 1841 and weighs 94,682 lbs. The diameter at the mouth is 7'8", with a height of 8 feet and a thickness of 1'5". It is the second largest bell in the whole country, as the largest bell in Myanmar is 'Mingun Bell' in Mandalay.

Myanmar people believe that after they pass away, nothing can be carried along and only their good deeds will remain sweet for the next existence. So, whenever you hear the tolling sound of the bell, please do not hesitate to whisper (even in your mind) "Sadhu, Sadhu, Sadhu..."

Lawka Pala Ogress

When you walk the pagoda along the north staircase of the pagoda, you will see the statue of Lawka Pala Ogress (လောကပါလမယ်တော်ကြီး) on the left side at the end of the stair case. There are a few ogre statues in Shwegadon as a decoration, but this ogress statue is not an ordinary one. It was built by the queen, Shin Sawpu, and donated as the guard to the pagoda at that time. Lawka Pala means 'guardian of the world'.

Lawka Pala Ogress

People come and pray to Lawka Pala ogress for their worldly wishes such as, "Kindly help me to get promotion and I will come to you with more offerings." When I took a photograph of her, I was told by the security guard, "You should first ask permission from her or your photograph will be blurred."

Thar Pike Kotaw (baby holding Brahma)

If you are longing to get a baby, you can go to Shwedagon and pray in front of the Brahma (higher celestial being) who is holding a baby boy (ဗြဟ္မာသားပိုက်ရုပ်တု). It is situated between the Tuesday and Wednesday corner of the pagoda. Married couples who do not get a baby or who wants a baby boy, come here and pray to that statue. Some couples have gilded that baby with gold leaf. At the right side of that Brahma, there is another standing Brahma holding flowers in his hand. If you want a baby girl, you can pray to the flower-holding Brahma. Twins? If you pray from the middle of those two Brahmas, you will get twin babies (a boy and a girl). Somebody said, if you pray for a baby there, your coming baby's birthday will be on the 7th day (starting from your praying day). For example, if you pray on a Sunday, you will get a Saturday-born baby, because the Brahma has to present your wish at the angels' conference and a one-week time is needed to get approval and obtain the grant.

Thar Pike Kodaw

Not only that if your children are disobedient or out of control, the parents can come and pray to 'Thar Pike Kotaw'. If your baby is sick or you believe that your baby is disturbed by spirits, you can also come and pray for their welfare here.

The Arrival of Theravada Buddhism to Bagan

In AD 1053, a learned monk from Thaton named 'Shin Arahan' (ရှင်အရဟံ) arrived in Bagan with the noble intention of introducing true Buddhism. At that time, Bagan (upper Myanmar) was influenced by the teaching of the Aris (who believed in Animism) and their religious practices were very much like playing athletic games or sports. King Anawrahta (အနော်ရထာ) had no admiration to the teaching and practice of Aris, who were like corrupt hermits. The worst thing was that a bride had to offer herself to the Aris on her wedding night in order to bear noble offspring. The King wanted to find a safe moral shelter for the people in his kingdom.

Photo: Ye Lwin Oo

Statue of King Anawrahta (AD 1044-1077)

King Anawrahta welcomed 'Shin Arahan' and was pleased with his introductory sermons on Buddhism. Shin Arahan became Anawrahta's spiritual teacher and a strong desire arose in the king's mind to introduce the Lord Buddha's sermons to his people. Now Anawrahta realized that apart from Three Gems (Buddha, Dhamma and Sanga), nothing else could give the true happiness to man in this world and the worlds beyond. At the same time, the venerable monk informed the king that the complete teachings of Buddha were in the 'Pitaka Thone Pon' (Three baskets of Buddha's teachings) which could be obtained from Thaton. So the wise king sent a mission with valuable gifts to the king of Thaton as a request for a set of the 'Pitaka Thone Pon'. Unfortunately, the Thaton king 'Manuha' turned down Anawrahta's request.

Sometimes wars are unavoidable in this world of desire. Anawrahta marched with great forces to Thaton. He conquered it and brought the 'Pitaka Thone Pon' back to his capital along with learned monks to preach to his people. After that, he united the Mon kingdom into his own kingdom and he converted the whole country to Theravada Buddhism, and purified the Aris and other spirit worshipping traditions. From that time onwards, Bagan culture was enriched by the infusion of Mon arts and crafts. Bagan was the golden era in Myanmar history. Anawrahta ruled his kingdom peacefully and passed away in 1077.

To sum up, it was not only the arrival of Shin Arahan to Bagan and the arrival of the 'Pitaka Thone Pon', but also Anawrahta's acceptance of the Lord Buddha's teachings which marked a turning point in Myanmar's religion and cultural heritage.

The Thirty-one Planes of Existence and the Way to Nirvana

When we talk about Myanmar, 'Buddhism' is an essential topic because it is deeply rooted in the Myanmar people's mind. A person in Myanmar may take refuge in other beliefs with his own reasons but if you peel off the skin, you are bound to find Buddhism underneath. So if you really want to understand a Myanmar, you should not neglect Buddhism because it is already influencing their day to day life, thinking, manners and attitudes. Let me explain a little bit about the thirty-one planes of existence in Buddhism.

The Thirty-one Planes of Existence in Buddhism

According to Lord Buddha's teaching, there are thirty-one planes of existence (သုံးဆယ့်တစ်ဘုံ) in this universe. Here, 'existence' means life or living.

When we look at the chart of the 31 levels of existence, the four lowest levels are all characterized by suffering. In the hell level, there are eight types of hell. The torturing in one layer and another are not the same. These hells are not an eternal hell like in Christianity. The victims are tortured for tens of thousands of years according to their sins but when the suffering for their demerits is over, they can move on to other existences. For example, in Buddha's Life time 'Azar Ta That' who killed his own father, the king, will be released from hell after suffering for sixty thousand years. Let's imagine one of the layers of hell. Giant hell dogs are chasing the victims. The victims are running on very hot ground. They are very exhausted and, finally, they have to climb up the trees which are full of thorns. They are bleeding and falling down. The hell dogs are waiting under the trees and the victims are eaten alive. Those things happen again and again until their sins are cleansed.

The animal world has a brutal nature and all are struggling in their own ways. The peta realm is the hungry ghost world and they are wondering in search of food all the time. They have very awkward forms. One type of Peta form has very big bodies with large stomaches. They cannot even carry their own bodies but they have thread-hole mouths and they can eat only a grain of rice each time. They are in a helpless situation! Asuras (demons) are spirits that sometimes try to haunt people and cause some disturbances. Both Petas and demons cannot be seen with laymen's eyes. Sometimes they can be liberated if they hear the sharing of merit of their human relatives after making donations.

We, human beings, exist in the 5th level. This plane is a mixture of suffering and pleasure. Some say, 'Man is less innocent'. It means that human beings can be naughtier and, at the same time, they can be wiser than other beings such as animals, which lack reasonable thinking. So, we have a great opportunity to try to reach the higher existences although we have to suffer from womb to tomb.

There is very little suffering and mostly pleasure in level 6 to 11. These beings are not born as babies. They appear in beautiful forms as adults and remain youthful all the time. All the Devas (male) look 20 years old and all the Devis (female) look 18 years old (nearest comparison is like the angels in Christianity). Myanmar people call them 'Nat' (these are divine Nats, not the same as the 37 indigenous nats). They dwell in golden houses with jewelled gates. Inside their great mansions there are beautiful gardens and fruit bearing trees; so many nice flowers are blooming in the garden; crystal water-falls are flowing; and sweet music is playing all the time. Even amongst those beings, there are different grades based upon their deeds from the past lives. They do not need to take food or discharge waste. Their energy is automatically refilled. The luxuries and pleasures are superior to what a human being can even dream of. All about the heavenly scenes are very splendid. But these are like baited and bloody traps because, while they are enjoying themselves all the time, they are apt to forget to practise the Dhamma (Lord Buddha's teachings). At any time, they can fall down to lower levels when the power of the past good merit is over.

In the sixteen planes from level 12 to 27, there are no females and all are males. They are called 'Brahmas'. There is no sex or attachment in these levels. They live pure and peaceful lives and are free from sensual pleasures. Those beings in heavenly realm have very light material bodies. They just have to think where they want to go and they are already there, like in our dreams or imagination. Their faces shine brightly and light up their surroundings. They occupy beautiful forms. Besides other wholesome deeds, deep practise of samahta meditation is essential to reach this plane. These planes are called Rupa-world where the 'Brahmas' live. 'Rupa' means physical form.

The beings from level 28 to 31 are in 'Arupa' worlds which mean that they have no bodily forms. They exist only in mental states. So those beings do not suffer physically. Life there is very peaceful, quiet and extremely long. The persons who reach certain stages of meditation and who have a great detachment to physical form reach these planes. One advantage of having no physical form is that they have no chance to commit sins, but one disadvantage is that they cannot hear the Buddha's teachings.

To sum up, we can go to high or low levels of existence and it is not necessary to go in an orderly or step by step manner. According to the strength of merits or demerits, a person may descend or ascend directly to a corresponding plane. It is also natural that if you fall down from a mountain, it is just a slipshod or jump but if you want to reach the peak, you have to try with might and main. There is one exception. They say that there is no direct fall from Rupa-loka or Arupa-loka (from 12 to 31), to the four misery planes. It means that there is an intermediate existence (5 to 11) for them before reaching the 4 lowest levels.

All in all, we human beings have the good fortune to be able to choose our course of actions in this existence which will pave the way to blissful or unhappy existences. Human beings have the opportunity to develop virtue and wisdom while in other planes, both lower and higher, remain constant in their unhappy or happy states.

Why are we in different levels?

Generally speaking, if your mind, speech and deeds are evil, nasty, or unwholesome and you continue constantly committing those acts, you will be reborn in lower levels. On the contrary, if you are virtuous, honest, and pure, and are constantly practising the noble acts of Dana (donation), Sila (morality) and Bhavana (such as spreading loving kindness), you are guaranteed to be reborn in higher and beautiful existences. Please see the details in the chart. This formula is a universal truth and it is neither a Buddhist belief nor an invention of the Buddha. But He first discovered the details when He became Enlightened under the Bodhi tree. We may notice that some people are born in wealthy or royal families and grow up in golden cradles while some in poor families have to sleep on gunny sacks on the ground. Even within the same family, some are wise, some stupid; some fair, some ugly. Why?. It is not the reward or punishment of someone. All those inequalities, Buddha explained, are the result of merits and demerits of one's past lives. It is a natural process of cause and effect and we cannot run away from it. For example, if you plant a mango tree, you will get mangoes; if you plant a neem tree, the tree will bear neem fruits one day. You cannot pray or cry to someone to bear mangoes from a neem tree. The actions which a person did will follow him as a shadow all the time.

Why do we wander in 'Samsara'?

Samsara is a Pali word which means, 'the cycle of 31 existences'. It is based on life, death and rebirth in any level. We (all beings) are travellers in this samsara (သံသရာ). As long as we are gripped by desire (like), aversion (dislike), and confusion, we cannot let go of our lives. The moment of death determines the nature of our next existence. In Buddhism, the art of dying is as important as the art of living. If we could completely purify the mind and eradicate selfish attachment, we would be self liberated and experience the peace and freedom of Nirvana.

Buddha said to His bhikkhus that those who reincarnate as human beings again are as little as the sands on His finger nail while those who go to the Apaya Bhumi (lowest four levels) are as much as the sands at the bank of 'Ganga River' because they do not know the four Noble Truths.

The *Four Noble Truths* (သစ္စာလေးပါး) are:

First Noble Truth	Dukkha (There is suffering).
Second Noble Truth	Samudaya (There is cause for suffering).
Third Noble Truth	Nirodha (There is cessation of suffering).
Fourth Noble Truth	Magga (There is a path leading to the cessation of suffering).

(If we describe the four Noble Truths from a medical point of view, we can clearly understand them as follows:

First Noble Truth is like the diagnosis of a disease.

Second Noble Truth is like the cause (pathology) of that disease.

Third Noble Truth is like the decision to cure the disease (or) to stop the things which encourage that disease.

Fourth Noble Truth is like remedy (or) taking the medicine.

Here, Buddha is like a Physician. He first found out the disease and realized which caused that disease. After that he decided to eradicate that disease and he formulated the remedy to cure the patients.)

The Four Noble Truths are the essence of Buddhism. After realizing the first three Noble Truths, we can simply follow the Noble Eightfold as a tool to climb to the higher levels and attain liberation (Nirvana). The Noble Eightfold Path comes from the last Noble Truth, 'Magga'. If you want to avoid bad karma, you must eradicate deluded thinking because all the roots of unwholesome actions come from it. It is a very fundamental and basic knowledge. The Noble Eightfold path is divided into three qualities – wisdom, morality, and concentration.

Noble Eightfold Path (မဂ္ဂင်ရှစ်ပါး):

Three Qualities	Eightfold Path
Wisdom *(panna)*	Right View
	Right Thought
Morality *(sila)*	Right Speech
	Right Action
	Right Livelihood
Concentration *(samadhi)*	Right Effort
	Right Mindfulness
	Right Concentration

What is 'Nirvana'?

In Oxford Dictionary, 'Nirvana' is mentioned as 'state of perfect bliss achieved by the soul'. In Buddhism, 'Nirvana' means saying 'goodbye' to the above mentioned 31 levels of life cycles (samsara). Nirvana in Pali language is 'Nibbana'. Human beings have to suffer as long as they are rotating in life cycles, regardless of power and wealth. Even if you reach high levels like paradise, you can fall down to the lower levels at any time if you make some mistakes, and you may not come up again. As long as rebirth continues into either low or high existences, we all have to suffer.

So, how can we reach Nirvana? It is a very serious question. Buddha passed through life after life before he attained Enlightenment. Even Buddha passed four Athin chay and 100,000 world-cycles (လေးအသင်္ချေနှင့်ကမ္ဘာတစ်သိန်း) (one world-cycle is equivalent to the beginning and the end of the world). When I was young I did not know how long the 'Athin chay' is. A learned person explained to me that if a person knows how long is 'one thin chay', he will say "If I have a chance to choose passing though those uncountable lives (or) swimming in the flaming seas and climbing the Blade Mountains along the universe to attain Nirvana, I will gladly choose the second one." Because one 'Athinchay' is the equivalent to one followed

Chart of the 31 Planes of Existence

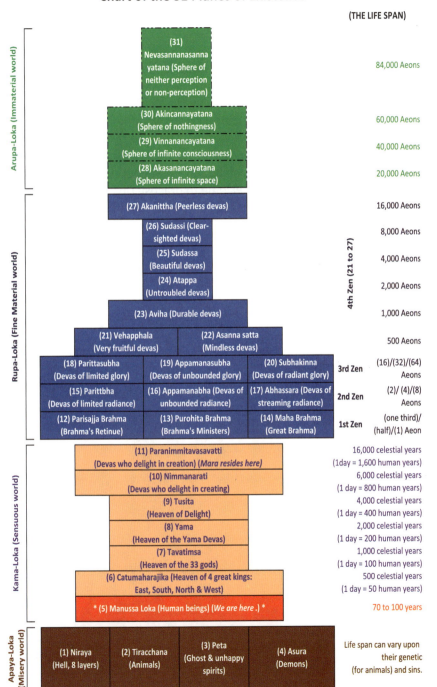

(THE LIFE SPAN)

Arupa-Loka (Immaterial world)

- (31) Nevasannanasanna yatana (Sphere of neither perception or non-perception) — 84,000 Aeons
- (30) Akincannayatana (Sphere of nothingness) — 60,000 Aeons
- (29) Vinnanancayatana (Sphere of infinite consciousness) — 40,000 Aeons
- (28) Akasanancayatana (Sphere of infinite space) — 20,000 Aeons

Rupa-Loka (Fine Material world)

- (27) Akanittha (Peerless devas) — 16,000 Aeons
- (26) Sudassi (Clear-sighted devas) — 8,000 Aeons
- (25) Sudassa (Beautiful devas) — 4,000 Aeons
- (24) Atappa (Untroubled devas) — 2,000 Aeons
- (23) Aviha (Durable devas) — 1,000 Aeons

4th Zen (21 to 27)

- (21) Vehapphala (Very fruitful devas) / (22) Asanna satta (Mindless devas) — 500 Aeons
- (18) Parittasubha (Devas of limited glory) / (19) Appamanasubha (Devas of unbounded glory) / (20) Subhakinna (Devas of radiant glory) — **3rd Zen** — (16)/(32)/(64) Aeons
- (15) Parittbha (Devas of limited radiance) / (16) Appamanabha (Devas of unbounded radiance) / (17) Abhassara (Devas of streaming radiance) — **2nd Zen** — (2)/(4)/(8) Aeons
- (12) Parisajja Brahma (Brahma's Retinue) / (13) Purohita Brahma (Brahma's Ministers) / (14) Maha Brahma (Great Brahma) — **1st Zen** — (one third)/(half)/(1) Aeon

Kama-Loka (Sensuous world)

- (11) Paranimmitavasavatti (Devas who delight in creation) (*Mara resides here*) — 16,000 celestial years (1day = 1,600 human years)
- (10) Nimmanarati (Devas who delight in creating) — 6,000 celestial years (1 day = 800 human years)
- (9) Tusita (Heaven of Delight) — 4,000 celestial years (1 day = 400 human years)
- (8) Yama (Heaven of the Yama Devas) — 2,000 celestial years (1 day = 200 human years)
- (7) Tavatimsa (Heaven of the 33 gods) — 1,000 celestial years (1 day = 100 human years)
- (6) Catumaharajika (Heaven of 4 great kings: East, South, North & West) — 500 celestial years (1 day = 50 human years)
- * (5) Manussa Loka (Human beings) (*We are here* .) * — 70 to 100 years

Apaya-Loka (Misery world)

- (1) Niraya (Hell, 8 layers)
- (2) Tiracchana (Animals)
- (3) Peta (Ghost & unhappy spirits)
- (4) Asura (Demons)

Life span can vary upon their genetic (for animals) and sins.

by one hundred and forty zeros of Aeons. As an ordinary person, I dare not imagine how long we have to float up and down in this Samsara.

Nowadays, we do not need to travel for such an uncountable endless journey nor do we need to swim in the flaming seas and climb the Blade Mountains of the universe. If we follow Buddha's guidance, and practise Dhamma correctly, Nirvana is within our reach. Lord Buddha is the spiritual teacher who showed the direct path to Nirvana. Nowadays, the new developments of the modern science are becoming better and better and never ending experiments are still going on in the outside world. Buddha is the perfect scientist of the inner world. Everybody is welcome to practise Dhamma without changing their uniforms or their religions. After that, to accept it or not is their own freedom.

Dear reader, which plane do you want to book for the next existence? It is better to prepare now before the unscheduled flight arrives. The choice is yours!

--⋈● ⫘ ●⋈--

37 Nats (Spirit Worshipping)

Although Theravada Buddhism has been widely spreading in Myanmar since the Anawrahta era, there are still Nat worshipping (နတ်ကိုးကွယ်ပသခြင်း). If you really want to know the Myanmar essence, 'Nat worshipping' should not be ignored too. There are 37 spiritual Nats in Myanmar. 'Nat' means 'god' in Myanmar language. But these 'nats' are not the same nats from the heavenly gods of 31 existences. These 37 nats are worldly spiritual nats. Those nats can help the people in worldly matters but sometimes they can give trouble too if people fail to pay proper respects to them. So nat worshippers are very scared of those nats and they dare not make any mistake or not to fail to keep their promises to them when they deal with those nats.

Beside the Buddhism, some Myanmar people still worship some of the nats for some reasons. As those nats are very sensitive, younger generation dare not discard the tradition and heritage of their older generations although they do not have deep belief in nat worshipping anymore. Unlike them, some people have a great faith in those worldly nats because they believe that those nats are very helpful to their business and that they bring luck and prosperity.

Nat worshipping is more popular in rural areas than urban places. Some worshippers celebrate small private 'Nat-pwe' (nat-festival) in front of their houses when they gain a lot of profit from their business. They hire the 'nat-kadaws' (nat-soothers) to entertain the nats and it takes about 3 days. The first is inviting the nats. The second day is nat feasts. Final day is the day for their departure. Normally nat-soothers are males but they apply the make-up and wear suitable dresses for each nat and behave in suitable manners and sing different songs for different kinds of nats. At nat-pwe, they all behave as if they were possessed by the real nats. Their songs consist of their backgrounds.

Actually, to be a nat is not easy. In their previous lives, those nats were human beings. They all have tragic stories. A nat must have the following characteristics while they were human beings.

- They were famous or popular.
- They had a supernatural power or strength.

- They were killed or unexpectedly died.
- Met violent or cruel death.

They have their own background stories:

1) **Thagyar Min** (သိကြားမင်း) - Actually, Thagyar Min is the head of the celestial beings (heavenly nats). His nature is quite different from those 36 nats. But the nat worshippers usually invite him with respect whenever they celebrate the nat festivals and they put him at the head of the 37 nats list too.

2) **Minmahagiri Nat** (မင်းမဟာဂီရိ) - His personal name was 'Maung Tint De' (means Mr. Handsome). His father is the famous blacksmith 'U Tint Daw'. He was extremely strong and he was able to break the tusk of a huge elephant. The king of Tagaung was so worried that he might usurp the throne that Maung Tint De was exiled from the village. The king selected his sister 'Saw Myat Hla' as his queen and used tricks asking her brother to come. When Maung Tint De came, he was arrested by the king's people and burnt him alive. When his sister saw that scene, she jumped into the fire with a broken-heart and both of them became nats.

3) **Golden Face Nat** (ရွှေမျက်နှာ) - She is the 'Saw Myat Hla', sister of Maung Tint De. As the above story, she jumped down into the fire. When people pulled her out of the fire, only her head was saved.

4) **Shwenabay** (ရွှေနဘေ) - was a beautiful woman of Mindon Village who married a *Naga* (Dragon). Later, her husband deserted her and she died of a broken heart. Another scripture says that she was actually the wife of Maung Tint De.

5) **Thone ban hla Nat** *(Beautiful in triple ways)* (သုံးပန်လှ) - She was a native of a Mon village called Takunnwan. She was beautiful in three different ways within one day. She was

given to King Duttabaung of Pyay, but the queen was jealous of her beauty and told the king that she was actually very ugly and so fat that she could not fit through the city gate. Hearing this, the king refused to marry Thonebanhla and she died in despair and shame. Another story said that she was the younger sister of Maung Tint De. She married King Samim Htaw Yama of Utthala and gave birth to a daughter, Shin Mi-hnè, but then died of a sudden illness.

6) **Shin Mi Hne (Ma Hne Lay)** (မနဲ့လေး) - She was the daughter of Thone ban hla. Two years after her mother's death, she died with deep grief and became a nat. Nowadays, when a baby is sick, the parents pray Ma Hne Lay to get well of their baby. She is the youngest among 37 nats.

7) **Shin Nyo** (ရှင်ညို) and

8) **Shin Phyu** (ရှင်ဖြူ) - Both were the sons of Maung Tint De and Shwe Na Bay. They were employed in king of Duttabaung's service. The king was so worried that they would usurp his throne that he asked the two brothers to fight to the end. Both of them died of exhaustion and became nats.

9) **Hti byu saung Nat** (Nat with White umbrella) (ထီးဖြူဆောင်း) - He was King Kyaungbyu, father of Anawrahta. He was dethroned by the two stepsons brought by Southern queen and forced him to become a monk. He died later and became a nat.

10) **Hti-byu-saung Medaw** (Royal Mother of Htibyusaung nat) (ထီးဖြူဆောင်းနတ်မယ်တော်) - She was the grandmother of Anawrahta, died of illness.

11) **Shin Mingaung** (ရှင်မင်းခေါင်) - He was king Kyizo who dethroned the king Kyaungbyu. He was hit by an arrow of a hunter and died. Actually, that hunter released his arrow to a deer in the forest.

12) Shwe Phyin Gyi (ရွှေဖျင်းကြီး) and

13) Shwe Phyin Lay (ရွှေဖျင်းလေး) - Both of them were sons of Byatta, the royal messenger, and Me Wunna, a flower-eating ogress from Mt. Popa, during the reign of King Anawrahta of Bagan. They were killed for neglecting their duty to provide a brick each thus leaving gaps in Taungpyone Pagoda, which was built by King Anawrahta.

14) The Mandalay Grandpa (မန္တလေးဘိုးဘိုး) - He was killed by the royal order of King Anawrahta because he could not well-manage Shwe Phyin Gyi and Shwe Phyin Lay (above two brothers) who neglected their service in building pagoda. He was assigned to take care of two brothers after their father's death.

15) The Dwarf nat (Shin Kwa nat) (ရှင်ကွနတ်) - She was the sister of Mandalay Grandpa. She was killed together with her brother for protecting the two brothers by hiding them (Shwe Phyin Gyi and Shwe Phyin Lay).

16) Nyaung Chin Oh nat (ညောင်ချင်းအိုနတ်) - He was a descendant of King Manuha of Thaton in Bagan. He died of leprosy during the reign of King Anawrahta.

17) Min Si Thu nat (မင်းစည်သူ) - His name was Alaungsithu, King of Bagan. He was the grandson of King Anawrahta and assassinated by his son Narathu (1167-1170) who usurped his throne.

18) Maung Shin nat (The swing rider nat) (မောင်ရှင်) - He was the grandson of King Alaungsithu. While he was a novice, he fell down from the swing and became a nat.

19) Min Kyaw Zwa nat (မင်းကျော်စွာ) - He was also known as U Min Kyaw, he was the son of the Lord of Pyay and Kuni Devi. He was a drunkard, cock fighter, and excellent horseman. He was killed by the devils who had been his victims.

20) **Aung Zwa Ma Gyi nat** (အောင်ဇွာမကြီး) - He was also called Bo Aung Zwa, and a commander of King Narapatisithu of Bagan (1173-1210). He was killed by the king when he showed disrespect to the king, because the king failed to keep his promise of rewarding him with one of his maids.

21) **Shwe Sit Thin nat** (ရွှေစစ်သင်) - He was the son of Bagan King Sawmonnit (687-730). When his father sent him to the battlefield, he was playing fighting cocks and he was imprisoned and died.

22) **Mother of Shwe Sit Thin nat** (ရွှေစစ်သင်နတ် မယ်တော်) - She died of heartbreak over the sorrowful plight of her son.

23) **Lord of Five Elephants** (ငါးစီးရှင်) - He was the son of Thihathu. He became king Kyaw Zwa after his father's death and got five white elephants. He reigned nine years and died of illness.

24) **Mintaya Nat** (မင်းတရား) - He was the King of Innwa, was hunting in the forest where he met a fairy, and went insane when the fairy disappeared. While he was in this state, one of his followers, Nga Nawk, murdered him.

25) **Maung Pho Tu nat** (မောင်ဖိုးတူ) - He was a tea trader during the time of King Minkhaung of Innwa. He was bitten by a tiger on his way to the Shan State and became a nat.

26) **Anauk Mi-pha-yar** (Western Queen) (အနောက်မိဖုရား) - She was queen of King Minkhaung I of Innwa, daughter of the Shan chief Tho Ngan Bwa, and mother of Min Yè Kyaw Zwa. She died of a heart attack after being startled by seeing Min Kyaw Zwa (U Min Kyaw) on a magic stallion in a cotton field.

27) **Lord of White Elephant of Aung Pin Le** (ဆင်ဖြူ၍ရှင်) - He was the son of King Minkhaung of Innwa (1401-1422), killed by an arrow released by his enemy the Sawbwa of Ohnbaung at Aung Pinle.

28) **Shin Kone** (ရှင်ကုန်း) - She was a maid of King Thihathu. She accompanied the king to the battlefield and she died on her

.... return to the capital.

29) **Shwe Nawrahta nat** (ရွှေနော်ရထာ) - Grandson of King Minkhaung II of Innwa (1481-1502). His servant tried to assassinate the king, but was caught and put to death. Because of Shwe Nawrahta's involvement in the plot, he too was put to death.

30) **Min Ye Aung Din nat** (မင်းရဲအောင်ဒင်) - He was the husband of Princess Shwe Sin Tu, daughter of King Thar Lun of Innwa and the queen, who was daughter of Sawbwa of Monè in the Shan State. He died from an excess of opium smoking.

31) **Maung Min Byu nat** (မောင်မင်းဖြူ) - He was a son of King Innwa and died of excessive drinking of alcohol.

32) **Shin Daw nat** (ရှင်တော်) - He was a young novice monk of Innwa and died of a snake bite.

33) **Tabin Shwe Hti nat** (တပင်ရွှေထီး) - He was the King of Taungoo (1512-1550), became a drunkard and was assassinated by a servant who was drunk also.

34) **The lady of North** (မြောက်ဘက်ရှင်မ) - She was the wet nurse of King Tabinshwehti, and a native of North Kadu. She died in childbirth.

35) **Shin Min Gaung of Taungoo** (ရှင်မင်းခေါင်) - A minor governor of Taungoo and son of Min Yè Theinkàthu, the royal attendant, he died of illness.

36) **Thandawgan nat** (သံတော်ခံ) - A royal messenger of King Minkhaung of Taungoo, his given name was Yè Thiha. He went into the forest to gather flowers, caught malaria, and died.

37) **Yunbayin (King of the Yun)** (ယွန်းဘုရင်) - was Mekuti, the captive king of Chiang Mai, who died of illness during the reign of King Bayinnaung of Hanthawaddy (1551-1581).

The History of 'Taungpyone' (Nat Festival)

The 'Taung pyone' nat festival ('တောင်ပြုံး နတ်ပွဲတော်) is very popular in Myanmar. Every year, the festival time falls in the Myanmar month of Wakaung (August). Devotees from all over the country flock there to make donations and pay respects to their respective nats.

Taungpyone is situated 9 miles away from Mandalay. The tradition of Taungpyone is based on some tragic stories.

Byatwi and Byatta

Let us draw the reader's attention to the topic 'The arrival of Theravada Buddhism to Bagan'. Do you think that King Anawrahta conquered Thaton capital easily? As a great fighter, he used different strategies in different battles to win. But unlike previous battles, this time his people had to face with some mysterious incidents. When Anawrahta's soldiers tried to climb up the wall of the city, they were beaten by powerful unseen forces. The soldiers ended up with hysteria, or high fever and the King could not ask them to do again. It was beyond his understanding.

So, Byatta was assigned to investigate the situation. It was he who was familiar with the capital because he was an exile from Thaton. Byatta went there and observed the area near the city wall. He was not attacked but suddenly a vague figure, which he realized was his late brother 'Byatwi' who had been killed by the King of Thaton, appeared. Byatta was very frightened but tried to be calm himself and face his brother. As 'Blood is thicker than water', Byatwi did not harm his brother despite the fact that he was a powerful spirit. He said that he was in helpless situation because the Thaton king had poured his blood all along the city wall. He was assigned to protect the city and he could not be liberated. But he could reveal one secret. Due to the shortage of his blood, there was a narrow space about the size of a sitting hen forming a gap at one corner of the city wall. He said that the gap was defenceless and that his power did not extend to that place. Byatta grieved for his brother and brought the secret information to the king.

Once Anawrahta knew of the weakness, he changed his strategy and conquered Thaton. Anawrahta raided Thaton and brought three repositories of Buddhist Scriptures (Pitaka Thone Pon) and some learned monks to Bagan. Unfortunately, Byatta lost his life in this bloody battle. He left behind two sons called 'Min Gyi' and 'Min Lay'. Anawrahta continued to take care of the two brothers and later put them under his employment.

Why Byatwi could not be liberated:

One day, two brothers from India were floating along a river after being shipwrecked. A hermit noticed and saved the two brothers, and provided them with food and shelter at his monastery. The brothers were 'Byatwi' and 'Byatta' (ဗျတ်ဝိ နှင့် ဗျတ္တ). They served the hermit by running errands for him. One day, the hermit took them to the forest to forage for food.

They found a small, lifeless, golden colored body under a tree. The hermit knew straightaway what it was and he explained to them that it was the shell of 'Zawgyi' (a powerful alchemist who always wear red robe and carries a magic cane in his hand.) He can fly up the sky like a bird; travel under the water like a fish; go underneath the earth. In fact, he can create whatever he wants! A Zawgyi usually wanders deep inside the forest in search of rare herbs. The small body is called 'Zawgyi Pho Win Thar' (ဇော်ဂျီဖိုဝင်သား). The hermit understood that whoever ate that would gain a supernatural power, although it was not as great as that of a real Zawgi.

They brought it to the monastery since the hermit intended to give this priceless food to the King. He kept it and fell asleep due to the fatigue of travelling into the forest. The aroma of the food soon attracted the two brothers and they could not help tasting a little bit. The taste was very wonderful and they found themselves eating the whole thing!

The two brothers felt a strange feeling and their bodies became lighter. When they jumped, their body lifted up into the sky, and when they leaned against a tree, it fell down. Since they wanted to tease the hermit, they lifted a stone slab ten cubits in length and eight cubits in breadth at some distant place and put it at the foot of the stairs of the monastery. (One cubit equal to one and a half feet). When the hermit woke up, he realized what had happened!

They became very famous among the villagers for their extraordinary power and the news reached King Manuha of Thaton. The king was frightened that they might usurp the throne. So one day, he ordered that they be killed and offered a high reward for their heads. However, nobody could arrest them. The wise men counselled that their power would not be effective if they were put under a women's lower garment, like a longyi (sarong). Byatwi had a lover in town and her name was 'Ma O Zar'. He often came to see her. So the king's men plotted to arrest him, as they had been ordered. Once Byatwi entered into the town, they covered him with a woman's sarong and arrested him. (The superstition 'Man will lose his power if he walks under a women's hanging longyi' came from this story.)

Although Byatwi was arrested, nothing could kill him. So, the commanders tried to break his will by saying that a man should not give his heart to a woman who had betrayed him. They insinuated that Ma O Zar had laid a trap for him to be arrested due to her lust for the King's reward. Byatwi did not trust them. He said that his love for Ma O Zar was so strong that if she personally came and gave him 'a quid of betel and a cup of water', it was enough for him to die.

The King's people used deception again by telling Ma O Zar that her lover was pardoned by the king and longing to see her. Ma O Zar was overjoyed and prepared to see her hero at once when she received the news but she was told, "You should not go empty-handed. Don't you think you should bring a quid of betel and a cup of water for your tired lover?" She brought it, handed to him, and spoke sweet words to her lover without knowing

Min Gyi, Min Lay and their Mother

she had been deceived. Love-sick, Byatwi took what she had handed him. He could not hear her words anymore and his heart was filled with pain, greater than the cruel torture of the king's people. Finally he died as he let go of his power after receiving the gifts from Ma O Zar. However, Byatwi could not yet be liberated. The wise men advised the King that the flesh and bones of the supernatural Byatwi should be buried at the four corners of the city walls and his blood should be poured drop by drop along their entire length. The king listened and did it. In this way, Byatwi could not escape and his spirit was assigned to protect the city.

His brother 'Byatta' ran away from Thaton and took refuge in Bagan and became one of the best men in King Anawrahta's court. While he was serving there, he fell in love with 'Mae Wunna', a flower-eating nymph. He met her each day when he went to the forest to pick flowers for the queen. They had two sons named Shwe Phyin Gyi and Shwe Phyin Lay. Later they were known as Min Gyi and Min Lay in Taung Pyone. They have a different story too.

Min Gyi and Min Lay

When their father 'Byatta', who was Anawrahta's best man, lost his life in the battle at Thaton, King Anawrahta continued taking care of them. Min Gyi and Min Lay were popular, not only due to the fame of their father (who had supernatural power), but also as a result of their own youth and glamour.

King Anawrahta's group, including the two brothers, stayed in Taungpyone to supervise the building of a 'Wish-fulfilling pagoda'. This pagoda was being built with the participation of everyone. Everyone was delighted to contribute a brick and, after the pagoda was completed, the king would come and see the pagoda. People who made a wish and prayed at this pagoda would have their desires fulfilled.

Since Min Gyi and Min Lay were young, their spirits were lifted and they were curious to wander about the nearby villages while they were stationed there. Min Lay saw the village belle 'Ma Shwe Oo', whose father was the head of the village. He could not control his admiration for her although she was already betrothed to another. It became difficult for Min Gyi to control his brother. He did not want his younger brother to become like their Uncle Byatwi, who worshipped love and lost his life. While everybody's attention was on building the pagoda, Min Lay's mind was entirely occupied with courting Ma Shwe Oo while Min Gyi tried to control his younger brother. It caused them to forget their duty to contribute a brick. The pagoda was nearly finished.

The king arrived to inspect the pagoda. The king paid respects to the pagoda. When he checked the pagoda, he saw that there was a space where two bricks were missing. Why? At the same time, with the king's permission, the head of the village told the

The Wish-fulfilling pagoda built by King Anawrahta

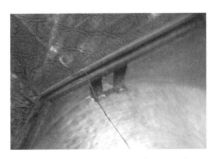

Two Empty Spaces inside the pagoda

king about Min Lay's aggressive advances on his daughter. The King decreed an order to cane them as a punishment. But they were killed by the king's people. (According to local gossip, it was plotted by a few people of Anawrahta due to their jealousy towards the two brothers. When Anawrahta ordered to cane the two brothers, they ensured that the two brothers met their end.)

Before the king left for Bagan, the spirit of the two brothers asked a favour of him. Since they had no place to dwell at the moment, they begged him to forgive their faults and bequeath a place for them. The king was so touched to hear this that he declared without hesitation that the Taungpyone area was for them. Since that day onward they became the lords of Taungpyone. Later, Taungpyone becomes like the head quarter of all the nats. Till now, the spaces of two bricks are empty in that pagoda and nobody dares to fill them. When the nat soothers sing a song for them, they sing with a sorrowful tone that they were killed due to their negligence in contributing their two bricks. Isn't it pitiful?

Mahawthahta

Last week, a friend of mine visited me. While we were having a chit-chat, she remarked that nowadays people are addicted to Korean movies which are presented by Myanmar Radio and Television. While they are watching those movies, they cannot talk well and when she makes a phone call to her friends and relatives, their mind is half absorbed in the movie. Unlike them, she has a great liking of 'Bao Jintian' movies (which are the old Chinese movies about the judgement of problems) which were presented by MRTV before. My talkative friend looked a little bit angry towards those people with whom she could not talk as much as she wished. She praised Bao Jintian (ပေါင်ချိန် ဇာတ်လမ်းတွဲများ) (in the movies, some people called him 'black face' as he was born with a half moon on his forehead like a prophet). She was of the opinion that more movies like 'Justice Bao' should be presented on television rather than romance or dramas so that people can improve their sense of justice from such educational movies.

That night, after recollecting her observations, I suddenly remembered the Mahawthahta Jataka, there was a young, wise man called 'Mahawthahta' (မဟော်သဓာ) about whom we learnt in our high school textbook.

Once upon a time, King 'Widayharit', who ruled the 'Meikhtila' capital in the 'Widayharit' country had a strange dream. In his dream, he saw the four huge fires were flaring upon each side of the capitals' walls. In the middle of the four huge fires, a small fire like a firefly appeared and went straight up into the sky until the whole universe was illuminated. After illuminating the whole sky, that small sharp fire fell down to the ground and all of the angels and human beings paid homage to the small fire with flowers and incense. The small fire did not make the people hot, despite walking inside it, and they felt very peaceful. The king woke up from that dream and was frightened. The next morning, he asked the prophets about it. The prophet, 'Theynaka' interpreted it and pronounced, "My Lord, please do not worry. It is a very good dream. The four huge fires represent four of us who are now serving near you. The small, sharp fire means a wise man will appear in the near future and, although he is very young, he will be wiser than the four of us". The king was very excited by the prophet's prediction. "Where is that wise man now?"asked the king. The prophet replied, "He is now either in the womb of a mother, or he has just been delivered".

In eastern village of that country, there was a very wealthy man named 'Thiriwuddana'. His wife 'Thumana Dewi' got pregnant and a few months after the king's dream, she delivered a baby boy. Thagyarmin (the king of celestial beings) put a medicinal stick in the baby's hand. The baby gave it to the mother to cure all sorts of diseases. That medicinal stick was like a panacea and all diseases were cured just by smelling or taking a little bit of water after putting that stick in the water. His father's seven year old migraine disappeared too. The father considered that his son was not an ordinary baby. He was blessed by heavenly beings and that was why they gave this medicinal stick to the baby. So he gave the baby the name 'Mahawthahta'. According to the father's inquiry, there were one thousand babies who were delivered on the same day as his son, and they all became friends of Mahawthahta.

When Mahawthahta was seven years old, his personality was very admirable and glamorous. He instructed a great carpenter to build a playground and resting place for their group. At the same time, Mahawthahta decided to make a garden and a public lake, too. The design Mahawthahta created was very splendid and looked like the 'Nanda' garden in heaven. People came to admire Mahaw Thahta's garden and they found that it could quench their physical and mental tiredness of life and they became very peaceful.

The king could not forget his dream. Everyday, he was waiting expectantly as to when the fifth wise man would appear. So, one day he asked the four wise men, "It has been seven years already since my strange dream. So the four of you should go in the four directions of the country and find the wise man for me, in accordance with my dream." The prophet who went to the east of the capital saw the resting place for travellers which Mahawthahta had built. Once he saw that, he straightaway knew that the architect must be a wise man because it was like an angel's garden, which was beyond the dreams of a normal human architect. According to his inquiry, people explained that the garden was built by Mahawthahta, who was only seven years old. So, he presented that news to the king and they realized that Mahawthahta was the fifth wise man. Naturally, the king wanted to bring him to the palace but the prophet, 'Theynaka', advised the king to wait and observe Mahawthahta's skills more and more.

Here, I will present three problems which Mahawthahta solved:

Solving the problem of the mother of a son

One day a woman, carrying her baby, came to Mahawthahta's lake to take bath. After giving a bath to her baby, she laid her baby to sleep near the lake and she took a bath, herself. At that time, an ogress saw the baby and desired to eat it. So, she disguised herself as a woman, came nearer to the baby, and asked the mother, "This baby is very cute. Is it yours?". The mother said, "Yes". The ogress cradled the baby and said, "I want to carry the baby for a while." When the mother allowed her, the ogress carried and pretended to pacify the baby for a while. Then, she ran away, taking the baby. The mother chased her and asked the ogress, "Where will you take my son?" The ogress replied, "Where is your son? This is my son." They argued and reached the gates of Mahawthahta's playground.

Mahawthahta invited them to come in and asked, "Why are you arguing?" The ogress said, "I was carrying my baby and walking. This unknown woman came up to me and accused me of taking her son." The mother explained what happened, too. After closely observing the two women and their behaviour, Mahawthahta, at once, realized which was the mother and which was the ogress. He asked them, "Will you accept my judgement?" Both women said, "Yes."

Mahawthahta marked a line on the ground. He let the ogress hold the two hands of the baby and mother hold the two feet of the baby and said, "Both of you pull the baby. The winner will be the mother of the baby." First, the two women pulled the baby. The baby cried loudly, due to the pain. That crying made the mother's heart very painful. As she could not stand her baby's crying anymore, she released her hands and stood aside in sorrow. At that time, Mahawthahta looked at the public and asked "Who truly loves the baby, the mother or the other woman?" The people answered "Only mothers love their babies so much."

"So, what do you all think? Is the winner the mother, or the woman who gives up pulling the baby is the mother?"

The public answered at the same time, "The woman who cannot stand the baby's cry must be the real mother."

He asked again, "Do all of you know the woman who stole the baby?" When the people said that they did not know her, Mahawthahta explained, "This woman is not a human being. She is an ogress." The people asked, "How do you know?" Mahawthahta explained, "You see this woman. She never blinks. Her eyes are red. She has no pity for the baby. According to this evidence, I can say that she is an ogress." The ogress admitted that what Mahawthahta said was correct and that she stole the baby because she wanted to eat him. Mahawthahta taught her, "You have committed so many sins in your previous lives. That's why you became an ogress. If you do not stop committing sins, how will you ever escape from this lower existence?" He extracted a promise from the ogress not to kill others and released her.

The mother was very grateful to Mahawthahta and said, "My lord, you saved my son's life. I pray for you to live longer." She was very happy and went back to her village carrying her baby.

After hearing about Mahawthahta's judgement, which was duly reported by the prophet, the king wanted to bring Mahawthahta to the palace. But the prophet, 'Theynaka', said that it was not enough yet, and he advised the king to test Mahawthahta's wisdom by sending him another problem.

Choosing the cutch (Acacia catechu) stem, top or base

One day, the king made a smooth stem, about nine inches (9") in length, from the cutch tree. He sent it to the eastern village and ordered, "I heard that the people from the eastern village are very wise. So differentiate this stem. Which side is the top and which side is the base? If you cannot differentiate between the two, the whole village will be punished."

So the villagers brought the problem to Mahawthahta's father with a hope that the son may be able to solve it. The father asked

Mahawthahtar

his son whether he knew the solution or not. Actually, Mahawthahta knew, straightaway, once he touched the cutch stick but he wanted to prove it in front of the people. So, he asked them to bring a cup of water. He tied a string in the middle of the stick and put it on the surface of water. One side sunk down. Then he asked the public, "Which part of the tree is heavier? The top or the base?". The public answered at the same time, "The base is heavier than the top." Mahawthahta made a mark indicating the base and the top and he let the people send it to the king. The king was elated with Mahawthahta's intelligence and he tried to bring Mahawthahta to the palace. As usual, the prophet, 'Theynaka,' insisted on sending one more problem to test Mahawthahta's skill.

Putting the silk inside the royal ruby

One day, the king ordered the village where Mahawthahta was staying to put a silk thread inside the royal ruby, which had 8 curves inside. The ruby was worn by all the previous kings. The silk thread was now very fragile and nearly broken, and the king could not wear it. Actually, the king had arranged to kill two birds with one stone - testing Mahawthahta's skill and putting the silk thread inside the ruby. Once again the king threatened that if they could not accomplish this, the whole village would be punished. As it was a very difficult task, the villagers were in a state of despair. "Even putting a thread into a needle hole is not easy. How can we put this silk thread within the 8 curves of the royal ruby?" So, news of the problem eventually reached Mahawthahta.

Mahawthahta told them not to worry and asked them to bring some honey. First, he applied honey to the old thread and placed it in front of a red ants' nest. Soon, the ants came out and ate the honey. Due to their lust, they ate the honey-soaked-thread, too. Then, on the other side of the ruby, he put more honey. But on this side, he put a fine strand of new silk thread into the hole. So, after eating the honey on the other side, the ants entered back into the ruby and returned to the other side. In doing so, they carried the new thread along their way back to their nest. In this way, the silk thread was successfully put into the royal ruby. Mahawthahta asked the villagers to send it to the king. The king was very impressed with Mahawthahta's wisdom.

▸▸ *If you want to read more about Mahawthahta's judgement skills, I would recommend you to find the 'Ten Great Jatakas' (Zat Kyi Se Bwe) books.*

Seven Birthdays and Their Characteristics

Whenever I tell the people that I am a Friday-born, their first response is either "Are you sure? Did you check in the calendar?" or "Friday-borns are very talkative. Why are you so quiet?" or "Your name starts with 'M', so we think you are a Thursday-born". At such a time, I have to explain to them that when I was young, I looked very much like the picture of the baby on the 'Meiji Milk Powder' tin box. So my aunty gave me that name, 'Meiji' and 'Soe' is my father's name. To pronounce it easily, they spelt my name 'May Ji'. As a result of the combination of these three words, some of my friends tease me, "Were you very naughty to your mother when you were young? That's why your mom gave you that name?" (ငယ်ငယ်တုန်းက အမေကို ရှိကျပြီး ဆိုးလွန်းလို့လား). Because 'May May' means mother in Myanmar language. 'Ji' and 'Soe' both have similar meaning of naughtiness although they have their own homonyms, too. (Later, I came to know that 'Meiji' is the name of the young Japanese emperor in ancient time who was enthroned in his teenage and transformed Japan into a modern industrialized country.)

According to them, "It is good for Friday-borns to be talkative because the more they talk, the more they will be prosperous!"

In this way, when we hear a person's name, we know at once on what day he was born and we can roughly predict about his characteristics. (Please see the following chart). When you go to a pagoda, you will see people pouring water at their birthday corners, offering flowers, candles lights, and incense sticks.

A mother and son offering water at Monday corner.

Seven Birthdays and Their Characteristics

No	Birthday	Symbol	Lucky stone	Name starts with	Direction	Planet	Characteristics
1	Sunday	Garuda	Ruby	Any vowel, a,e,i,o,u (အ)	North East	Sun	Too sensitive, (if he/she has curly hair, not too sensitive)
2	Monday	Tiger	Pearl	Ka, kha, ga, gha, nga (က ခ ဂ ဃ င)	East	Moon	Organized persons but sometimes Jealous
3	Tuesday	Lion	Thandar (Coral stone/ red color)	Sa, hsa, za, zha, nya (စ ဆ ဇ ဈ ဉ)	South East	Mars	Stubborn
4	Wednesday (am)	Elephant	Emerald	Ya, Wa, la, (ယ ၀ လ)	South	Mercury	Quick temper
4	Wednesday (pm)	Elephant (taskless)	Emerald	Ya, ra (ရ)	North West	Rahu	Quick temper (Mild)
5	Thursday	Rat	Oattha phaya (Topaz)	Pa, pha, ba, bha, ma (ပ ဖ ဗ ဘ မ)	West	Jupiter	Harbour a grievance
6	Friday	Guinea-pig	Diamond	Tha, ha (သ ဟ)	North	Venus	Very talkative
7	Saturday	Dragon	Sapphire	Ta, hta, da, dha, na (တ ထ ဒ ဓ န)	South West	Saturn	Hot-tempered

They believe that by doing these kinds of good deeds, they will gain the fortunate results and their misfortunes will be decreased.

Knowing your weekly birthday (Sunday to Saturday) is important in Myanmar peoples' lives such as when to go to a pagoda, an astrologer, or choosing a marriage partner, a wedding day, giving birth, giving a child's name, building a house, or a ground-breaking ceremony, etc..

Compatible pair of Days for marriage ('Oothar Seinpan, Danhla Koshar') (ဦးသာစိန်ပန်း၊ ဒန်းလှကိုရှာ)

Here, a verse 'Oothar Seinpan, Danhla Koshar' was made for the people to remember easily. Let's see; 'Oothar' represents 'Sunday and Friday" etc ...

- Sunday and Friday
- Tuesday and Thursday
- Saturday and Wednesday (morning)
- Monday and Wednesday (evening)

Incompatible pair of Days for Marriage ('Dhammar Thawka, Innwa Yarzar') (ဓမ္မသောက အင်းဝရာဇာ)

- Saturday and Thursday
- Friday and Monday
- Sunday and Wednesday (morning)
- Tuesday and Wednesday (evening)

The effect for the couples with the same Birthday

Monday and Monday	- Wealthy (It means that if husband and wife are both Monday borns, they will be wealthy.)
Tuesday and Tuesday	- Anxieties

- Wednesday and Wednesday - Worries
- Thursday and Thursday - Happiness
- Friday and Friday - Good opportunities
- Saturday and Saturday - Loss in Business
- Sunday and Sunday - Evergreen Love

Good Days to get married

If you get married on ~

- Sunday - You will get a good husband/wife.
- Monday - Unstable marriage
- Tuesday - Money and good partner
- Wednesday - Scarcity
- Thursday - Get properties
- Friday - Free from danger
- Saturday - Marriage cannot last long

Good days to wash hair (Oh-Si-Tee) (အိုးစည်တီး ပြီးအောင်လျှော်)

Sunday, Tuesday and Saturday are the good days to wash hair. People can remember with a verse (Oh-Si-Tee). Oh represent 'Sunday', Si represents 'Tuesday' and Tee represents 'Saturday'.

On the contrary, there are unlucky days to wash hair. It is "Ka-Yin-Tha-Mway" (ကရင်သားမွေး ခေါင်းမဆေးရ). It represents 'Monday-Wednesday-Friday-Thursday'.

Even nail-cutting has lucky days and unlucky days

Tuesday and Saturday are good days to clip the nails and the rest are not good days. But Monday is neutral.

If you clip nails on Tuesday, you will have good health and on Saturday, you will win over your rivals.

Unlucky days for hair-cutting

(မွေးနေ့ သောကြာ၊ တနင်္လာ ကေသာဆံဖြတ် မပြုအပ်)

One should not have his/her hair cut on Monday, Friday and his/her own birthday. (Another meaning to the above verse is that the Friday-born person should not have his/her hair-cutting on Monday.)

Good days for ploughing (for farmers)

Monday, Wednesday, Thursday and Fridays are good days to plough.

Lucky days to start building a house (For engineers, carpenters and house owners)

If you build a house on ~

- Sunday – You will be in trouble.
- Monday – will be rich soon
- Tuesday – abundance of food and crops
- Wednesday – will be prosperous
- Thursday – Happiness
- Friday – will get a lot of servants
- Saturday – Very wealthy

The sayings are correct or not (ကာမသားစကားမမှန်၊ ဦးစံရာလာမှန်စကား)

Sometimes, we are unsure whether what a person says is correct or not. At such a time, you can apply this formula.

'Kar Ma Thar', Sakar Mahman, 'U San Yar Lar', Hman Sakar. It means if a person gives information or gives you a promise on Monday, Thursday and Friday, it is not reliable. But on Sunday, Tuesday and Wednesday, you can take it seriously.

Basic Myanmar Astrology (Mahabote Pillar)

Mahabote Pillar (Basic Myanmar Astrology) (မဟာဘုတ်တိုင်ထွန္နည်း) is mainly utilized when we wish to calculate one's past, present and the future based on the hours and day one was born. In this way, we can know the advantages and disadvantages of an individual.

First, write down the year one was born according to the Myanmar era and divided the number by seven.

The remainder will be 1 or 2 or 3 or 4 or 5 or 6 or 0. If the remainder is zero, we take it as 7.

According to the remainder number, we can construct the Mahabote pillar with reference to the following verses.

Remainder 1	Aung 1	Lan 4	Htu 7	Sit 3	Thu 6	Gyi 2	Pwe 5
Remainder 2	Gyi 2	Pwe 5	Aung 1	Lan 4	Htu 7	Sit 3	Thu 6
Remainder 3	Sit 3	Thu 6	Gyi 2	Pwe 5	Aung 1	Lan 4	Htu 7
Remainder 4	Lan 4	Htu 7	Sit 3	Thu 6	Gyi 2	Pwe 5	Aung 1
Remainder 5	Pwe 5	Aung 1	Lan 4	Htu 7	Sit 3	Thu 6	Gyi 2
Remainder 6	Thu 6	Gyi 2	Pwe 5	Aung 1	Lan 4	Htu 7	Sit 3
Remainder 0	Htu 7	Sit 3	Thu 6	Gyi 2	Pwe 5	Aung 1	Lan 4

Example (1): A person was born on 15 Full moon day of Tabaung (Sunday) at 6 am in the year 1279.

1279 divided by 7 (the remainder is 5).

Here, 1 represent for Sunday, 2 Monday, 3 Tuesday, 4 Wednesday, 5 Thursday, 6 Friday, 7 or 0 Saturday.

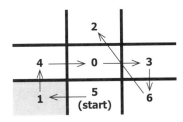

Example (2) : We can draw for a Thursday-born (the remainder 3) person as follows:

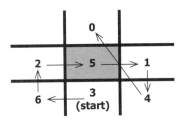

Table of Houses

Adipati		
Ah Tun	Thike	Yarza
Marana	Binga	Puti

So, according to Mahabote pillar, the first person was born in the house of Marana (Death and Wandering) and the second person was born in the House of Thike (Treasure). The table of the Houses is fixed and you have to adjust the remainder table which is not the same with each person.

Those born in the House of the sickly and infamous (Puti)

If a person was born in the House of the sickly and infamous, he will be without fame. He is not polite and the deliberation will be abrupt. When young, one will be very sickly and his parents will have to look after with anxiety. He shall wander about to earn one's living. He will get married with a person from another place. If a woman, she will get married to a man of one of these places. He will have to wander about a great deal. He is liable to keep one's secret and find fault with other people. If Puti-borns move from one's native place to another place and get married, one can be famous.

Those born in the House of the sickly and Loss (Binga)

If a person was born in the House of the sickly and loss, he/she will be very sickly from infancy. He will cause anxiety to his parents and relatives. He will have to face with losses many times in property, jewels, gold and silver. He will have a weak heart and will be easily frightened. He will do things very impulsively. When that person gets older, he can become a leader or head of an organization.

Those born in the House of the Death and Wanderings (Marana)

If a person was born in the House of the Death and Wanderings, he will have many diseases. He is likely to be short lived and died early. If he does not die early, one can become a rich man, a holy man, a noble man or a man of wisdom. If a woman, one can become a spouse of a man in power or a nun. There is a saying for Marana borns "If one dies, it will become earth but if one is alive, he will be elevated to greatness." (Thay Yin Myay Gyi, Shin Yin Shwe Htee) (သေရင်မြေကြီး၊ ရှင်ရင်ရွှေထီး). He will help his parents, teachers, relatives and friends. He will cause great anxiety to his parents. He will be shy. His hair may be coiled or may have sulky state of mind. He will speak the truth but he will not be eloquent. He will be honest and he will not stand to any nonsense. He will admit the truth.

Those born in the House of Fame (Ah Tun)

If a person was born in the House of Fame (Ah Tun), he will be famous. His state of mind will be active, quick. He will be courageous and brainy. He will be diligent and self reliant. He will get rich. He will be proud. He will be full of authority, conversant in literature and a good speaker.

Those born in the House of Treasure (Thike)

If a person was born in the House of Treasure (Thike), he will be rich throughout his whole life. That person will become a man in power or a holy man. He will have a sense of shame or fear. He will be generous and willing to donate. He will be educated and clever. He will be revered by others. He will have a great deal of business ideas. He will be soft and tender. He will have many friends. He will be successful by giving words of advice. He will be a good speaker and will become a lecturer.

Those born in the House of the Ruler (Yarza)

If a person was born in the House of the Ruler (Yarza), he will attain a lot of property, jewels, gold and silver and will enjoy his riches like a king. He will take interest in industrial affairs and likely to become an industrialist. He will make friends and work with those in power. He may be stern but honest.

Those born in the House of the Chief (Adipati)

If a person was born in the House of the Chief (Adipati), he will be famous. He will have livelihood with knowledge of speech. He may become a trader. Being a good speaker in a grand style, he can become a lecturer. He will seek special knowledge. His business could be accomplished successfully due to his zeal and diligence. His mind is straightforward and steady. He will have many friends and will be a chief among them.

➤ *Remark: Generally speaking, those who are born in Puti, Binga and Marana Houses are liable to meet with Poverty. It is a poor horoscope. Those who are born in Ah Tun, Thike, Yarza and Adipati will be rich. It is a rich horoscope.*

But there are some exceptions.

Although Puti, Binga and Marana borns are sickly and poor, but, if they are born on Monday (2), Wednesday (4), Thursday (5) and Friday (6), their adversity in life is not too severe and they will be less afflicted by sickness. Only the Sunday, Tuesday and Saturday borns are bound to be sickly.

Although in the House of Ah Tun, Thike, Yarza and Adipati are said to be rich, but if they are born on Sunday (1), Tuesday (3) and Saturday (7), they may be poor.

Zodiac Circle

According to Myanmar Astrology, a person's planet is circulated in a clockwise direction in accordance with the following chart. For example, a 25 years old Sunday-born is now in Tuesday planet after staying 6 years in Sunday plus 15 years in Monday. He has to stay 8 years in Tuesday. He can check strong point and weak point of Tuesday planet so that he will know what to do and what not to do while he is in Tuesday planet.

Sunday (6 years)	Monday (15 years)	Tuesday (8 years)
Friday (21 years)		Wednesday (17 years)
Rahu (12 years)	Thursday (19 years)	Saturday (10 years)

The influences of the Sunday Planet

If your zodiac enters the Sunday planet, you will be cheated or things will be stolen. Your mind will be disturbed by your spouse. You will lose properties or four-legged animal at home such as, cow or buffaloes. You will have to wander within one year due to unsettlement. You should not accept a visitor with a brown complexion, curved nose and heaped forehead. He may bring danger to you. Women may disturb you. You may suffer from stomach or gas pain. Avoid going to south and north-east places. Avoid eating the foods starting with Sunday names in Myanmar pronunciation such as 'coconut', 'egg', etc... (Note: If the name has two or more syllables you must take first syllable for the animate and the last syllable for the inanimate.)

The Influence of the Monday Planet

A young maiden will come into your life. You will get inheritance from the east. It is a wise choice if you go and work in the east. The farm, land or jewelleries will come to you as inheritance. You will make donations. You will win in legal matters. Single persons can meet with a lover wherever they go. Don't accept if a pregnant woman comes from the north. If you do business together with Monday and Thursday borns, you will get prosperity.

The Influence of the Tuesday Planet

You will have to face with legal matters, fighting and arguments for the other people's spouses. Avoid going to the south east and north-west or you will meet with enemies. Single persons will meet with competitors in love affairs. Things will be stolen. You may get bleeding or arrested. Business is not smooth and you may incur loss. There will be sickness and eye problem. Be careful how you talk. There may be misunderstanding between lovers.

The Influences of the Wednesday Planet

Under this planet, the inheritance from the south place will come to you. You will receive the things with the Wednesday names in Myanmar pronunciation such as cart, boat, gold, farm, etc. You will suffer from gas pain in chest or abdomen. Fate will smile on your love affairs and will get married. Avoid the foods which start with Wednesday names such as watermelon, lime, pumpkin, pork etc... Do not accept the visitor from north east or west or you will be cheated.

The Influences of the Thursday Planet

You will have to travel a lot. If you are single, you will get married with a lover from the west. Prosperity from east-west will come to you. You will receive properties like farm, land or garden from south or east. But you will be disturbed by a woman from south-west; do not go to that direction. You will get inheritance. You will be admired by other people.

The Influences of the Friday Planet

You will have to travel a lot. You will be rich. You will receive farm, crops, cow, buffaloes, elephant or house from the north. Single people will get good husband/wife. You will get promotion under this planet. Poor ones will get rich. You will get a new house. If you are a monk, you will get a new monastery and your glory will rise. A lot of admirers will be around you.

The Influences of the Saturday Planet

If your zodiac enters this planet, don't go to the south west; if you go, you will get bleedings, get arrested or face with the legal matters. Don't do trading business or selling/ buying farm, land, cow or buffaloes. You will incur loss. You should not go to the far places from native land; you will meet with danger or lose money or stolen. You will get disappointment in woman matters or face legal matters.

The Influences of the Rahu Planet (Those born on Wednesday evening)

You have to worry a lot. You will get misunderstanding from your seniors such as parents or teachers or boss. You may get divorced. You have to move to other place. You will lose cow, buffalo, property or jewellery. You will be disturbed by the thief, liar or the government people. There may be traitors from your relatives. You will be accused. Get sick. Avoid going to the west.

Making 'Zartar' Tradition (ဇာတာဖွဲ့ခြင်း)

Zartar-front and back side

In ancient time, the tradition of making one's 'zartar' (horoscope) is very popular. After a child was born, the parents usually asked the reliable astrologer to make a 'zartar' for their baby. They carefully kept it until the baby was old enough to keep it himself. Zartar is engraved on the palm leaf. On the 'zartar' a person's detailed horoscope is written on one side and on the other side is included a person's name, date of birth, time and place he was born in detail. Even though a person has passed away, the rest of the family keep his zartar as a memento. In ancient time, people usually kept the zartars of all family members at the altar like a treasure.

Some people make their 'zartar' on brass/copper sheet. The 'zartar' for the royalties were specially engraved very beautifully and ornamented. Zartar is naturally not to be seen often or to use it. Only when necessary, a person shows its own zartar. For example, if a person is in difficult situation or important occasions such as getting married or wanting to make important decision, he goes to the astrologer to check his horoscope by showing his zartar. Zartar is very helpful to the astrologers too because he does not have to calculate the inquirer's horoscope from the beginning or he does not have to ask his date of birth in detail. All basic information is on the zartar already and he can instantly predict the inquirer's destiny.

Zartars on palm leaves

The Ten Flowers of Art

Culture is the treasure of a country and Myanmar is rich in its own culture and architecture which has developed over more than a thousand years. There are ten main kinds of Myanmar traditional arts which we call the '**Ten Flowers**' (ပန်းဆယ်မျိုး). It is a good metaphor because 'Pan' directly translates as 'flower' in Myanmar language, but it is also used to describe the making of decorative arts or, as a generic term, for traditional arts and crafts. Most of these arts began to emerge during the Bagan era. The original touch of those olden days can still be seen in upper Myanmar, especially in Bagan and Mandalay. The Ten flower arts are as follows:

- Panbe (ပန်းဲ) (the art of the blacksmith)
- Pantain (ပန်းထိမ်) (the art of the gold and silver smith)
- Pantin (ပန်းတဉ်း) (the art of bronze casting)
- Pantaut (ပန်းတော့) (the art of making floral designs using masonry)
- Pantamault (ပန်းတမော့) (the art of carving stone)
- Panyan (ပန်းရန်) (the art of bricklaying and masonry)
- Panbu (ပန်းပု) (the art of wood and ivory carving)
- Panpoot (ပန်းပွတ်) (the art of turning designs on a lathe)
- Panchi (ပန်းချီ) (the art of painting)
- Panyun (ပန်းယွန်း) (the art of making lacquerware)

1. Panbe (the art of blacksmith):

Panbe is the art of making utensils for the household, military weapons, and farming tools such as body armour, swords, royal daggers, scissors, sickles, hammers, axes, etc. This art is also well known as the work

Traditional Panbe

of beating iron to get a desired shape after heating it. Myanmar's blacksmiths are famous in South East Asia.

2. Pantain (the art of gold and silver smith):

It was written as 'Pan Htyan' in old inscriptions. 'Htyan' means the creation of artistic ornamentation with gold and silver. Goldsmithing is the art of making earrings, bracelets, pendants, necklaces, etc. Silversmithing is the art of making prize cups, shields, silver belts, and others silverware. A Pantain master says "Sometimes, people misunderstand us and believe that we look at

silver smith

the jewellery with lust because those are precious things. Actually, we are craving only for the designs. Only our professional peers can understand the way we look."

Pantin

3. Pantin (the art of bronze casting):

There are three products in Pantin : copper, bronze and brass. This is the art of making bronze statues by a lost wax process, such as Buddha images and other figures such as bells. The bells in pagodas are an outstanding product of Pantin.

4. Pantaut (the art of making floral designs using masonry):

This is the art of building temples, pagodas, monasteries, and other buildings with bricks and mortar. It is very popular in Myanmar. Myanmar traditional stucco carving emerged before the Bagan period and it improved during the Bagan, Innwa, Amarapura and Yadanarpon periods.

Pantaut

5. Pantamault (the art of carving stone):

Carving Buddha image

'Tamault' comes from 'Tamo' and it means 'stone' in the Mon language. Pantamault is the art of skilfully carving sculptures from stone, such as Buddha images, standing figures, and decorative pillars and obelisks. Most of the Pantamault works can be seen in Mandalay.

6. Panyan (the art of bricklaying and masonry):

Panyan

It also includes carving and making reliefs of stucco and cement on arched entrances and on the walls of temples, religious edifices, and some buildings.

7. Panbu (Wood and Ivory carving):

Panpu

This is the art of making standing figures, embossed figures, wall hangings, floral designs, folding screens, and furniture from wood and ivory. The main tool of the Myanmar woodcarver is the chisel, made of iron with a wooden handle, and a wooden mallet.

8. Panpoot (the art of turning designs on a lathe):

Panpoot on Lathe machine

Myanmar utensils are so essential that even the Royal household cannot function without this art of turnery. Royal regalia, such as flower or betel trays with stems, ceremonial food containers, veranda posts, chair legs, bed legs; and crafts basically rely on turnery. This work is commonly known as 'rubbing the woods on the turner's lathe'.

9. Panchi (the art of Painting):

It was found as Pan Hki in old inscriptions and stands for the art of expressing one sided vision. Water color paintings are made on paper and cardboard while oil paintings are made on cardboard and canvas as well as on the walls of religious edifices. The artists paint live figures for human portraits, animals,

Panchi

objects, scenery, and photos. Nowadays, Myanmar paintings have become very popular in the international market.

10. Panyun (the art of making lacquerware):

Panyun

The making of lacquerware is based on bamboo, wood and lac (the sap of a tree, Myanmar people call it 'sis-se'). Yun means the incisions made upon the plain lacquerware with a sharp iron stylus to make all kinds of patterns and then applying colour to the grooves. The most popular products are monk's bowls, betel boxes, cheroot boxes, etc.

* These ten flowers art can be noted down in short form as '**Be-Tain-Tin-Taut-Mault-Yan-Bu-Poot-Chi-Yun**'. Researchers say that Myanmar has 3000 ancient inscriptions, not including those that have been damaged, and this represents the richest heritage of ancient inscriptions of all in Southeast Asia.

Besides the ten flower arts, there are some other popular Myanmar arts. All are amazing with their own unique styles.

Pottery (အိုးလုပ်ငန်း): Nowadays, the pots are used not only as water and food containers but also as decorations in guest rooms. Myanmar's handmade pots are very popular for their good appearance and reasonable price. You may notice that all Myanmar pots are very cute in their own way. Today, the main pottery works can be found in Nwe Nyein village, near Kyauk

Myanmar Pots

Myaung, a river-side town near Shwebo, and Twante, near Yangon.

Hmansi Shwecha

Mosaic (မှန်စီရွှေချ): Myanmar people know this art as 'Hman Si Shwe Cha'. Experts make the glass that is to be embossed or embedded in various sizes and shapes forming circles, squares, triangles, and ovals with valuable gems or semi-precious gems and pearls. You can see these arts in palaces, museums, old monasteries, and some royal buildings.

Tapestry (ရွှေချည်ထိုး): This art needs a lot of patience and time because it is all handmade needle work. The clothing worn by the kings, queens, and other royal family members were made of Tapestry (Shwe-chi-htoe). Foreigners have a great liking for this art, especially the colorful designs of the tapestry bags.

Tapestry

Gold foil

Gold Foil Making (ရွှေဆိုင်းလုပ်ငန်း): This is the art of making very thin gold leaf, especially to gild the pagodas and Buddha images. When you go to a pagoda, you will see that some people are gilding the Buddha images and praying. So, we can say that this is a noble art.

Wall Painting, Bark Painting, and Bottle painting (နံရံဆေးရေး၊ သစ်ခေါက်ပန်းချီ နှင့် ပုလင်းပန်းချီ): These are modern arts as there is a saying, 'Art improves with age'. These arts are amazing too and are attractive in the international market. This art is made on walls, on tree bark, and inside glass bottles.

Bottle painting

Gemstone painting

Palm Portrait and Gemstone Painting (ထန်းရွက်ပန်းချီ နှင့် ကျောက်စိမ်းပန်းချီ): These two arts are not purely paintings. They are mixed with a portraits skill. The artist has to create a portrait with leaves or gems upon the painting. People fall in love with those portrait paintings, too.

A Myanmar lady wearing Chaik Longyi

Silk Weaving (ပိုးယက်ကန်းထည်များ): For important and auspicious occasions, Myanmar people proudly wear locally woven silk. They call them 'chaik' and a Mandalay chaik longyi (ချိတ်လုံချည်) is very much appreciated by both men and women. Depending upon its design and quality, the price is high as well. Although availability of modern textile is on the rise with so many designs both local and from abroad, 'Chaik' can still win the Myanmar people's hearts.

Myanmar Chaik

Rattan/caneware (ကြိမ်ထည်ပစ္စည်းများ): Cane products are widely used in Myanmar, especially house-hold and office utility items such as baskets, chairs, table trays, cane balls, hats, penholders, photo and mirror frames, hand fans, floor mats, and partitions. Previously, it was made by village people and now this business has extended to the towns as small cottage industries.

Cane Products

Myanmar now exports cane/rattan products to other countries such as Holland, Germany, and France and has now become an important factor in Myanmar's economy.

Pathein Umbrella (ပုသိမ်ထီး): Making umbrellas with Myanmar traditional designs originated in Pathein (Ayeyarwady Region). So, it is popularly known as the Pathein Umbrella. The skeleton of the umbrella is made of bamboo and it is then wrapped in paper. After that, a colourful design is painted on the paper and it is put under the sun to get dry. Slowly, the makers began to become more innovative and they replace the paper with cloth, silk, or cotton canopies to make the umbrellas more durable and attractive. The whole system is made by hand and they have proven very attractive to foreigners as souvenirs, or to display in a lobby or on a lawn.

Pathein Umbrella

Myanmar Jade and Oyster Shell Carvings (မြန်မာ့ကျောက်စိမ်း နှင့် ကနကမာ ပစ္စည်းများ):

Myanmar is famous for its mineral resources, the ruby lands in Mogoke (Mandalay Region), and the jade mines in Phakant (Kachin State).

Every year, Myanmar obtains a large amount of foreign exchange from jade auctions as Myanmar Jade is well known in the international market. The combination of good quality Myanmar jade and the modernized workmanship from outside countries, especially China, results in excellent sales of these products.

Myanmar Jade

The world's biggest natural pearl originated from Myanmar and was found on the 19th of April, 2001. It was discovered during oyster fishing near Zardatgyi Island, Kawthaung Township. Its surface looked liked a brain, the colour was silvery and lustrous. It weighs (168.98) grams and measures (62mm x 50mm x 31mm). After taking out the precious pearls from the oysters, the mother-of-pearl shells can also be appreciated. Oyster shell carving is very attractive in its own way, too. It can be carved as portraits or as kitchen utensils, such small spoons, forks, knives, tooth-pick boxes, pepper containers, and ladies-ware like hairpins, hand chains, bracelets, etc. Nice products of oyster shell carving can be seen in the Bogyoke market in Yangon.

Oyster shell carving

Traditional Music, Dance, and Puppetry

Music is the universal language. They say that even a tree or an animal can respond to music. Music was started by mothers who tried to soothe their babies to sleep.

Myanmar Musical Instruments

Each country has its own national cultural heritage and musical instruments. Myanmar is no exception. There are basically five kinds of musical instruments. They are Brass, String, Leather, Wind, and Clapper.

A Myanmar orchestra is known as a 'Hsaing Waing' which literally means a drum circle suspended within a frame. Basically a Myanmar Hsaing Waing consists of seven sections: namely, drum circle, brass gong, rectangular gong, base drum, cornet oboe, clapper, and cymbal. The drum player is the leader of the Hsaing Waing.

A Myanmar Hsaing Waing is decorated with floral designs and mythical figures. However, although it is a beautiful ensemble made up of brass, leather, wind, and clapper instruments it does not include the traditional string   instrument. I would like to explain a little bit about the famous Myanmar harp, the 'Saung'.

The traditional Myanmar harp (String instrument) came into existence in AD 802 during the 'Pyu' kings. It is made of Cherry wood. Its body is shaped like a hollow boat. The hollow body is covered with deer skin. The strings are made of silk. According to the silk

Myanmar Orchestra

string's size and length, it produces different and beautiful tones. In ancient times, it included seven strings but over time it developed to include 16 strings. Its length is 32 inches. The Myanmar harp is played in a sitting position and held against the bosom.

Today, harps are being used not only as musical instruments but also as artefacts to decorate sitting rooms or other dwelling places, like hotel lobbies.

There is a very interesting riddle about the 'Myanmar Harp':

Myanmar Girl with harp

- *It lands on earth, but it is not a bird.* (မြေမှာသက် ငှက်လည်းမဟုတ်)

- *It is held against the bosom, but it is not a baby.* (ရင်မှာထား သားလည်းမဟုတ်)

- *It has a long beard, but it is not a Babu.* (မုတ်ဆိတ်ဖွား ကုလားလည်းမဟုတ်)

- *It has a curling tail, but it is not a monkey.* (အမြီးကောက် မျောက်လည်းမဟုတ်)

- *It sings a sweet melody, but it is not a maiden.* (အသံသာ ကညာလည်းမဟုတ်)

(*Babu – Indian man with a long beard)

Traditional Dance

Myanmar dance looks easy but, actually, it is not as easy as one might imagine. The dancers need to keep smiling, all the time, while they are dancing. Some dances require the dancer to sing, as well. Every part of the body, especially head, waist, feet and hands, need to move rhythmically according to the music. The costume for traditional dancers is made by special design and it covers nearly the whole body. Female dancers need to wear several layers. Nowadays, Westerners are also learning Myanmar dance. It is not only entertaining

Myanmar Traditional Dance

but also a good form of physical exercise. Myanmar has many races and each race has its own traditional dances.

There are different styles of dancing:

Bagan Dance : Bagan dances are slow and subtle. The dancers wear costumes like ancient royalities.

Ogre Dance: An ogre (Bilu) is a demon and can disguise itself in many forms. Ogre dancers wear the bilu mask and hold a knife. Ogre dance can be seen in the Ramayana drama. Dasagiri is the popular ogre in this drama who steals away the princess Sita - the lover of Rama, by disguising himself as a hermit while Rama was trying to catch the golden deer, which was in disguise as the sister of Dasagiri. Some writers say that the love of Dasagiri towards Sita is greater than that of Rama.

We can also see Rama's dance in the Ramayana drama, which originally came from ancient India. The dancers have to wear the masks of Rama, Lakkana, Sita, Dasagiri, the hermit, and the golden deer.

Kainnara and Kainnari Dance: These are an ancient couple of mythical birds. They have a human head and body, with wings. They are the symbol of true love. According to the traditional tales, they cried for 700 days and nights because of one night's separation due to heavy rainstorm and floods. The dancers dance with bird-like movements while accompanied by music.

Nat-kadaw Dance: The Nat-kadaw (spirit soothers) dance is to entertain or please the nats. The dancers wear a red headband and a tightly knotted red scarf around their chest. They dance as if they are possessed by the spirit of the nat. The dance is very serious. Sometimes they dance in a very rough manner according to the individual character of each of the 37 nats.

Oil Lamp Dance: This is a popular dance among the Myanmar traditional dances. The dancers perform as if they were making an offering light to Lord Buddha. While they are dancing, the performers' hands are always upturned to balance the oil lamps they are holding. They try to keep the flame alive until the end of the dance.

U Shwe Yoe and Daw Moe Dance: This performing couple dance with humour to entertain the crowds and volunteers who have completed digging a well or repairing a road. This dance is open to the public and can be seen along the roadside, too. The couple wear awkward costumes and sport funny faces. U Shwe Yoe is an old bachelor who is courting Daw Moe, a spinster, but she turns down his proposal with sarcastic words. Sometimes, both dancers are males resulting in an even more humorous performance.

Zat Pwe and Anyeint Dance: A Zat Pwe is an all night performance which continues until early morning, but Anyeint can end anytime after midnight. We can see traditional solo dances and duet dances in a Zat Pwe. The Zat Pwe and Anyeint are composed of many programs such as a stage show, an ancient drama, a modern drama, and duet dances which are performed by actors, actresses, singers, comedians, villains, and so on. Some people are addicted to watching Zat Pwe until, after a few nights, their eyes become like a panda's eyes!

Zawgyi Dance: A Zawgyi is a folk character in Myanmar tradition. He is an alchemist who usually wanders in the deep forest to find medicinal plants. We can see him depicted in a happy mood with a magic wand in his hand. With a touch of his magic wand, female shaped fruit becomes a real and beautiful lady who can fulfil his worldly desires. He usually wears a red coloured robe.

Zawgyi

Puppet Dance: Puppeteers manipulate the strings of the puppet making it appear as if it were alive, like a human dancer. In return, the human dancers enjoy dancing in a style reminiscent of puppets. Which one do you think is more difficult?

Puppets

Puppets are one of the tourist attractions in Myanmar. Traditional Myanmar puppet theatre (yoke thay) dated from the 15th century. In the 19th century, it reached the peak of its popularity. Some say that the custom of puppeteering started from within the royal family, when people in the palace tried to entertain the king's children, in former times.

The head, hands, and feet of the puppets are tied to the associated body parts. These parts are made of wood and clay. Then, the strings are attached across the piece and the puppet is dressed like a human dancer corresponding to its specific character. Most puppets have eleven strings. Five of these strings are attached from the head, shoulders, and rump to a wooden cross piece. The upper arms, thighs, and hands are operated with the six remaining strings which hang loose and are draped over the cross piece.

Myanmar Puppetry

Normally the puppeteers are required to stand behind a half curtain. Singers sit next to the puppet players and sing or speak according to the drama's script. In rural areas, puppet-shows can be seen at the pagoda festivals. In towns, some big hotels arrange puppet-shows to entertain their guests or upon a customer's request.

Actually, the art of puppeteering is not easy. The puppeteer has to manipulate all strings of the dancing puppets. Their talents are admired by both locals and foreigners. My personal curiosity about the puppeteers is whether they personally know how to dance or not. A puppet player confided to me that it is not necessary for them to know how to dance and that practise makes them perfect.

Flowers and Festivals in the Myanmar Calendar

There are twelve months in the Myanmar Calendar as with the Western calendar. But, every 4 years, there are thirteen months i.e. 2 months in 'Waso'. At that time, we say First Waso and Second Waso. Myanmar people call it 'War Htat' (ဝါထပ်) (War means Waso, Htat here means again, or overlapping). According to an old saying, if it is a War Htat year, there will be flooding or heavy rain in the rainy season. The Myanmar calendar is based on the cycles of the moon. Every month has its own waxing moon days and waning moon days. This means that after fifteen waxing days, there will be the full moon day and after every 14 or 15 waning days, there will be the new moon day. Every Myanmar month has its own festival.

There is a Myanmar saying "If you do not know the season, you may check with the flowers" (ရာသီမသိ ပန်းနဲ့သိ). In the Myanmar calendar, there are 12 months and so let's see which flowers bloom in which season:

1)   **Water Festival (Myanmar New Year):** This is the most popular festival in Myanmar. It falls in mid April. Water festival draws

No	Myanmar	Flowers	In Western Calendar	Festivals
1.	Tagu	Kantkaw, Yinkat	April-May	Water Festival (Thingyan)
2.	Kasone	Sankar flowers	May-June	Banyan Watering Festival
3.	Nayone	Jasmine and Mulay	June-July	Ti-Pi-Ta-Ka Examination (on the Buddhist Scriptures) (Sar Pyan Pwe)
4.	Waso	Ponnyat flowers	Jul-August	Waso Robe Offering
5.	Wakaung	Khattar	Aug-September	Sar Yae Tan Mae Pwe (Maha dote)
6.	Tawthaline	Yinnmar	Sept-October	Regatta Festivals
7.	Thadingyut	Five kinds of Lotus	Oct-November	Lights Festival
8.	Tasaungmone	Khawei	Nov-December	Kahtein Robe Offering
9.	Nattaw	Thazin	Dec-January	Literary Festival
10.	Pyatho	Kwarnyo	Jan-February	Equestrian Festival
11.	Tapotwe	Paukle	Feb-March	Htamanae (Glutinous rice) Festival
12.	Tabaung	Padauk, Tharaphi and Ingyin	Mar-April	Pagoda Festivals/Feast

everybody's attention, young or old, and the whole country is very excited when they think about the water festival. It does not fall annually on the same day. You have to check with the Myanmar calendar. Historically, every year, the royal astrologers (*Ponna*) from Mandalay calculated the details about the coming Myanmar year before the Water Festival. Events such as what time Thagyarmin (King of the celestial beings) will

Padauk Flower (Symbol of Water Festival)

come down to earth, what kind of animal he will ride, what is likely to happen, which products will be prosperous (or not), what sort of weather conditions (such as droughts or floods), what diseases will be prevalent, and so on. It is called the 'Thingyan sar' (Water Festival Prediction) and many, especially old people, take it very seriously. Thagyarmin usually comes down by riding something and holding something in his hands. For example, if Thagyarmin comes down to earth by bestriding a cow or a buffalo, the coming year will be abundant with rice or crops; if he rides a dragon, heavy rain; if a Garuda (mythical bird), it will be very windy or stormy. If he holds fire in his hand, it is a symbol of war or crisis; if he holds some

Water Festival during Bagan Era

flowers in his hand, it will be a peaceful and an auspicious year.

The king of the gods personally comes down during the water festival to take note of those who is doing good deeds and who is not. He brings two kinds of papers - one is made from gold sheets and one from a dog's skin. He writes down the good people's names on the gold sheets and the bad persons on the dog's skin. He observes very closely what people are doing during the Thingyan. If the people are religious and taking Sabbath, giving donations, releasing animals such as birds or fish, paying respects to seniors and elderly, he notes down those people's name on the gold paper. Even notorious people are very careful during these days because they are scared that their name will be listed on the dog's skin.

(One wonderful thing about Water Festival is the 'Thingyan Moe'- Water Festival Rain. Sometimes nature is very wonderful and beyond people's understanding. Water Festival is in the middle of the summer but every year, 2 or 3 weeks before Water Festival, the rain falls without fail. It is called 'the prelude or welcoming rain to the Water Festival'. At that time, we get the sweet aroma of the earth. People become very alert and excited about the New Year. It looks like the rain refreshes everybody and gives them strength to celebrate the Water Festival to its fullest. After the rain, the Padauk flowers start to bloom and, hence, the Padauk flower is a symbol of the Water Festival. They say that the Padauk is a very punctual and faithful flower. They bloom once in a year during Water Festival. Myanmar people usually say, "The Padauk flowers are blooming. Today is a good day!")

According to the old saying, "Human beings have been commiting sins the whole year". To cleanse those sins, they spray each other with water to symbolize that they are not carrying those sins or bad habits into the New Year. Water refreshes the people's mind and body so that in the New Year they can start afresh with a new mind and body. At this time, *Thagyarmin* comes down from heaven to the earth. You may see a small flower pot in front of every Buddhist's house to welcome Thagyarmin. Water Festival lasts for 4 days (5 days in some years) and the following day is the New Year.

For youngsters, this festival is a great opportunity to enjoy life to the fullest and to act crazy. Thingyan songs are on the air for a

Ingyin flowers

few months prior to the festival and people are very much amused. You may see pandals in every quarter and on every road. Even the small streets have their own small pandals. Some pandals are very big. Every government ministry, most of the companies and associations build their own pandals. Water pipes are placed on the front line of the pandals and girls can be seen standing ready to spray water upon cars and people who pass by the pandals. Everyone gets soaked.

The older people go to the monasteries to take Sabbath or to the meditation centres. During this opportune time, some young people make merit by washing the old people's hair very tenderly, clipping their nails, and paying respect with some food, clothing, or other. In this auspicious time, people set free some animals such as birds, fishes, and cows. Some make snacks like 'Mont lone yay paw' and donate them to monks and laypeople.

On New Year's evening, people prepare flower pots with some flowers and leaves, including thread, sand, and water, to be placed where monks will recite Suttas together. Every quarter has its own places to recite. At the end of the monks' recitation, the laypeople bring those holy pots back to their homes and spread the sand and water on the surrounding fences to dispel evil and put the flowers in each corner of the fences. They keep the thread for the babies to wear for good health. Those recitations (Suttas) are meant to dispel evil forces and afterwards they beat empty barrels or some utensils which can make the loudest noise possible. At the same time, in some quarters, people make fires (especially in the villages), to scare away the evil spirits or ghosts, so that the coming year will be very safe and auspicious.

2)   **Banyan Watering Festival**: This festival falls on the full moon day of Kason, the second month of the Myanmar calendar. The full moon day of Kason is a day of three-fold significance – the day Buddha was born, the day He attained Enlightenment, and the day of His demise. On that day, people go to a pagoda to water the roots of the sacred Bodhi or Bo tree representing the tree where Buddha attained Enlightenment while meditating under it.

3) **Ti-Pitaka Examination**: Nayon is the time of holding the Ti-Pitaka Examination Festival. That holy examination is for monks and nuns who participate as the sons and daughters of Lord Buddha. The examination period and ceremony that followed is called 'Sar-pyan pwe'.

Khattar Flowers

4) **Waso-Robe Offering Festival**: The full moon day of Waso is the beginning of the Buddhist Lent. During the 3 months of this Lent period, marriages, or moving house are discouraged for laymen, and moving from one monastery to another, or travelling for an overnight stay are prohibited for monks. During this month, people donate robes to the monks.

5) **Maha-Dote Festival**: The Maha-dote Festival is celebrated in Wagaung. In Lord Buddha's lifetime, 'Maha-dote' was the name of a very poor man who became very rich after offering meals to Lord Kassapa Buddha. Lord Kassapa Buddha accepted only his offerings while wealthy persons were trying to make offerings to the Buddha thinking that Maha-dote could not afford to donate meals to the Lord Buddha due to his poverty. During this month, every house is assigned to take care for the monks' breakfast or lunch. Not only that, but people go to their village monastery to contribute their donations to a long queue of monks, who also come from nearby villages. It is also called 'Sayey tan mae pwe'.

6) **Regatta Festival**: Tawthalin is the time for the Royal Regatta Festival. In the Western calendar, it is in September and boat races are held in practically every river and lake throughout the country.

7) **Festival of Light**: The Light Festival falls in the month of Thadingyut. It is also the end of the Buddhist lent (from July to October). This festival lasts for 3 days – the full moon day, and the days before and after the full moon day. Starting from the evening, you can observe that the whole town is full of beautiful lanterns. The pagodas are crowded with people who donate candle lights. It is not only a time of joy, but also a time for thanks giving and paying homage to elders, teachers, and parents, requesting forgiveness for whatever misdeeds they may have committed in the past so that they will not carry these sins into the future.

Actually, this festival originated from the time when people welcomed back the Lord Buddha with offerings of lights when He descended from the Tusita Heaven after He stayed there during the whole Lent period and preached to celestial beings, including His mother, who was reborn in this heaven.

8) **Kahtain-robe offering Festival**: It is the time to weave the 'Mathoe Thingan' (Everfresh Robe) to donate to the Buddha. Groups of young women work hard weaving the saffron-colored robes throughout the whole night and, the following full moon day, offer it to the Buddha. On that day, the groups of weavers compete with each other as to which group will finish first while a traditional music troupe plays to encourage them. People donate Kahtain robes to the monks in this season. It is their belief that by doing this act of merit, a place in heaven is reserved for donors and the door to hell is automatically shut down.

Fire balloons festival at Taunggyi

Tazaungmone is full of colourful activities. On the full moon night, naughty young people can behave as thieves and they move things from one house to another. They may write down on a signboard in front of a spinster's or old bachelor's house, 'Husband/wife is urgently required' and other such practical jokes. All herbal plants are most effectively harvested during the Tazaungmone full moon night. This being so, people eat Mezali (*Cassia siamea*) bud salad as medicine. Streets, houses and buildings are full of colourful lights and people release fire balloons, too.

9) **Literary Activities**: In the Myanmar calendar, the ninth month is Nattaw (December) and it is the time for literary activities, honouring those to whom honour is due from the times of the Myanmar kings. Awards ceremonies in various fields of literary work are usually held on the first day of the waxing moon in Nattaw. Writers and poets travel all over the country to meet their readers and hold seminars, discussions, and talks on various literary subjects.

10)   **Equestrian Festival**: Pyatho is the time to celebrate the Royal Equestrian Festival. In ancient times, people showed off their abilities in the presence of the king and queen, such as martial arts, and the games played while riding horses. All were amazing. The custom of holding an equestrian festival is now being revived and promoted by the government.

Equestrian Festival in ancient time

11)   **Hta-ma-nae Festival**: Hta-ma-nae is a popular Myanmar food made of glutinous rice and this festival falls in Tabotwe. Many hands are needed to make it. The rice is first soaked in water to get soft before they start cooking it. A group of women prepare the ingredients, such as peeling ginger, slicing coconuts, and heating up the peanuts. When everything is ready, a giant, concave iron pot is placed over the fireplace and oil is put in it. When the oil becomes hot, ginger is the first to go in, second is the glutinous rice, and then two or three strong men, each with a huge wooden ladle, begin to stir the rice thoroughly. While they are stirring the rice,

A group of people making Htamanae

sliced coconuts, roasted peanuts, and salt are added, one by one. Roasted sesame seeds are added last and the flavour of 'Hta-ma-nae' depends on the sesame seeds. It needs not only strength, but also skill to have a good taste and a good mixture.

12)   **Pagoda Festival**: Tabaung is the month of the Pagoda Festivals. Myanmar is the land of pagodas and each pagoda has its own festival days. But most of the pagodas' festivals fall in Tabaung, the last month in the Myanmar calendar. This festival may be compared to the carnivals in Western countries. Pagoda Festivals are the most picturesque sight of Myanmar and they widely represent a part of the Myanmar people's lifestyle and enjoyment. The Pagoda areas are crowded with many consumers' goods shops, toy shops, food stalls, merry-go-rounds, magic shows, puppet shows, the famous Zat pwe (dramas), and Anyeint. It is the time of enjoyment for both young and old.

Night scene of a pagoda festival

Language and Literature

Myanmar language

According to the historical record, Myanmar literature is more than 1000 years old. The Myanmar language has 33 letters in it while the English has 26. There are also 12 vowels. Here is the chart of Myanmar alphabet and numbers.

က	ခ	ဂ	ဃ	င
စ	ဆ	ဇ	ဈ	ဉ
ည	ဋ	ဌ	ဍ	ဎ
ဏ	တ	ထ	ဒ	ဓ
န	ပ	ဖ	ဗ	ဘ
မ	ယ	ရ	လ	ဝ
	သ	ဟ	အ	

0	1	2	3	4	5	6	7	8	9
၀	၁	၂	၃	၄	၅	၆	၇	၈	၉

The arrangement of a simple Myanmar sentence is *subject-object-verb* while English sentence is *subject-verb-object*. For example:

I go to school (in English). Kyuntaw Kyaung thot thwarthi.' (in Myanmar). 'Kyuntaw' means 'I', 'Kyaung thot' means 'to school' and 'thwar thi' means 'go'.

There are 'loan words' in Myanmar language too. For example;

- ☞ The words such as 'driver' 'radio' 'telephone' came from the English language.

- ☞ 'Samsara' 'Dukkha', 'Nibban' derived from the Pali language.

- ☞ 'Prata', 'Coolie', originated from the Indian language.

- 'Zayat', 'salaung', 'kadaw' came from the Mon language.
- 'Eukyarkway' 'htawlargyi' 'kawpyant' are adopted from the Chinese language.

There are different styles of speaking in the Myanmar language. When Myanmars speak with monks or the ancient royal family, they cannot use the normal usages. They have to use a very polite usage. For example, 'Hote kei' means 'yes' in Myanmar language. Instead of 'Hote kei', they say 'Tin Pa phayar' to monks and 'Hman hla pa phayar' to the ancient kings. Instead of 'Thay thi' ('die' in Myanmar language), they say 'Pyan lun taw mu thi' for the monks and 'Nat ywa san thi' for the kings.

The followings are some simple domestic usages:

- (မင်္ဂလာပါ။) Mingalarbar! - Hi, Hello. Auspicious day! (You can use this greeting anytime, anywhere except in sad occasions).
- (နေကောင်းလား။) Nay Kaung Lar? - How are you?
- (ဘယ်အချိန် ရုံးသွားမှာလဲ။) Bae a chain yone thwar hmar lae? - What time will you go to office?
- (ကားခဘယ်လောက်လဲ။) Kar kha bae lauk lae? - How much is taxi fare?
- (ရွှေတိဂုံဘုရား သွားချင်တယ်။) Shwedagon Phayar thwar chin tae - I want to go to Shwedagon pagoda.
- (ကယ်ပါအုံး။) Kae par ohn - Help me!
- (သူခိုးဗျို့၊ သူခိုး။) Thakhoe! Thakhoe! - Thief! Thief!
- (ဒီနားမှာ ကောင်းတဲ့ မုန့်ဟင်းခါးဆိုင် ရှိပါသလား။) De nar mhar kaung tae Mohinga sai shi lar? - Is there any good Mohinga shop nearby?
- (ကျေးဇူးတင်ပါတယ်။) Kyay zu tin bar tae - Thank you.
- (တာ့တာ။) Tah, tah! - Bye Bye!

Usages and Dialects - Myanmar people call each other's name by prefix according to their age or rank. If the person is about the age of an uncle or father, they prefix 'U/Daw' (means Mr./Mrs.) or uncle/aunty. Among friends or someone of the same age, they refer to a nick name without any prefix. If the person is older, they prefix

'Ko' for male and 'Ma' for female (mean brother/sister). Normally, they never call an elder person by his nick name although they are friendly. Sometimes you may hear the habit of calling mother/father or grandpa/grandma to old strangers, especially in villages. For example, if the old woman's name is Daw Sein, young people may call her 'A May Sein' or 'A Phwar Sein' with love and respect. 'A May' or 'May May' means mother and 'A Phwar' or 'Phwar Phwar' means grandma in Myanmar language.

As Myanmar has a lot of regions, there are many dialects as well. You can guess a person's native heritage if you listen to their tone or pronunciation of the Myanmar language. In each region, their speaking styles of the Myanmar language are different and each tribe has their own peculiar way of pronunciation. For example, people fromTaungoo pronounce 'sh' sound for both 'ch' and 'sh'. If they say "Chit tae" (Love you), you will hear "Shit Tae" (Scratch you). They are not aware of their own regional pronunciation until people from another town cannot help smiling upon hearing their mispronunciation. When they say "Bar hin chat lae?" (What curry do you cook?), you will hear "Bar hin shet lae?" (Which curry is shy?)

In the English language, the pronoun 'I' can be used for both sexes. But in Myanmar, 'Kyun-taw' is the pronoun for a man and 'Kyun-ma' for a woman. If a girl uses 'Kyun-taw' in expressing herself, you can be sure that she is from Mandalay. The women from Mandalay usually refer to themselves as 'Kyun-taw'. It is distinctive to the very lovely and outstanding dialect of Mandalay.

'Ma Shi Buu' means 'do not have' and 'Ma Thi Buu' means 'do not know' in the Myanmar language. Rakhine people, however, omit the last word 'Buu'. They usually reply 'Ma Shi', 'Ma Thi', etc...'Sar' means 'eat' in the Myanmar language, but people from upper Myanmar say 'Iway' instead of 'sar'.

In ancient times, the royal family called their mother 'Mae Mae'. Nowadays, we call mother 'May May'. But in Myeik and Dawei regions, that usage is still common in some families. In Myeik, they say 'Kyay Pyar' instead of 'Pike San'. 'Pike san' means 'money' and 'kyay pyar' means 'coins'. So both usages have similar meanings.

In Myanmar language, there are some terms which cannot be directly translated into the English language. For example the saying,

'Thabeik hmauk' in Myanmar means 'boycott' in English. 'Thabeik' means 'monk's bowl' and 'hmauk' means 'turn down'. Myanmar people often use to say, 'arr nar tae'. The nearest expressions of 'Arr nar tae' are 'I'm afraid' or 'I do not want to bother you'. Actually, the saying 'Arr Nar Tae' is very difficult to translate it into other languages as it has very subtle meanings and cultural nuances. Normally, they use it when they owe some small gratitude to each other or after doing a small mistake.

Slang usages (Slanguages) : Most of the slang usages can be heard when young people or very close friends talk to each other freely. However, there are some popular slanguages which are used by both young and old people. For example, 'Bae Oo' means 'Duck egg' in the Myanmar language. But nowadays people call the police 'Bae Oo' (ဘဲဥ) behind their back as the round white hats they wear look like duck eggs. The word 'Boe Taw' (ဘိုးတော်) is used for their boss or employer or an old senior person as 'Boe Taw' is the name of the one of the ancient Myanmar kings 'Boe Taw Phaya'. Not only that, Boe Taw is the royal usage for 'grandpa' in ancient time and 'Bwar Taw' means 'grandma'. 'Bike nar tae' means 'tummy pain' in the Myanmar language but people use its meaning as 'urgently in need of money'. For example, "He will sell his house/car for a reduced amount because he is in 'bike nar tae' now." The usage 'Bike nar tae' (ဗိုက်နာတယ်) is popular among businessmen who are in the property business.

Myanmar people enjoy using the riddles too. It is an enjoyable custom in rural areas where under the moonlight, a person makes riddles and the rest of the people have to find the answers. While most of them are still brainstorming, a person can say the right answer and they all become very happy and smile. *For example:*

- *(The answers are below and before you check the answer, please think yourself for a while.)*

1) 5 persons bring it, 32 persons grind it, then fold it with a mat, and put it into a cave. What is it?
2) It appears once a year, like a prince holding white umbrella. What is it? (Hint: an edible thing)
3) Nobody washes it, but it is very white.
   Nobody fills it, but it is full of water like angel's well.

What is it?

The answers:

1) *'Eating rice with hand'. The reason is Myanmar people take rice with their hand. So, 'five persons' means 'hand or five fingers', '32 persons' means '32 teeth', 'fold with a mat' means 'tongue' and 'put it into the cave' means 'throat'.*

2) *'Mushroom'. It appears only in its seasonal time and looks like a white umbrella.*

3) Coconut

Myanmar Literature

Myanmar literature is more mystical and deeper than Western languages. Like English literature, Myanmar literature has drama, poetry, novel, short stories and prose. Literary Criticism is taught in the University level.

Myanmar literature has been handed down from generation to generation as Myanmar passed through the eras of Bagan Era, Pinya, Innwa, Taungoo, Nyaung Yan, Konbaung, Colonialism (before Independence), and after Independence.

As 'Pen is mightier than sword', Myanmar literature reached its climax under the colonialism due to the strong emotion that aroused a patriotic spirit. A lot of talented writers appeared during that time.

Most of the dramas are played about real stories of Buddha's 550 previous lives. These stories are extracted from '550 Nipattaw'.

Short stories like 'Akha mae Coolie htan chin a kyo' (The benefit of being a volunteer coolie) by U Pho Kyar (1891-1942) and 'Bilatpyan Mg Thaung Pe' (England-return Mg Thaung Pe) which is extracted from the novel 'Shwe Pyi Soe' by U Latt are still popular till now because they are not only educational but also very entertaining.

James Hla Kyaw's (1866-1919) 'Ko Yin Mg, Ma Mae Ma' and P. Monin's (1883-1940) 'Nay-yi-yi, Nay-nyo-nyo' novels were the masterpieces of those writers.

Theippan Maung Wa (1899-1942) and Shwe Oo Daung wrote

some popular dramas. Literary alchemist 'Saya Zawgyi (1907-1990)' transmitted the old records into poems and essays which gave Myanmar history a new outlook for young people. Thakhin Kotaw Hmine (1876-1964) and Hmawbi Saya Thein (1862-1942) are the outstanding writers of 20ᵗʰ century.

In Myanmar history, there are many poets, too. Some poets were great fighters from the royal military service like 'Natshinnaung (940-974)' and 'Nawadaygyi (860-950)'. Natshinnaung is famous for his romantic love poems. Some great poets were monks like Shin Maha Rahtathara (830-892), Shin Maha Thilawuntha (815-880). Some were ministers like Myawaddy Mingyi U Sa (1128-1215), Wungyi Padaytha Yaza (946-1016) and Latwae Thondara (1085-1161). Ma Mya Kalay (1171-1207) and Hlaing Htaik Khaung Tin (1195-1237) were two famous poetesses of the royal family.

Myanmar poems are very subtle and deep. That is one of the difficulties in translating poems from Myanmar to English. For example, when we read a poem, we can see the scene in our mind's eyes and we can get the smell of crops or flowers. But how can we translate this to readers of the English language?

'Mya Zedi Stone inscription' (Rajakumar stone inscription)

They say that Myanmar literature started from the stone inscriptions. The 'Mya Zedi' Stone inscription (မြစေတီကျောက်စာ) is the earliest stone script according to historical record. It was situated in the compound of 'Mya Zedi pagoda' in Bagan. The writer was the prince 'Rajakumar. In this way, it came to be known as 'Rajakumar Stone Inscription'. It was carved around 474 according to the Myanmar calendar (1113 AD), one year after the prince's father passed away. He wrote it in four languages: Pyu, Mon, Myanmar and Pali. There were four surfaces on the stone and he carved one language on each surface.

Rajakumar (ရာဇကုမာရ်) was the only son of king Kyansittha. After Anawrahta passed away, Kyansittha ascended the throne and ruled Bagan. Rajakumar arrived at the palace when his father was bed ridden and at that time, the king had already made a decision to bestow his throne to the grandson 'Alaungsithu'.

Rajakumar according to Myanmar history was full of virtues. People knew him as a 'kind-hearted', 'dutiful' and 'noble-minded' son. In Myanmar history, there were some princes who usurped the thrones of their fathers, but Rajakumar had a noble character. When he knew that his father had already decided to give the throne to his grandson, not even a single thought of anger entered his noble mind. His mind had already been tamed under the guidance of his monk teacher and religious mother when he was growing up in his home village. Not only that, he sold all of the treasures which he had inherited from his mother and he made a gold Buddha image as a donation for his dying father. After that, he wrote the 'Mya Zedi' Stone inscription as a record of his donation. Under the guidance of his religious mother and the teacher-monk, he recognized the gratitude towards his parents and arranged this donation to repay his gratitude to his father.

Carving stone inscriptions started to be popular during Bagan era. There are three characteristics of a stone inscription:

1) About a donation - It is for the people to rejoice and share merit

2) Prayer   - It is their wish and main intention

3) Curse   - It is to prevent harm from the destroyers

Here is the direct translation of the 'Rajakumar stone inscription':

❑ In this auspicious time, I pray to Buddha.

❑ 1628 after the Lord Buddha's time, a virtuous king 'Sri Tribhuvanadityadhammaraj' ruled 'Arimaddanapur' capital.

❑ The name of a dear wife of that king was 'Trilokavatamsakadevi'.

❑ She had a son named 'Rajakumar'.

❑ The king gave his beloved wife three villages. After she passed away, the king gave these three villages and her jewelleries to their son 'Rajakumar'.

❑ After ruling 28 years, the king was going to pass away.

- His beloved wife's son 'Rajakumar' made a Gold Buddha image to repay his gratitude to his father.

- He handed that Buddha to the king. The king rejoiced at his donation by saying "well-done, well-done" when he said :

- "I, your slave, made this Gold Buddha for my lord; the three villages of slaves which my lord gave me, I gave to this Gold Buddha."

- He made his donation by water dropping in front of seven great monks named 'Shin Sri Mahather', 'Shin Sri Muggaliputtatissatther, 'Shin Sri Sumedha, 'Shin Sri Brahmapal', 'Shin Sri Brahmadiv', 'Shin Sri Son' and 'Shin Sri Sanghasena'.

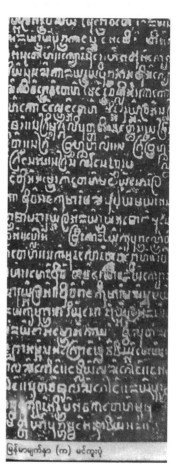

Myazedi Stone Inscription in Myanmar Language

- After that, 'Rajakumar' enshrined this Gold Buddha and made a stupa.

- He donated three villages named 'Sakmunalon', 'Rapay' and 'Henbuiw' to that pagoda by water dropping and then Rajakumar pray:

- "May this meritorious work, performed and accumulated by me, be the cause of my attaining Omniscience! Whosoever, be he my son, or grandson, or any other relative, with evil intent and unbelieving mind should oppress those slaves, dwellers in the three villages, whom I have dedicated to the cave-pagoda and the gold image of the Great Sage, may this vile person be precluded from beholding the future Buddha 'Arimittiya'!

Proverbs

Proverbs were born from daily experiences, life's lessons and intellectual wisdom. Our great grandparents left those proverbs as a literary heritage for the young generations. Speeches, writings, discussions and day to day speaking become more effective by using the proverbs instead of long explanation. The followings are some well-known Myanmar proverbs and are easy to understand:

1. Ignorance is worse than poverty.

2. Even the god cannot fulfil a man's wishes.

3. Nobody can steal the golden pot of wisdom.

4. Can stand the heat on back but cannot stand the heat on ears. (means 'can work hard but cannot stand the frettings')

5. Trap the rabbit, but get the cat.

6. Regrets always come later.

7. Stay in suitable place than enjoyable place. (Do not chase after enjoyments)

8. If you are unaware, even a cave cannot be seen. If mindful, even a dew can be seen. (How terrible the unawareness is!)

9. A wise man never reveals his anger.

10. Do not try to cover the dead elephant with a goat's skin. (When a person is using the lame excuse, you can say this proverb)

11. Snake to snake, see the leg. (Snakes have no legs. But crooks can see what other crooks will do.)

12. The breeze can bring the scent of the flowers; the human beings bring each other's news. (If you want to know about a person, inquire among his friends)

13. Mango among fruits, pork among meats, tea among leaves (are the best)

14. You can stop speaking to someone, but you cannot stop being related.

15. Do use a needle in time, or you might need an axe later. (same as 'A stitch in time saves nine')

16. Collect the water while it rains. (Make hay dry while the sun shines.)

17. You can even be a God, if you try. (Everything is possible)

18. A person is fair among the lepers.

19. Old cows like tender grass.

20. Puppy licks your cheeks and ears if you give him favors. (Familiarity breeds contempt)

21. There's only 2 ways: go crazy, or go extraordinary! (Be somebody!)

22. You can pull back your hand, but not your committed word. (Be careful how you speak)

23. It's dress in a man, bindings in baskets' edging (are important)

24. Bone in chicken, gene in man. (that one must beware)

25. Before the bending arm straighten, or before the straighten arm bends (Death can come anytime).

26. It's like catching two eels at a time. (Doing two unsure things at a time, instead of doing one certain thing.)

27. Harrow before the cow.

28. Forget to bring the cow, when going out to plough. (when the most essential thing is forgotten, you can use this proverb.)

29. Oath in a king, promise in men. (are to keep)

30. Although silks are used, but Maung Pon still does not know how to play harp. (Waste of time and energy)

31. No more arrows, before getting into battle. (who wants to surrender before fighting)

32. Two may become enemies, when their ideas are the same.

33. If there are too many teachers or leaders with different ideas, the follower cannot do anything and learn nothing.

34. An unmarried woman is not honoured, even if she has 10 brothers.

35. A boat-load of fish gets spoiled, because of one Barbus fish.

36. You fail if you're afraid. If brave, you may become a king.

37. A genuine ruby won't sink in mud.

38. Fisherman near fisherman. Hunter near hunter. (choose your friends wisely)

39. One yard a day, Bagan won't move. (Do it a little every day, and you'll achieve)

40. A lawyer who has never been defeated. A physician who has his patients never die. (They never exist)

41. Seek wisdom like a beggar. (Be humble)

42. You cannot be lucky forever. (ups and downs in life)

43. Praise and blame last only seven days.

44. Do not retaliate hatred with hatred. (Because it will never end)

45. There is no escape for a criminal. (kings have long arms)

46. Ways will be found where there are needs. (where there is will, there is a way)

47. Once died, you know the price of a coffin. (gain lesson only from one's experience)

48. Like putting the bamboo quiver on the dog's crooked tail. (a person who goes back to his original habit all the time)

49. Take refuge in a hillock thinking that is a pagoda until a monitor lizard comes out from it. (illusions)

50. Money will not stay with the stupid person.

51. Toddy (liquor from palm tree) reveals the theft of a buffalo. (A drunkard cannot keep the secret)

52. Dry paddy after the sunset; ploughing the field when the rainy season is over. (for a lazy person)

53. Nobody is to be blamed but yourself. (When we trace the beginning of the problem, we find that the source of the problem comes from us).

54. Stupid person gets the idea when it is too late.

55. Picking up the frogs and putting them into a bag with a hole. (cannot save the money)

56. While the cat is away, the mice are very playful.

57. If you are in a hurry, use the old road. (May be the new road is not familiar to you and you may be delayed)

58. Only when you stumble, you remember your mother. (One's mother is ignored until one is in trouble)

59. If you offend the teacher, the spear will pierce your throat.

There are true stories behind some proverbs. For example:

Once upon a time, a cowboy saw that an egret was catching a fish. Before eating the fish, the egret lifted it up and caught it with his beak. After seeing that, cowboy got an idea and he first practised like that egret with a bamboo stick. When he became confident, he used the spear instead of the stick. He played it in front of people and people were amazed. He became popular for his stunt and that news reached the king. He performed well a few times in front of the king and the king was so pleased that he gave the cowboy a lot of rewards. The king became curious and asked, "Where did you learn this?" The cowboy did not want to admit that he learnt it from an egret. He feared that the king would look down on him because his teacher was a bird. So he answered, "It is my own innovation." After giving that lie, when he performed the next time, the spear pierced his throat and he died.

The proverb "If you offend the teacher, the spear will pierce your throat." (ဆရာကို အာခံလျှင် အာခေါင် လုံစူးတတ်သည်။) originated from that true story.

မြန်မာ့ရိုးရာစကားပုံများ

၁။ မရှိတာထက် မသိတာခက်

၂။ လူ့အလို နတ်မလိုက်နိုင်

၃။ ပညာရွှေအိုး လူမခိုး

၄။ ကျောပူတာခံနိုင်တယ် နားပူတာမခံနိုင်ပါ

၅။ ယုန်ထောင် ကြောင်မိ

၆။ နောင်တဆိုတာ နောင်မှရ

၇။ ပျော်ရာမှာမနေနဲ့ တော်ရာမှာနေ

၈။ သတိမမူ ဂူမမြင်၊ သတိမူရင် မြူ‌တောင်မြင်

၉။ လူလီမှာအမျက်၊ အပြင်မထွက်

၁၀။ ဆင်သေကို ဆိတ်သားရေနဲ့ မဖုံးနဲ့

၁၁။ မြွေမြွေချင်း ခြေမြင်

၁၂။ ပန်းသတင်းလေညှင်းဆောင်၊ လူသတင်းလူချင်းဆောင်

၁၃။ အသီးမှာ သရက်၊ အသားမှာ ဝက်၊ အရွက်မှာ လက်ဖက်

၁၄။ မခေါ်ဘဲနေလို့ရမယ်၊ အမျိုးမတော်ဘဲနေလို့မရပါ

၁၅။ အပ်နဲ့ထွင်းရမည့်ကိစ္စ ပေါက်ဆိန်နဲ့ပေါက်နေရဦးမည်

၁၆။ မိုးရွှာတုန်း ရေခံ

၁၇။ ကြိုးစားရင် ဘုရားတောင်ဖြစ်နိုင်သည်

၁၈။ အနုတောမှာ လူချော

၁၉။ နွားအို မျက်နှ‌ကြိုက်

၂၀။ ခွေးကလေးအရောဝင် ပါးလျက်နားလျက်

၂၁။ ထူးလျှင်ထူး မထူးလျှင်ရှူးလိမ့်မည်

၂၂။ လက်ကျွံလျှင် နတ်လို့ရ၊ စကားကျွံလျှင် နတ်လို့မရ (သေချာစဉ်းစားပြီးမှ ပြောပါ)

၂၃။ လူမှာအဝတ်၊ တောင်မှာအကွပ်

၂၄။ လူမှာအမျိုး၊ ကြက်မှာအရိုး

၂၅။ ကွေးသောလက် မဆန့်မီ၊ ဆန့်သောလက် မကွေးမီ (အနိစ္စသဘောတရား)

၂၆။ ငါးရှဉ့်နှစ်ကောင် တစ်ပြိုင်တည်းမဖမ်းနဲ့

၂၇။ နွားရှေ့ထွန်ကြူး

၂၈။ လယ်ထွန်သွား နွားမွေ

၂၉။ မင်းမှာသစ္စာ လူမှာကတိ

၃၀။ ပိုးသာကုန် မောင်ပုံစောင်းမတတ်

၃၁။ စစ်မရောက်ခင် မြားကုန်

၃၂။ အကြံတူ ရန်သူ

၃၃။ ဆရာများ သားသေ

၃၄။ မောင်တစ်ကျိပ်ရှိသော်ငြား၊ လင်မရှိလျှင် မတင့်တယ်

၃၅။ ငါးခုံးမတစ်ကောင်ကြောင့်၊ တစ်လှေလုံးပုတ်

၃၆။ ကြောက်လျှင်လွဲ၊ ရဲလျှင်မင်းဖြစ်

၃၇။ ပတ္တမြားမှန်ရင်၊ နွံမနစ်

၃၈။ တံငါနားနီး တံငါ၊ မုဆိုးနားနီး မုဆိုး

၃၉။ တနေ့တလံ၊ ပုဂံဘယ်ရွှေမလဲ

၄၀။ မမှားသော ရှေ့နေ၊ မသေသော ဆေးသမား

၄၁။ ပညာရှာ၊ ပမာသူဖုန်းစား

၄၂။ ကံအမြဲ မကောင်းနိုင်

၄၃။ ချိုးမွမ်းခုနစ်ရက် ကွဲရဲ့ခုနစ်ရက်

၄၄။ ရန်ကိုရန်ချင်း မတုန့်နှင်းနဲ့

၄၅။ ရာဇဝတ်ဘေး ပြေးမလွတ်

၄၆။ လိုလျှင်ကြံဆ နည်းလမ်းရ

၄၇။ တစ်ခါသေဖူး ပျဉ်ဖိုးနားလည်

၄၈။ ခွေးမီးကောက် ကျည်တောက်စွပ်

၄၉။ ဘုရားမှတ်လို့ကိုးကွယ်နေ၊ ဖွတ်ထွက်မှ တောင်ပို့မှန်းသိ

၅၀။ လူမိုက်နှင့်ငွေ အတူမနေ

၅၁။ ထန်းရေမူး ကျွဲခိုးပေါ်

၅၂။ နေဝင်မှ စပါးလုန်း၊ မိုးလွန်မှ ထွန်ချ

၅၃။ ဘယ်သူမပြု မိမိမှု

၅၄။ လူမိုက်နောက်မှ အကြံရ

၅၅။ ပလိုင်းပေါက်နှင့်ဖားကောက်

၅၆။ ကြောင်မရှိ ကြွက်ထ

၅၇။ အလျင်လို လမ်းအိုလိုက်

၅၈။ ခလုတ်ထိမှ အမိတ

၅၉။ ဆရာအာခံ အာခေါင်လုံစူး

Life-time Occasions

Wedding

Marriage is the second most serious thing which Myanmar people consider as a matter of life and death. Parents play a vital role in their children's marriage. 'Setting a suitable marriage for children' is one of their main duties and without the parents' agreement, the wedding is far off. There are some stories that, in the old days, the boy had to work in the girl's house for about 10 years so that the parents could observe him very well. If they liked the boy, they agreed to bestow their daughter to him. They said that in olden days, the couple had to observe each other for 3 years before marriage. Myanmar parents want to see their children 'Riding elephants and surrounded by horses' (ဆင်စီး မြင်းရံ) instead of 'Elephants stepping and horses kicking' (ဆင်နင်း မြင်းကန်) in married life. As they are conservative people, they believe that there are three things in life which cannot be erased or undone after committing: 'Marriage, building a pagoda, and getting tattoo'. That's why they are very careful about married life.

Myanmar bride and groom

In ancient times, regardless of appearance, a wife was chosen by checking the kitchen at her house and a husband was chosen by checking at his bed. If the mother in law to be was invited to the girl's house, she would go to the kitchen first and observed how her future daughter in law handled the kitchen, how clean the kitchen was and so on. Because kitchen was the place where the money flowed out everyday and it was important for a wife to cook proper and healthy food for the whole family. The kitchen should be clean and there should be no wasted food over. If she could cope well with kitchen matters, it was not much to worry for other things. If the girl's parents wanted to know the habits of their son-in-law to be, they asked someone to quietly check the bed of that man. They said that after a man got up from bed, if he kept his bedding properly in a high place, he came from a holy existence; if he kept those things on his bed, he came from human existence; but if he did not keep the pillows properly, did not fold his blankets and did not take off his mosquito net (chin htaung) it meant he came from animal existence.

Wedding ceremonies can vary from one place to another depending upon their status or financial strength. Nowadays, there are a lot of places to celebrate, such as hotels, monasteries, churches, town halls, at the boat club or at their own houses. Before the marriage, as usual, both sides have many decisions to make at the engagement ceremony, such as when or where the wedding will take place, how many people they will invite, what kind of foods they will offer to the guests and after the marriage, where the couple will stay, etc. If the girl's side accepts the engagement, it means that the marriage is fifty percent sure because if the girl's side does not agree, even the engagement will not happen. Then they choose an auspicious day to celebrate the wedding by consulting with an astrologer or monk. It is also a great opportunity to let people know their wealth and status. They may print all the degrees they have achieved and positions of the whole family in the wedding invitation card. Weddings can be celebrated anytime except during the Buddhist Lent, which lasts about 3 months from full moon day of Waso to full moon day of Thadingyut, (roughly from mid July to mid Oct).

The wedding day is a very exciting day. Normally, the boy's side has to bear the expenses. If it is a Hotel wedding, they will hire a music band and popular singers; they will invite honourable persons to show off their important contacts; they will decorate themselves with many jewellery to show off their wealth; and you will see a lot of nice flowers on the stage and tables. First, the announcer will introduce both families to the guests by microphone from the stage. He/she praises both sides as best as they can, after that he invites the bride, groom, and parents to come up on the stage. They exchange the wedding rings with the assistanceof an honourable guest and then the guests can eat while being entertained with music. Gifts are received at the entrance of the wedding hall. A city wedding will last only about one and a half to two hours (as another wedding is going to occupy the hall) but a village wedding can last about half a day. Besides the wedding ceremony, wealthy people can hold a wedding dinner at a restaurant on that night. Here, when you give a wedding gift, you should not give a knife or scissors, or something like that, because they are superstitious and it is their belief that those are the symbol of fighting or quarrelling and their marriage cannot last long. After they get married, it is not necessary for the Myanmar ladies to put husband's name behind their names or to change their names.

You may see a strange custom taking place after the wedding. Some close friends and relatives queue at the door of the wedding chamber asking for a 'bride price' from the young couple by barring them with gold chains. They barter the amount until everyone is satisfied and finally the newly-wed couple is allowed to enter their room.

Naming ceremony or Giving birth

Myanmar people have no preference in having a baby boy or girl. They appreciate both equally. They say, "a boy is like strength for parents while a girl is like an umbrella to them". But there is also a counter saying to this. "A boy becomes a tiger, if he is not good, and girl becomes fire" (လိမ္မာရင် အား မလိမ္မာရင် ကျား) (လိမ္မာ ရင် ထီး၊ မလိမ္မာရင် မီး). In ancient times, when a baby was born to a wealthy family, they invited a learned person. He put some gold ornaments into a clean cup, together with water, to wash the baby's hair and to give shower, so that the baby would be rich. When you go to admire the newborn baby, you should not say, "the baby is so fat" or "so heavy", because if you say like that, an ogre may hear and come to harm the baby. That belief comes from an ancient story about an ogre and a baby (please read the story about 'Manussiha' under the Shwedagon Pagoda chapter). Some people celebrate a naming ceremony for their baby, 'Kin Poon Tat Mingalar', on the 100th day after the delivery day. The Myanmar naming system is quite independent. It is not essential to include father's name. For example, the names of U Zaw Win's children can be 'Nay Toe', 'Thuzar Tun', 'Su Myat Noe', etc... Instead of putting the father's name, they are more concerned about choosing a proper name according to their birth date. For example, Monday-born babies should start their names with Ka, Kha, Ga, Gha, Nga (က၊ ခ၊ ဂ၊ ဃ၊ င) etc. (Please see the detail in the chapter 'Seven Birthday and their characteristics'.) For example, 'Kyaw Thu', 'Khin Khin Htar' and 'Graham' are the names of Monday-borns. To get an auspicious name for their baby, they are anxious to consult with an astrologer or a monk.

Novitiation Ceremony (Shin Pyu)

This is a holy ceremony. A boy's life has two auspicious times while a girl has only one. It means a boy has 'Novitiation and wedding' ceremonies in his life time. They believe that sending their son to enter the monkhood is the same as booking a place in paradise after their death; or at least they close the gates of hell. A boy can be a novice at the age of 9 -10 years when he is ready to learn how to wear the robe, not to take food after 12 noon, and other Buddhist precepts.

The village novitiation ceremony takes two days. The first day is 'Ahlu-lay' (small feast) and the second day is 'Ahlu-gyi' (great feast). On the first celebration day, the boy is dressed up like a prince. He goes to the monastery riding a beautiful elephant or horse and is protected by a white umbrella. (He looks like an ancient king visiting the town with many followers). Those novice-to-be are called 'Maung Shin Laung'. Poor people, if they cannot afford to hire a horse or an elephant, carry their sons on their shoulder or on bicycles. They say that a 'Maung Shin Laung' should not touch the ground. In urban places, people can use the cars instead of the horses or elephants. Many people, including his parents, are around him. They are

Novitiation ceremony in village

wearing very nice clothes, too. You may see joy mixed with pride on the parents' faces for their treasured son when they send him to the monastery to be a novice. When they reach there, the monk shave the boy's hair and the parents hold a white cloth to catch his hair

Maung Shin Laung

before it drop to the ground. The monks teach him everything - how to wear a robe; how to behave; all the do's and don'ts in accordance with the Buddha's teaching. Prayers and Buddhist chants add to the moment. The 'Sayadaw' (chief monk) gives the novice a new name called 'Bwe'.The duration of the novicehood is usually from at least three days to a week. After becoming a novice, he is regarded as a higher person in a religious way (like Baptism in Christianity). Some novices stay in the monastery for a long time and they can become monks when they are twenty years old.

There are precepts for the novices:

1) Not to kill other's life
2) Not to steal
3) Not to commit sexual relations
4) Not to say a lie
5) Not to drink alcohol
6) Not to eat after mid-day
7) Not to sing, dance, play on any musical instruments
8) Not to use cosmetics or beautify the face
9) Not to use too comfortable bed and sitting places
10) Not to touch money and precious thing's such as gold and jewelleries

Among the above Ten Precepts, no. (1) to (5) are obligatory for all layman Buddhists but not to commit 'sexual misconduct' instead of 'sexual relations' and No. (6) to (10) are additional for the novices and nuns.

Some wealthy families hire a traditional music band and dancers for the night time of the novitiation ceremony to entertain the people. In a village, it will take nearly the whole day. They build a pandal infront of the house and, according to the tradition of the village, everybody comes and helps them. If their compound is not big enough to build a temporary pandal, it can be built at the village monastery. The ceremony is like a feast for the whole village. They provide food for nearly the whole day, including a heavy lunch. In addition to the meal, they offer Myanmar snacks, plain tea, green tea leaf salad (Laphet Thoke), betel-quid, and cheroots, too. If a poor family cannot afford the novitiation ceremony for their son, they celebrate together with another two or three families, or more. In a village, some poor people borrow money from others to celebrate the novitiation for their children and as a result, they owe a great debt.

In some families, if there is no boy, they can put a girl into the nunnery. But to be a nun is not compulsory like becoming a novice.

Funeral

As most Myanmar people are Buddhists, they believe that death is just a threshold to another life. They believe in rebirth. Although sometimes you may fail to attend a wedding, you should never fail to show your face at a funeral or the bereaved family will feel upset due to your negligence. If you cannot attend for a sound reason, it is better to send a card, flowers, or a message. There is a saying among Myanmar people, 'Funeral one time; monastery ten times' (မသာတစ်ခေါက်၊ ကျောင်းဆယ်ခေါက်). It means that the merit amount you gain from sending a dead person to a cemetery one time is equivalent to going to monastery ten times to take the Sabbath.

Ferry fare – As they believe in rebirth they put a 25 pya coin in the corpse's mouth to pay the ferry fare when he goes to the next world. He has to travel life after life. That habit is still valid until now. Once it is certain that he is no longer alive, by checking with the doctor, they wash the body clean and put on his favourite clothing. If it is a woman, make up can be applied, according to their request, before passing away.When a Myanmar Buddhist dies, it is necessary to invite the monks three times for 'Thet pyauk swun' (သက်ပျောက်ဆွမ်း), 'Myay Kya Swun' (မြေကျဆွမ်း) and 'Yet Lae Swun' (ရက်လည်ဆွမ်း). As soon as a person is dead, a monk from a nearby place is invited urgently and offerings given for 'Thet pyauk swun' (praying for the spirit which leaves the body). In front of the house, they put a small signboard by writing the name and age of the dead person. A pot of plain tea and black watermelon seeds are offered at that house until the funeral. At night, the windows and doors are opened so that the spirit of the dead person can wander around the house and card playing is allowed at night so that there are people at the house. They keep the deceased for 3 to 5 days before cremation. On the funeral day, three or five monks are invited to pray for the deceased. It is called 'Myay Kya Swun' (praying for burying the dead).

After the funeral, they bring back some dirt from the funeral ground or a leaf near the corpse to the house so that the dead knows his way home from the cemetery. It means the spirit of the deceased can stay at home for a week. On the 7th day, 'Yet Lae Nay', a group of monks are invited and given offerings for 'Yet Lae Swun' and the monks pray for the dead person. Without 'Tharanagon thone par' (taking refuge in three gems; Buddha, Teachings, and Order), it can never be a complete Myanmar Buddhist funeral.The monks recite it for him to reach a higher existence. In addition, the spirit can accept the donation for him/her to reach to a higher existence. The monk calls the name of the deceased and says loudly, "May the deceased and all beings share in the merit that their relatives are doing now." Not only that they allow him to go free by saying, "You can go anywhere you wish and you don't have to dwell at home anymore". If the deceased is in government service, it is very important that his/her department announces, "You are now liberated and nothing concerned with our association anymore" so that the spirit can be free and he no longer feels that he is still in service. Monthly and annual donations for the deceased person are made in remembrance of the bereaved family.

Phonegyi-Pyan (ဘုန်းကြီးပျံ) - means monk's funeral. It is quite different from a layman's funeral. If a sayadaw, the Abbot, of a monastery passes away, the whole village may come and cry to offer their condolence. Contributions from the whole village are collected depending upon their financial status. They say that 'Phone Gyi Pyan' cannot be celebrated during Buddhist Lent period. They will keep the body for about one week or 10 days (sometimes they keep for a few months depending upon the rank of the monk). If

A Pyre preparing by the villagers for Phonegyi Pyan cremation

the body is to be kept for a long period, the internal parts of the body are taken out and preserve the corpse. It is put inside a glass coffin which is decorated elaborately. The pyathatt (pyre) is built outside of the village for the cremation (please see in the photo). The mourners also come from the nearby villages. They will perform funeral rites like a festival to pay their last tribute to their beloved sayadaw. Monks' funerals are usually crowded with people who come to see the entertainment like dramas, traditional music band, shops, and some gambling. 'Aye-yin-kyuu' (အေသင်ကျူး) (dirge recitation by professional mourners) is essential at the abbot's funeral. She will sing a funeral song in tears and praise the virtue of the departed monk and sometimes with a short drama about the departed monk. On the final day, the performance becomes the highest. She has to perform as if she refuses to give up the Sayadaw's body when the holy beings are coming down to take it to their Heavenly home. It is like a tragic drama. As their performance is very touching, it can move the audience to tears. Sayadaw's coffin is carried from the monastery to the cremation place (outside of the village) on a barge and only the monks can carry or handle sayadaw's coffin from one place to another. The cremation is done in the late afternoon. The next morning, people go to that place to pick up the bones. Some say that when a few great monks pass away, their bodies remain unrotten and even the hairs grow as if they were still alive. It means that they had gained a certain stage of meditative power.

Mode of Eating, Dressing, Behaviours and Habits

Table Manners

You may see in villages, a Myanmar eating table, which is a round wooden one with short legs so that no chairs are needed. The family sit on mats or stools and have their meals together. Whenever they take meal, they take off their slippers (except on some occasions) to pay respects to the meal because food gives energy for humans to live. Myanmar meals are very simple. Every meal consists of rice and curry. They take meals three times a day- breakfast, lunch and dinner. Although they take rice and curry for lunch and dinner, breakfast will be of a variety of foods, such as fried rice, mohinga, steamed sticky rice, coconut noodles, ekyarkway and tea, prata or dumplings. As Myanmar lies between two big countries, China and India, they enjoy Chinese and Indian food, too. The way they cook their own food is not as spicy as Indian food nor as sweet as Chinese food. Myanmar curries are a mixture of those two types except a little bit oilier.

Myanmar Eating table

The eldest person sits nearest to the altar side. 'First come, first serve' is not a custom of Myanmar eating tables. The other persons should not take the meal unless the eldest do. But if you first serve a spoonful of curry to the eldest person, to show him respect, the rest can start eating. It is considered impolite to talk too much while eating. If you are thinking of taking more rice, do not eat all the rice from the plate, a fistful amount should be left or it will lead to poverty.They use a plate to put the rice and bowls to put the curries. Spoons are used to serve the curry. Normally, they take the rice with their hands and a fork and spoon are not needed. This tradition is rarely followed in rich families and in urban areas. Taking rice with the hands is also considered paying respect to the rice. As they are conservative, they (except the most sociable) are not used to talking too much with strangers. You may notice that manner especially at dinner parties. Some may be stuck in silence while the foreigners are discussing all manner of topics at such occasions.

Myanmar curries are very simple to cook. Within a few days, you can learn to cook many kinds of foods from Myanmar's kitchen. They do not need many cooking utensils except for a stone mortar and pestle (ဆုံနှင့် ဆုံကျည်ပွေ့) to pound the garlic, onion, and ginger. The basic style of Myanmar cooking is:–

Stone mortar and pestle

- Before cooking, apply salt to the meats, a little bit of turmeric powder and seasoning powder can be added and then left for a while.

- Pound the ginger, garlic and onions with a stone mortar

- Cut the tomatoes into small pieces.

- If everything is ready, put the cooking pot on the stove. When the pot becomes hot, first pour in some oil, as much as you like. When the oil is hot, add the mashed ingredients and fry them for a few minutes. Then, add the tomatoes to form a paste and add color and then continue to fry for a while. Finally, you can put all sorts of meats and cook until these become tender. (If you would like more color, you can add chilli powder. Some people also put shrimp paste according to taste).

Clothing

Myanmar men and women wear a longyi or htamane similar to the sarong in Malaysia. On special occasions, they wear good quality textiles like silk. Men wear a Tai-pon (traditional jacket) and women wear long sleeves with a traditional Chaik longyi. Normally, they wear a cool or thin type of textile due to the country's warm climate.

A Singaporean visitor once asked me whether Myanmar men wear underpants or not when they wear longyi. When they take shower in a village, where a private bathroom is not available, women tie their htamane up to the armpits. They are very simply contented people. They do not keep many clothes at home. They keep only a few sets of clothing to wear on special occasions and some for daily wear. Excessively revealing or inviting styles of women's clothing are rarely found.

A Myanmar lady in olden days

Women, either young or old, apply Thanakhar paste (which can be obtained by grinding the bark of a Thanakhar tree with water on a circular slab of stone) which makes the skin cool and complexion fair. It can be called Myanmar traditional make–up. Myanmar women like to put flowers in their hair. You may see all the women putting decorative flowers in their hair on important occasions such as a graduation ceremony, wedding ceremony, and other special events. They believe that flowers are auspicious things, good in both appearance and scent. One of my foreigner friends told me that when she attended a Myanmar wedding, she was very worried lest she be stung by a bee which was flying around the beautiful big flowers in the hair of the lady next to her.

Behaviour and Habits

You may think that Myanmar people are very friendly and concerned persons because when they meet you at meal time, they may greet you by asking, "Have you eaten?". If the answer is positive, they continue, "What curry have you eaten?". If the answer is negative, they may play host to you. When they bump into each other on the street they say, "Where are you going?"or "Where have you been?" instead of saying, "Hi" or "Hello".

You may often hear them say, "Arr Nar Tae" (အားနာတယ်) among members of Myanmar society. This habit causes misunderstanding to foreigners who are staying or doing business in Myanmar. Because

A Myanmar Woman

of this 'Arr Nar Tae' mind, sometimes simple things can become complicated, although they are simple minded people. 'Arr Nar Tae' roughly means "I feel bad" or "I don't want to bother you" in English.

Genuineness is common in Myanmar people. They are not used to tact or pretence in relationships, even in the business field. A foreigner says that the mood of Myanmar people can easily be read on their faces, such as when they are in a happy mood, or experiencing sorrow, like, or dislike.

Greeting by hugging is not practised and greeting by kissing is regarded as Western culture. You may not see kissing in public even between a man and his wife. Women seldom shake hands when they are introduced to another person, she just smiles and nods her head.

When you explore the countryside by car or train, you will see paddy fields, buffalo carts, small bales of dry hay near small huts, and evergreen trees everywhere as Myanmar is an agricultural country. You can enjoy the fresh air and natural, simple sight-seeing. Pagodas and monasteries are everywhere along the way as Myanmar is a devoutly Buddhist country.

One lovely nature of Myanmar's people is that you do not have to make appointment with them when you want to pay a visit. They will never get angry if you visit their house without informing them in advance. They will welcome you. Not only that, they may offer you a meal with pot luck if you reach them at their eating time. They love to be hospitable. But you must also keep in mind that they may, too, pay you a visit without prior notice.

By nature, they are helpful people. They never hesitate to direct you when you ask for an address. They are very willing to let you know if you ask where there is a good Mohingha shop or a good astrologer. They never hesitate to help you if you fall down on the road or if a baby is crying to find his lost mother or has lost his way home.

The followings are some etiquette for the young Myanmar people to observe:

- You should not step on the shadow of elder people or monks. If they unintentionally step on it, they have to say 'Kan dawt, Kan dawt' (ကန့်တော့၊ ကန့်တော့) (means 'pardon me').

- Do not interrupt while elder persons are talking.

- A young person must bend his/her body when they pass in front of an elder or senior person.

- When they give or hand something to an elder person, they give it by holding it either with both hands or with the right hand supported by the left.

- The youngest person has to wash all the dishes of the elders after eating together.

- Although they can take rice with the right hand, they should not take the curry with their hands.

- When you take rice with your hands, the rice should not be too much and only a moderate mouthful should be put into your mouth at one time.

- If the curry you want is out of your reach, politely ask another to serve it for you.

- Before they go out on a trip, they usually pay respect to their parents for a safe journey.

- Young people usually carry the bags of their parents or seniors when they walk together.

- When you talk with elder persons, don't talk standing on one leg, or lean on the table, or put your hands on the waist. You must talk to them properly with due respect.

Duties and Responsibilities; The Eighteen Noble Arts

The tie between parents and children among Myanmar families are very strong. The parents think that their responsibilities will never end. They are ready to sacrifice for their children their whole life no matter how old or how ungrateful their children may be.

The five duties of parents are:

1) To guide their children away from wrong doings
2) To show the correct ways
3) To give them education
4) To provide them investment
5) To arrange suitable marriage

Let's see the five duties of children too:

1) To look after the parents
2) To take responsibilities for their parents' affairs
3) To perpetuate the family
4) To be worthy of one's inheritance
5) To perform works of merit on their parents' behalf

There is a saying, "If we compare the parents' gratitude; the highest Mt. Myintmo becomes the horn of a cattle; the ocean becomes water from the buffalo's footprint; the universe becomes a leaf of plum tree".

As Myanmar people are very conservative, the duties between husband and wife are quite strict. Living together between unmarried couple is unacceptable and the adultery is a shameful matter in Myanmar society.

The five duties of the husband are:

1) To love and adore his wife
2) Not to ignore her
3) To avoid adultery

4) To endow her what you have earned
5) To please her with clothes and ornaments

In return, the wife has:
1) To manage efficiently all domestic affairs
2) To look after the relatives of both sides
3) To be faithful to her husband
4) To keep the property safe
5) No to be lazy

Among teachers and pupils, they have their own respective duties.

Teacher's duties:
1) To train them to be disciplined
2) Not to withhold some knowledge
3) To send them to better places (upon the student's own aptitude)
4) To admonish and encourage them
5) To protect them from wrong ways

The following duties are expected from the students:
1) To be diligent
2) To listen to the teacher's advice
3) To greet him with delight when he comes
4) To learn what he teaches
5) To respect and look after them

The duties between friends:
1) To be generous
2) To have sympathy
3) Doing business together
4) Talk friendly
5) To be faithful

The duties of a master/employer to servants:
1) To give enough food
2) To manage them properly
3) To cure if they are sick
4) To share some necessary things
5) To let them go out sometimes

From the servants/employees:
1) To sleep later than the employers
2) But to wake up earlier than their masters
3) To take only what the boss gives
4) To work things well with loyalty
5) To acknowledge the master's goodwill

Five duties of the Dayakar (laymen) to the monks or religious teachers:
1) To keep admiration in mind
2) Do his necessary things
3) Talk with respect and polite words
4) Invite to house when necessary
5) Donate as much as possible

There are six duties of the Monks or hermits:
1) To prevent from wrong doings
2) To direct the correct way (with the religious knowledge)
3) Preach new sermons
4) But repeat the old preachings too if necessary
5) To show the way to heaven
6) To be kind to all beings

There is a general saying in Myanmar relationship, 'Pay respects to the elders; admiration for the same age; be kind to the younger' (ကြီးသူ့ကို ရိုသေ၊ ရွယ်တူကို လေးစား၊ ငယ်သူ့ကို သနား). As long as you obey that adage, every relationship will be smooth.

The 18 Noble Arts

In olden days, all princes of Myanmar royal families and all noblemen from the wealthy families have to learn 18 Essential Arts. It was known as 'Ahtar Ratha Set Shit Yat' in Myanmar language. But girls are less likely to concern themselves with these subjects. The 18 subjects are:

1. Astrology
The study of the supposed influence of the stars on human destiny.

2. Law
The study of rules established by custom, agreement, or authority.

3. Arithmetic
The study of mathematics and calculating by means of numbers such as addition, subtraction, multiplication, division and so on.

4. Yoga
The study of exercises for the relaxation of body and mind.

5. Do's and Dont's
The study of a subject learning about etiquettes among the human society. It is also known as 'Lawka Niti' in Myanmar language.

6. Science
The study of the substances, identification, experimental investigation, and theoretical explanation of phenomena and sometimes practical laboratory.

7. Music
The study of the art of arranging sounds through melody, harmony, rhythm, and tone.

8. Algebra
The study of a branch of mathematics which is used with letters or alphabet to represent the numbers and quantities.

9. Martial arts
The study of the physical arts for combat or self-defence.

10. History
The study of common records of past events (of a country or a person, etc.).

11. Astronomy
The study of the stars, moon and planets.

12. Poetry
The study of the beautiful word arrangement which comes out from the poet's emotion.

13. Physiology
The study of the bodily functions of living things and their parts.

14. Pretence
The study of the quality or state of being pretentious; ostentation.

15. Disciplines
The study of training to be orderly for moral or mental improvement.

16. Literature
The study of writing and learning especially novels, poetry and dramas.

17. Grammar
The study of how to use and combine the words correctly to form sentences.

18. Mantra
The study of sacred verbal formula to pray repeatedly or incantation for mystical potentialities.

Thirty-Eight Auspicious Deeds

At the time when people wondered how these Thirty-Eight auspicious deeds (သုံးဆယ့်ရှစ်ဖြာမင်္ဂလာ) appeared, Ashin Ananda explained to them, 'I have heard that: At one time the Buddha was staying at the Jetavana monastery of Anathapindika in Savatthi. Late at night, a certain deva (male celestial being), whose surpassing beauty illuminated the whole Jetavana came to the Blessed One. Standing in a suitable place, he respectfully addressed the Glorious One in this verse':

'Many men and devas, desiring happiness, have pondered on the question of blessing, but could not get the right answer. May you please, O Venerable One, tell me what is the noblest of blessings.'

(For twelve years, men and devas had tried in vain to discover the basis of prosperity and happiness. The Lord Buddha has expounded such a basis comprised of the Thirty-Eight auspicious deeds, which can remove all evils and bring about prosperity and happiness to both men and devas.)

Those Thirty-Eight Auspicious Deeds are:

1) Not to associate with fools
2) To associate with the wise
3) To honour those worthy of honour
4) To live in a suitable locality
5) To have done good deeds in the past
6) To set oneself on the right course
7) To be possessed of vast learning
8) To be possessed of skill
9) To be well trained in discipline
10) To have pleasant and good speech
11) To support mother and father
12) To cherish wife and children
13) To have an unconfused occupation
14) To give alms

15) To live righteously in accordance with the Dhamma
16) To help relatives
17) To do blameless deeds
18) To cease from sins
19) To abstain from sins
20) To refrain from intoxicants
21) To be vigilant in righteous acts
22) Reverence
23) Humbleness
24) Contentment
25) Gratitude
26) Listening the Dhamma at proper times
27) To be patient
28) To be obedient
29) To meet with holy persons
30) To discuss Dhamma at proper times
31) To restrain from worldly pleasures
32) To live a holy and pure life
33) To have insight knowledge of the 'Four Noble Truths'
34) To realize 'Nibbana' for oneself
35) A mind that is unshaken by contact with worldly conditions
36) A mind that is sorrowless
37) A mind that is passionless
38) A mind that is secure

►► *Regardless of age, religion and caste, those who obey and do the above auspicious deeds will gain prosperity and happiness everywhere.*

Thanakhar, Ngapi, Toddy and Chewing Betel-quids

Thanakhar

Thanakhar (သနပ်ခါး) is a kind of fragrant paste which is obtained by grinding the bark of the Thanakhar tree on a circular, flat stone with a little bit of water. It is white-yellowish colour. Sandalwood is the nearest similarity to Thanakhar. The Thanakhar tree (*Limonia acidissima*) can be planted in a dry zone. So the best quality Thanakhar is obtained from Shwebo, Pakhoku, and Shinmataung. When I was in University, one of my classmates applied Thanakhar every day. She was very good looking with her unique style while other University students applied make up. She was popularly known among the men as the 'Shwebo Princess'.

Thanakhar and Kyauk Pyin

The advantages of Thanakhar are many. Women apply it not only for beauty but also for improving skin complexion because it can make the skin cool. It is the best skin protection in hot weather. It can be used as a medicine for small insect bites from mosquitoes, ants, etc. It can be utilized for mild skin problems like pimples and

Thanakhar Girl Applying Thanakhar To Mr. KB Tan

acne. Myanmar mothers feed a little bit of Thanakhar to their infants to be healthy. Even some men apply Thanakhar at home to make their skin cool. Thanakhar can be applied all over the whole body.

Myanmar women young or old like to apply Thanakhar. Some make a leaf shape, circular shape, or heart shape and apply it on their cheeks resulting in a beautiful appearance. Although modern cosmetics are in abundance, Myanmar women are still in love with traditional Thanakhar. Nowadays, they make the Thanakhar with modern methods to preserve it longer and it is packed in plastic boxes. In this way it is very convenient for women to bring Thanakhar when they go out on a trip. Applying Thanakhar is very compatible with Myanmar weather and the women who have to work in direct sunlight, such as construction workers, or paddy transplanters, apply very thick thanakhar on their faces. There are so many Myanmar songs which praise Thanakhar, such as the Thanakhar on a mother's cheek, or Thanakhar on a lover's cheek.

After a tiring day, before you go to sleep, take a shower, apply Thanakhar all over the whole body and go to bed with a mild, natural fragrance and cool feeling. It will give you a sound sleep and nice dreams!

Ngapi

Ngapi (ငါးပိ) is a preserved food made from either small fish or shrimps. As most of the people from rural areas are poor, Ngapi is very convenient food for them. It can be kept for a long time without refrigeration and it is very easy to cook quickly.

There are two main types of Ngapi: 'Seinsar Ngapi' and 'Yaygyo Ngapi'. Seinsar Ngapi which is a major product of lower Myanmar, especially in the Myeik area, which is made of preserved shrimps. Yaygyo Ngapi, on the other hand, is made of small, preserved fish and is characterized by a strong, fishy smell, and salty taste. They put a little bit of Seinsar Ngapi when they cook Myanmar curry to have a better taste. It can be heated and pounded along with chilli and garlic to create 'Ngapi htaung'. Ngapi Yaygyo has to be boiled and filtered for bones. Then, powdered dry prawns and chillis are added to become 'Ngapi Yay'. It becomes a type of fish gravy. It is like a thick soup,

Small Fishes under the Sun

but not meant for drinking. They take it with variety of vegetables, some fresh, some raw, or boiled. Some are preserved, such as cucumbers, bean sprouts, boiled watercress, or egg-plant. Those vegetables eaten with Ngapi yay are called 'Toh-za-ya' (တို့စရာ). When they preserve the small fish to make Ngapi, some liquid drops to the bottom of the pot and it is used as a fish paste. It can also be put into curry when they cook and then it is called fish sauce (Ngan Pyar Yay). Similarly, we can obtain Ngan Pyar Yay (Shrimp Sauce) out of Seinsar Ngapi.

In the delta area, we can also get a good quality of shrimp paste (Ngapi Seinsar), fish paste (Ngapi Yaygyo) and salted dried fish (Nga chauk). Not only that, but when they preserve the good quality fish together with some rice it becomes 'fish cake' (Nga chin). It is sour and salty. Fish cake can be taken as salad by mixing it with sliced onion, chilli, coriander (Nannan pin), and oil. Some big fish can also be preserved as Ngapi-gaung'.

In the rainy season, when the fish are very active and abundant, the fishermen catch a lot of them. In villages, nearly every house preserves Ngapi for their own use in big earthen pots. They put as much small fish inside the pot as possible by pressing them together with salt and in that way it can last until the next season. That's why, the expression 'Ngapi theik, Nga chin theik' (press like Ngapi and Nga chin) can be used in a crowded bus when the bus conductors ask the passengers to go in despite the fact that the bus is full already. Besides their own use, some people can sell Ngapi at the market to get some extra income. So they do not need to worry about curry problem as in most of the villages the market is not available. Before they put the small fishes and salt into the big pots, the small fishes are put under the sun for one or two days. (Please see the photo.).

Ngapiyay and Tohsayar

In U Thagadoe's book, 'Sulanaphar and other herbal medicines' on page 163, he mentioned that Ngapi is rich in vitamin D and can help with physical growth and brain development. He recommends that parents should let their babies eat a little bit of Ngapi in their young age. As Ngapi is made from the whole body of small fish, eating Ngapi means you will attain the energy of the whole body of the fish, even the bones. So, we should not regard 'Ngapi' as a poor man's curry and we can appreciate it as one of the favourite curries of the Myanmar people. In Myanmar restaurants, it is customary to offer 'Ngapi Yay with 'Toh-za-ya' as a side dish.

Toddy

Nature provides us with food, clothing, and shelter. Toddy (ထန်းရည်) comes from the spadix of the toddy palm. Toddy palm or palmyra palm trees are everywhere in Myanmar's rural areas. The palm tree climbers climb up the palm trees, one after another, in the early morning. Some can climb about 50 palm trees a day. They bring some earthen pots and a knife along with them. When they reach the top of the trees, they pounded and cut the top of the spadix and put the pots under it to get the toddy (palm sap). It is called 'Htan yay' in the Myanmar language. Morning toddy is soft and sweet similar to sugarcane juice. If you wait longer, until the afternoon, it becomes stronger and the taste changes. The longer you keep it, the stronger the taste like wine. By evening, the taste is the strongest and the sweetness disappears, becoming a type of liquor. You should not keep toddy overnight because sometimes you may get diarrhoea as it becomes more fermented. You should always take it fresh within the same day. Women take the morning toddy and men, who like the strong taste, take the afternoon toddy. After selling out all the afternoon toddy, the work of a palm climber is finished and the next day, he repeats his routine work again.

When they boil the morning toddy in a big pot over an open fire, they get jaggery (palm candy). Jaggery is very medicinal. It can assist in digesting foods quickly and it can diminish toxicity. So, if you suffer from food poisoning, you should take a lot of jaggery. You may find a jaggery bottle if you check the kitchen of Myanmar houses. Jaggery is served in Myanmar restaurants as a snack after a meal.

So palm climbers earn their living by selling toddy and jaggery. Not only that, but their families also make palm cake (Htan thee moh). It is made of the yellow colored, outer shell of the palm fruits. The inner flesh of the fruit kernel can be taken fresh. We can get 'Htan thee moh' in the morning market. It is nice, too.

So if you want to forget about the world for about half a day, you can go to the palm fields and take a drink of strong toddy to get some relief from your stress and strain. When I was in University, I learned the poems of the Persian, fatalist poet, Ohmar Khayyam (1048-1131). He usually praised the virtues of wine and love in his poems. The following verse is extracted from Ohmar Khayyam's Rubaiyat, which was translated into English by Edward Fitzerald (1809-1883).

A Toddy Climber

Ah, my beloved, fill the cup that clears

Today of past regrets and future fears-

Tomorrow?---Why, tomorrow I may be

Myself with Yesterdays' sev'n thousand years.

If there were to be such a chance, I would like to bring that great poet to the shady palm fields and let him have a sip of toddy. Then, I would like to inquire whether he wants to amend his poem to 'Love and Toddy', instead of 'Love and wine'.

Chewing Betel-quid

When I was in the Middle School, our history teacher gave us some general knowledge in the class. She said, in ancient times, when there were no cosmetics, women (including the royal family) chewed betel-quid to color their lips red. They beautified themselves with natural things. But, if not only the lips, but the teeth become red, will it be good looking still?

Kun ait

Some say that the habit of chewing betel-quid (ကွမ်းဝါးခြင်း) arrived Myanmar, together with Buddhism, from India. It is one of Myanmar's ancient customs that if a guest comes, the host serve him with plain tea, betel-quids, cheroots, etc. In ancient times, most Myanmar, even the royal family, took betel-quid. Small pieces of betel-nut are put in betel leaves and eaten together with some paste of limestone, cumin, tobacco, and cardamom seeds as desired. In villages, they keep betel-nut and leaves in a box to offer guests (please see in the photo). The betel box (kun-ait) is made of copper or aluminium. The box has three layers. The tool to cut the betel-nut (called 'kun-hnyat'), betel-nut, and small limestone box are in the top layer. Tobacco is in the middle layer, and the betel leaves are in the lowest layer.

There are some sayings related to betel-quid: 'Kun-taung-kine', 'Kun-ta-yar nyet' period, 'Kun-ta-yar and yay-ta-hmote' and so on. 'Kun-taung-kine' means a belle (the most beautiful girl) of the village and its direct Myanmar meaning is 'holding the betel-box'. Because in a village if there is a ceremony, like novitiation, all the beautiful girls are invited to walk ahead in a long queue holding things like betel boxes, robes, etc. 'Kun-ta-yar nyet' is a period of time and it refers to about 10 to 15 minutes within which time a betel-quid is chewed well. In ancient times, some people said to each other, "Please wait for me for about a kun-ta-yar-nyet period. I am busy now!" 'Kun ta-yar and yay-ta-hmote' means 'A quid of betel and a cup of water'. That saying comes from the story of Byatwi. (Please read the story of Byatwi under 'Taungpyone/Nat festival').

Betel-nut and leaves are very medicinal, too. If you suffer from dysentery or diarrhoea, put the betel-nut in water for a few hours until the liquid become acrid tasting and drink it. If you are coughing, you can take the Myanmar medicine 'Yet sar' together with betel leaves. Some people give a bath to their baby with betel leaves water to take out the heat from the baby's body. Some highway drivers chew betel-quid to prevent sleepiness. Some say that chewing a little bit of betel-quid can make the teeth strong. But everything has a limit, as the saying goes, 'An overdose is dangerous while a moderate amount is medicine'. As betel-quid is taken with lime (limestone), if you take too much, you may get a stone inside your body (like a gall stone, urine stone, kidney stone) and your teeth will get ugly. A person says that he can stand not taking a meal but he cannot stand with no betel-quid to chew.

Betal-quids for sale

Nowadays, the City Development Committee is promoting a campaign to get rid of the habit of chewing betel-quid with a view to keep the city clean. They will charge a fine if people spit after chewing betel-quid in public places.

Games and Sports

"Let the children be happy". Basically a happy childhood will not be complete without playing games. The more they play, the more they will be intelligent, more cheerful and more encouraged to do the good things in the future. Roughly speaking, games are for the children and sports are for the adults. Games have less discipline and more freedom while sports have a lot of disciplines to observe. Both games and sports can make a person fit in body and mind.

Games

Most of Myanmar games are played in the open air and need no uniform. There are a few popular games.

a) **Htoke See Htoe** : It needs two teams consisting of 4, 5 players 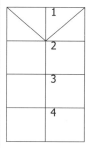 in each. Before the game is started, they draw the marked off areas as shown. People from one team have to stand on the lines and catch another team who are trying to pass through the lines from the beginning to the end. If someone is caught, they start the game again by changing the run.

A group of children playing Htoke See Htoe

b) **Di- Htoe** : A person has to pursue other players by shouting "Di" continuously until one of them is caught. If he/she can catch a person, she can be liberated and it is the latter's turn to shout and catch them again. Some players can shout 'di' for so long and they can catch more than one person within one chase.

c) **Shwe Swon Nyo Bar Lo Loh Wae** : It is a kind of tagging game, too. One player tries to catch the player who is at the end of the long queue facing him. Normally, they put the youngest or the shortest person at the end of the queue while the front people are covering him/her not to be caught by the single opponent who is acting as Shwe swon Nyo (Golden kite). It is a very cute game. Before they start the tagging, it is customary to make some questions and answers such as :

Golden Kite Game

- A group of people : "Golden kite, why are you flying?"
- Single Opponent : "Because I want Ma Htwe Lay (youngest lady).
- People : "We did not bring Ma Htwe Lay."
- Single : "I see her behind"
- People : "Ma Htwe's flesh is very bitter, what will you do?"
- Single : "I will wash it with the creek water."
- People : "If the creek water becomes dry, which water will you use?"
- Single : "I will wash it with river water."
- People : "If the river water becomes dry, which water will you use?"
- Single : "I will wash it with sea water."
- (Finally) Single : If I cannot find any water, I will catch Ma Htwe Lay now. (And they start tagging.)

Those people in the queue make excuses not to catch Ma Htwe Lay and that the opponent also has to find water to wash her bitter flesh from creek to sea. It is like a word contest and finally when the

Fighting Cock Game

single opponent cannot find any water to wash, he tries to catch the youngest one. After catching Ma Htwe Lay, the game has to start with a different opponent again.

d) Kyet Pha Khut (Cock style fighting) : This game originated from rural areas. A group of children are watching while two children (especially girls) are moving their legs in sitting position on the ground like the two cocks fighting. The watchers from two sides chant in unison to excite their competitive spirit while they are competing. They are watching anxiously who will get tired and give up first:

"Our cock will win and get the award of the golden cup and your cock will lose and deserve only a copper cup!"

The other games like "Nyaung Bin Ta Sei" (Banyan Ghost), "Laik Oo Phwat Tan" (Hiding the tortoise's eggs), "Ta Pyar Hnit Pyar Pe Lin Pyar", "Wine Kyi Pat Pat Du Wai Wai" (players link hands and move in), "Pazun Sait", "Tai Oo Tann" are popular among the young children.

e) **Lun Swe Pwe (Tug of War)** : People play this game with an intention to invite the rain. They believe that after playing this game, rain will come within a few days. We can see this game in drought areas of upper Myanmar. This game is very simple. Two groups of people try to pull the big rope from opposite side with standing position on the ground. The line is marked in the middle of the two groups as the territory. They compete as to which side is stronger and if one side can pull the rope to their own side, that group will be the winner.

f) **Chaw-Tine-Tet- Pwe** : It is climbing up to the greasy pole. The participants are male adults and this game can be seen in village pagoda festivals, Thadingyut and Tasaungmone festivals. People have to climb up to the standing big bamboo which is about 15 yards long. People make it smooth first by applying it with the pork fats to

Chaw Tine Tet Pwe

become slippery and the reward money is put at the top of the bamboo together with a small flag for the winner. The saying 'Unity is strength' proves in this game. One climber alone cannot reach as it is very slippery. So the climbers team up with each own group. They step on one's shoulder and they finally reach the goal. Some clever groups wait until the bamboo become less slippery while the other group are striving.

Sports

Cane ball

Chinn Lone : Chinlone is a rattan/cane ball and a few men stand in circle and try to keep the ball in the air by using any part of the body except the hands. It is a pure traditional sport, very simple and inexpensive. So everybody (nowadays women) can play it anytime, anywhere. Unlike other games and sports, this sport has no opponent, only a group of people play together and if the ball fall down to the ground, they start the play again.

Thaing : Thaing is Myanmar martial art for self-defence and sometimes it can be played with swords. The Thaing players usually wear the traditional dress of Shan race such as Shan trouser and Shan shirt as this kind of dress is a good match with that sport and comfortable to play. Both men and women can play it.

Playing with Cane Ball

Boxing : Myanmar has its own style of boxing. You can see the Myanmar boxing plays at the pagoda festivals and on some occasions. The matches are accompanied with the traditional orchestra to encourage the boxers and to excite the audience.

A Myanmar Bed-time Story

Everybody has a longing for their own childhood. When I reminisce about my childhood, a bedtime story comes to my mind which I would really like to share with the readers.

Ma Htwe Lay and the Snake Prince
(မထွေးလေးနှင့် မြွေမင်းသားပုံပြင်)

Once upon a time, there was an old woman who regularly came to the Fig tree (Tha Phan) (သဖန်းပင်), (*Ficus glomerata*) near the river to pick up its fallen fruits. She had three daughters. One day, she came to the usual place and found no Tha Phan fruits. The next day, again, she could not find any fruits and she became very upset. While she was sitting at the root of the tree in despair, she heard the sound of "Shwee—shwee". She looked up and there was a big snake resting in the tree. She was very frightened and said, "Oh, Snake Prince, if you want my eldest daughter, please drop a Tha Phan fruit for me". A fruit dropped. And then she asked again, "If you want my second daughter, please drop another one". Another fruit was dropped. And then she asked again, "If you want my youngest daughter, please drop another." This time, the snake shook the tree with his big tail and all the fruits dropped to the ground. The old woman was very happy. She gathered a lot of Tha Phan fruits and quickly went back home.

On her way back home, there was an old tree stump and it asked her, "Oh, you are carrying a lot of Tha Phan fruits, would you please share one with me?" After giving one Tha Phan fruit to the old tree stump, she said, "If a snake asks about me, please do not let him know that I go back home this way. Show the snake the other way." Then, she continued on her way. Before she reached her house, she bumped into a cowboy. "There are a lot of Tha Phan fruits in your hands. It will be very kind of you if you would share one with me". The old woman bribed him with one and gave him the same warning.

The snake followed her. When he inquired about the old woman to the old tree stump, the stump replied as it was taught. But the snake said, "Why did you tell me a lie? I saw the Tha Phan fruit you got from the old woman. Correct?". The tree stump became so frightened that it admitted his deceit and showed the way to where the woman lived. In this way, the big snake reached the old woman's house and he hid in a big rice pot in the kitchen (in the village, they usually keep rice inside a big barrel shaped earthen pot).

Later, the old woman came to the kitchen to cook rice. When she tried to scoop up rice from the pot, the big snake coiled around her hand. The old woman was very frightened and she pleaded as before;

"Snake prince, if you want my eldest daughter, please uncoil from my hand one time. "The snake did.

She asked again, "If you want my second daughter, please uncoil from my hand one more time." The snake complied.

"If you want my youngest daughter, please uncoil from my hand once again." This time, the snake released her whole hand.

Now, the old woman dared not use anymore trick to deceive the snake. So, she called all her daughters and, beginning with the eldest one, asked,

"I had already promised the snake. If you pity me, will you marry him?"

The eldest one replied, "It is impossible for me to marry a snake."

When she asked the second daughter she replied, "I am so scared and I cannot accept him."

When she asked the youngest daughter, she said, "Mother, I am grateful to you and I will obey you."

The old woman was overjoyed with the youngest daughter's acceptance. She had saved her life.

So Ma Htwe Lay (means the youngest daughter) got married to the big snake. She treated the big snake as her husband and never failed in her duty as a good housewife.

At night, the snake prince slept inside a bamboo basket at the corner of Ma Htwe Lay's room. One night, she had a strange dream. In her dream, she was sleeping with a very handsome prince. She kept on dreaming the same dream every night. So one day, she asked her mother about the romantic dreams. The mother comforted Ma Htwe Lay and said, "Don't worry, I will ask a learned person to interpret your dream. Anyway, it sounds like a very good dream". That night, the old woman waited patiently and peeped into their room. What she found out was that, while Ma Htwe Lay was asleep, the snake's basket moved and a very handsome prince came out and lied down to sleep beside Ma Htwe Lay. While they were asleep, the mother tiptoed into their room and checked carefully. She found only the skin of the snake in the bamboo basket. She took the skin and quietly burnt it. Since the Prince had lost his skin, he could not go back to live as a snake anymore.

Ma Htwe Lay and the snake Prince lived happily together. They built a happy family life. They had a lovely baby boy. The prince adored his wife and baby very much and all the villagers called him "Snake Prince". But the prince told his wife a deep secret, and that was never to make him touch the blood of a snake.

As true love never runs smooth, problems started when the two elder sisters became very envious of Ma Htwe Lay's happy family life. So, they often complained to their mother and pestered her to find them nice husbands like the Snake Prince. One day, the old woman went out as she could not stand their complaints anymore. One her way, she found a big snake which was sleeping near the mount. She put it in the pa-choke (bamboo basket) and brought it home for her eldest daughter.

That night, she put the big snake in her eldest daughter's room. In the middle of the night, they heard the eldest daughter screaming, "Mother, please help me, the snake is swallowing my feet!" Her mother replied, "Don't be scared, he is just teasing you." Later, she shouted, "Mother, he has already swallowed my legs!!" Her mother comforted her in the same manner, without seeing them. Later, the daughter screamed, again, "Mother, he has reached all the way up to my neck!!!" Her mother told her, "You must be patient to get a nice husband like the Snake Prince." After that, she did not hear the daughter's voice anymore.

The next morning, the mother went to the eldest daughter's room to see the situation. She found the big snake was sleeping alone on the bed and his stomach was very bulky. She realized that the big snake had swallowed her daughter! The old woman was dumbfounded and cried for help. She asked the Snake Prince to cut open the big snake's stomach and take out her eldest daughter as fast as possible. The Prince refused. The old woman asked him, again and again. The prince refused several times and told her of his weakness. The old woman said, "It may be a lame excuse. You are the only man in the house and you are responsible for any matter in this home. Aren't you family minded?" The prince could not stand it anymore and he decided to help. He took a knife from the kitchen

Ma Htwe Lay pleading the Snake Prince to come back

and quickly cut open the stomach of the big snake to take out the eldest sister. The snake's blood splashed upon him.

They found the eldest daughter half dead and unconscious. Luckily, they were able to save her life, just in time. But what happened to the snake prince? While all their attention was on the eldest sister, the prince had slowly transformed into a snake after being touched by the blood of the wild snake. After seeing all that had happened, Ma Htwe Lay cried, mad with regret. The snake Prince looked at his wife for the last time and he seemed to be saying, "Goodbye, my love. I will never come back to the human world again."

He slowly, slowly, slithered into the forest. Poor Ma Htwe Lay followed him, carrying the little baby but the Snake Prince did not remember her anymore. She could not hear the villagers' warnings "Don't follow him. He doesn't recognize you anymore. You will be bitten." Indeed, when the snake turned and saw a crying woman following him, he tried to bite her. But Ma Htwe Lay raised the little baby in her hands and said, "This is your son. Don't you remember?" When he saw the baby, the snake could not bite her. But he turned and kept on going deeper into the forest. Ma Htwe Lay kept on following him. Whenever he tried to bite her, she raised the baby. The villagers watched this tragic scene until they disappeared out of sight.

▸▸ *When I was very young, after listening to this story, I got very angry with the old woman and the two elder daughters who had asked the Snake Prince to help them by killing the wild snake. Tears dwelled up in my eyes when I pictured the pitiful scene in my mind, imagining how the Snake Prince slowly crawled into the forest despite Ma Htwe Lay's pleading.*

In preparing this story, I had to question my elderly mother because I had already forgotten some parts of the story. She recollected her memory. Luckily, she could still remember most parts of it. So, I combined her recollections with the parts which I remembered, and the whole story was completed. This is one of my mother's favourite stories which she used to tell us as children.

⊷⊷ ⚙ ⊶⊶

Jewellery Rain

"When an old man dies, a library is lost". *(Tommy Swann)*

When I read this saying, I am reminded of my late grandpa, who often told us wonderful stories of Myanmar's ancient times. At that time, we relished listening to him with such curiosity that we forgot to blink!

One evening, he began telling, "Grandchildren, when we tell stories at night, the heavenly beings are very thankful to us because they are listening, too." "Now I want to tell you a true story called 'Jewellery Rain'."

"During the period when King Byamadat ruled the capital, 'Baranathi', there was a Ponna (ပုဏ္ဏား) (Brahmin) who knew a mantra which could make jewels rain down, including the nine most precious stones. He lived in a small village and had a young apprentice. One day, the teacher and his apprentice left for Seitadine village. On their way to that village, they passed through some forests. They bumped into a group of bandits called 'Peitha-naka-sawya' which included 500 thieves. The bandit leader captured both of them and said to the apprentice, "You go back and bring the jewels to us. We will keep your teacher for 10 days. If you dont come back in time, you will find only the corpse of your teacher." The student made a promise and quietly warned his teacher, "Master, please don't be scared. I will come back within a few days. The important thing is that according to astrology, today you can make the rain of jewels. However, please do not recite the 'Weidappa' mantra or else you will be in a great deal of trouble." Saying this, the young man left.

The teacher was tied near a tree. He was suffering, not only from hunger, but also from the bad weather and insect bites. That night, he could not sleep and looked up at the sky, helplessly. He found that the sky was full of sparkling stars and it looked like the stars were blinking at him. The old man was thinking, "my student reminded me not to recite the rain of jewels mantra but human life is most precious. I will make the jewellery rain fall and escape from these bandits."

The teacher asked the bandits why they had captured him. They replied that they wanted the jewels. So he said, "If you want the jewels, I can make the jewels rain down." At first, the bandits did not believe him. They thought the teacher was trying to trick them and said, "Are you sure? Don't deceive us. If you do, we will kill you". He replied, "I am not lying. Please untie me quickly. Give me new and clean clothing, nice flowers, and some scent."

The teacher made himself clean, changed into new clothing, put the flowers on his head, and applied some sweet scent. He gazed at the sky and recited many mantras. The bandits were looking at him with great interest. Slowly... slowly... the stars started to move and gather together. Those stars were stirring like a grinding machine in the sky. At that moment, the sky was filled with light. The old man kept on reciting. Not long after, the galaxy slid down to the ponna along the Milky Way and, reaching half way, fell to the ground as a rain of jewels. They found out that the jewels were all made into precious jewellery, such as rings, necklaces, pendants and ear-rings. All were made with the *nine precious stones. The bandits shouted like mad, "Hey, we are rich now. Pick up all these jewels."

The bandits released the old man and left the forest, carrying away the precious jewelry. On their way, the bandits met with another group, which consisted another 500 thieves. The first group was captured and the leader asked the second leader. "Why have you captured us?" "Because, we want the jewellery from you". So the first leader said, "If you want the jewellery, you need not capture us. You can ask the old man who is following behind us. He can make the jewels fall like rain."

So the teacher was captured, again. The second group leader asked him to make the jewellery rain. This time the teacher explained to him, "Sorry, according to astrology, the solar system allows the rain of jewels only once a year. If you want me to make the jewellery rain, you have to wait one more year." The bandit leader was very angry and he said "You stupid ponna! You just made the jewellery rain down for the other group. Why can't you make it rain down for us. We cannot forgive you". They killed him and quickly followed after the first group.

There was a big fight between the two groups. Finally, only two robbers were left. They carried a lot of jewellery away, together. On the way, they became tired and hungry. One of them asked the other to hide the jewellery in the bushes and wait there. He went to the nearby village to find food. On the way, he got an idea to put poison in the food for the other so that he could keep the whole treasure for himself. At the same time, the other one became very greedy gazing at all the precious jewellery. He thought to himself, "How nice it would be if I kept all those jewels for myself and nobody knows the truth. I must kill him first, before he kills me!" Soon, the other one came back after having his meal and brought the poisoned food for the thief who was waiting. Suddenly, the one who was waiting chopped the returning thief and consumed the poisoned food. Now, nobody was left.

Two days later, the apprentice arrived at the place where he had left his master and found his teacher's corpse along with those of all the bandits. The jewels were strewn near the two bandits. He realized the reality of the situation, as he was a wise person. He was so saddened. He buried his teacher's corpse and paid his last respects to his teacher. He carried some jewellery back to his town and peacefully lived the rest of his life.

From this experience he had learned two moral lessons:

"If a person cannot control his greed, it will lead to his destruction." and

"Knowledge is of no use without the power of reason."

►► *The nine types of precious stones (Nawarat Koe Thwe)* (နဝရတ်ကိုးသွယ်) *are: Ruby, Pearl, Coral, Emerald, Topaz, Diamond, Sapphire, Garnet, and the Cat's eye.*

Popular Foods and Snacks

In Myanmar, every region, every town has its own specialities. For example, Pathein is popular for Halawar, Shan state has a lot of tasty Shan foods such as Shan noodles, Tofu and Shan sour rice salad. Mandalay is popular for Nan kyi thoke and Myee shay. The following foods are generally accepted by the whole country.

Mohinga (မုန့်ဟင်းခါး): Mohinga is the favourite food of Myanmar

Mohinga

people. Mohinga in Myanmar is like 'Spagatti' in Italy and 'Sushi' in Japan. It is rice noodle eaten together with fish soup. Fish soup is cooked together with soft banana stems, onions, ginger, beans, lemon grass and other spicy things. Different region has different cooking style of Mohinga such as Rakhine Mohinga is known as Rakhine Monti, Myaung Mya Mohinga, Taungoo Mohinga, etc.

Ohn-noh-kauk-swel (Coconut Noodle) (အုန်းနို့ ခေါက်ဆွဲ): Its soup is made of coconut milk, chicken, onions and beans and eaten up with the flour noodle. In addition, people put fried beans, gourd fritter and boiled egg, chilli, lime in it and take it as they like.

(Both Mohinga and Ohn-noh-kauk-swel can be taken as breakfast. It can be served on some light occasions such as naming ceremony, donation ceremony, ground breaking ceremony.

Coconut Noodle

Kyar Zan Hin Khar

Kyar Zan Hin Khar (ကြာဖန်ဟင်းခါး): It is glass vermicelli soup cooked with chicken or pork including dried shrimp, dried mushrooms, egg, dried flowers and onions. The ingredients are put one by one in it. Some put chilli, lime and coriander leaves upon their liking. It is a good match to eat with Lime salad (Shauk Thee Thoke).

Nan Gyi Thoke

Nan Kyi Thoke (နန်းကြီးသုပ်): It is a big and round rice noodle salad with chicken curry, fried fish cake (*nga hpe kyaw*), onions, coriander, spring onions, duck egg, crushed dried chilli, dressed with fried crispy onion oil, shrimp sauce (Ngan pyar yay), lime and bean powder. Mandalay Nan Kyi Thoke is very popular.

Kauk Hnyin Paung

Kauk Hnyin Paung (ကောက်ညှင်းပေါင်း): It is taken as breakfast together with fried dry/fish or gourd fritters. It is steamed sticky rice (sometimes together with beans). Kauk Hnyin Paung can be of two types – white color and brown color. Along highway trip, when you stop your car in a small town, you may see the Kyauk Hnyin Paung vendors among other snack vendors who are asking you to buy. If you cook (not steam) sticky rice with water, oil, salt, sugar and a little bit of turmeric powder, it becomes 'Si Htamin'.

Shwe Yin Aye

Shwe Yin Aye (ရွှေရင်အေး): 'Shwe Yin Aye' in Myanmar means literally 'make the golden breast cool'. It is a cool sweet drink prepared of sago, gelatine, sugar and coconut milk. In addition, they put Kyauk-kyaw (Agar), bread, sticky rice, hmyawl (dried jelly stick) into the coconut milk and put some ice. Shwe Yin Aye sellers can make a lot of money especially in the Summer season.

Kyauk Kyaw

Kyauk Kyaw (ကျောက်ကျော): Kyauk-kyaw is made of agar. Agar is boiled with some sugar and needs thorough stirring on the stove for about 30 min. After that they make it cool to be congeal. They put some color for good appearance and coconut milk to get a nicer taste. Some people can make it two or three layers with different colors and is very attractive. On some occasions, it can be served as dessert.

Sanyon Makin

Sanyon Makin (ဆနွင်းမကင်း): Shwe-gyi (flour from the heart of wheat grain), coconut milk, sugar or jaggery are the main ingredients to make sanyon makin. Mix all those things and stir on the stove until it become thick. In addition, put some raisins and cashew nuts, butter in it. After that, pour in a wide and flat iron pan and bake with both upper and lower heat. Before pouring the paste, you need to put some oil first not to get sticky at the bottom part. It is a kind of pudding and a popular sweet dessert, too.

There are so many kinds of Sanyon Makin. If you make with Shwe Kyi, it is called Shwe kyi Sanyon makin. You can use bananas or potatoes or sweet potatoes or Yam or sticky rice instead of Shwe-kyi.

Htamanae

Htamanae (ထမနဲ): Please see under the chapter 'Flowers and Festivals in the Myanmar Calendar' in Tabotwe month.

Mont Lone Ye Paw (မုန့်လုံးရေပေါ်): It is known as 'Water Festival Snack'. It is small dumplings made with glutinous rice and inside is jaggery (Palm candy). First, the powder of glutinous rice and ordinary rice are mixed with 3:1 ratio and knead with some water to get paste. The jaggery is necessary and cut into small pieces of plum seeds measurement. Rice paste is flattened in the palm of the hands and those jaggery pieces are put in the middle and rolled to form a small ball. Put those small dumplings into the big boiling water pot and wait for a while. When some are afloat on the surface of boiling water means that those are cooked already. During water festival, every quarter make this snack and donate to other people

Mont Lone Ye Paw

too. As a practical joke, some women put chilli inside a few dumplings instead of jaggery. When they know that who is the unlucky one, there is a great laughter!

Pickled Tea-leaf Salad

Laphetthoke (လက်ဖက်သုပ်): Nobody denies if someone is offered the Laphet-thoke (pickled tea-leaves salad). Myanmar people say, mango is the king of the fruits and tea leaf is the king of the leaves. Especially the women like it very much and Myanmar people appreciate to take this salad either with meal or as a dessert. Ingredients are pickled tea-leaves, fried garlic, fried beans, sesame seeds, oil, chilli, dry prawns, sliced tomatoes and these are mixed together.

Bain Mont (ဘိန်းမုန့်): It is a kind of pancake made in Myanmar style with rice flour, palm sugar (jaggery), coconut chips and peanuts garnished with poppy seeds or sesame. So some people called it 'Burma Cake'. The paste of rice flour and liquid of jaggery are baked with upper and lower heat on the stove. The coconut chips, peanuts and poppy seeds are put over the cake for good appearance and good taste.

Jaggery (Palm Sugar/candy) (ထန်းလျက်): Jaggery is made from palm toddy and it is a kind of candy. Although it is a sweet dessert, it will never make you cough because it comes from the natural palm sap. Toddy is poured into the large bell-mouthed pan and boiled with open fire and need to be stirred until it becomes thick and sticky. After cooling it, you can

Jaggery

mould it into desired shape. Some people put scrapped coconuts in it to become the coconut jaggery. In some Myanmar restaurants, they offer you as a dessert to take after meal. Jaggery can be used as medicine too. It can help digest the food quickly and it can loosen the poisonous affect. Although taking food afternoon is forbidden to the Buddhist monks, they can take jaggery as a medicine. '

Mont Lin-ma-yar

'Mont' means 'snack' in Myanmar language. Other foods like Hnget Pyaw Thee Paung (ငှက်ပျောသီးပေါင်း) (steamed banana with coconut milk), Mont Phet Htoke (မုန့်ဖက်ထုပ်) (steamed sticky-rice powder mixed with jaggery), Mont Lat Kauk (မုန့်လက်ကောက်) (ring donut), Mont Oo Hnauk (မုန့်ဦးနှောက်) (steamed rice-powder), Mont Sein Paung (မုန့်စိမ်းပေါင်း) (Steamed

Toddy Palm Cake

rice cake), Mont Let Saung (မုန့်လက်ဆောင်း) (small pieces of boiled rice-powder paste in coconut milk or jaggery liquid), Mont Lone Kyi (မုန့်လုံးကြီး) (big glutinous-rice balls with sweet ingredients), Mont Lin-ma-yar (မုန့်လင်မယား) (rice based snack which has two halves), Kayay Kayar (ကရေကရာ), Yay Mont (ရေမုန့်) (water snack), Kauk Hlaing Ti Mont (ကောက်လှိုင်းတီမုန့်) (rice based snack in purple colour), Htan Thee Mont (ထန်းသီးမုန့်) (toddy palm cake) are popular too. Myanmar people are fond of making snacks in their free time or holidays or on some occasions, like full moon days or festival days. They make their favourite

Varieties of Fried Fritter

snacks, not only for their family, but they also donate it to the monastery and they share it to their neighbours too.

As Myanmar lies between two big countries China and India. The followings are the popular foods in Myanmar inspired by neighbouring countries.

Chinese inspired foods: Phet-htoke, Kaw pyant, Rice porrige (san pyote), Dumplings, Ekyarkway, Kyay O, Wetthar dote htoe, Si-chet kauk swe, Kaw-yay Kauk Swe.

Indian inspired foods: Samusa, Prata, Puree, Chaparti, To-Shay, Nan-byar, Biriani, Pharluda (cold drink).

Thai Papaya salad and Thai Sun Tan soup are popular too among Myanmar people.

Yay Mont

Kayay Kayar

Mont Sein Paung

Foods, not to eat together

Here is a list of the foods which should not be eaten together so as to avoid their adverse side affects:

1	Pomelo	Lime	Die
2	Star fruit	Chocolate	Die
3	Coconut	Honey	Asthma
4	Oyster	Beef	Die
5	Ice cream	Ginger salad	Die
6	Canned fish	Indian trumpet	Die
7	Banana	Palmyra nut	Die
8	Neem leaf	Chicken egg	Stiffness
9	Cucumber	Ice lolly	Asthma
10	Mangosteen	Sugar	Die
11	Lotus root	Beef	Die
12	Gourd	Parrot	Die
13	Chicken	Bitter gourd	Vomit
14	Pigeon	Ginger	Die
15	Land crab	Mushroom	Die
16	Pumpkin	Pigeon	Die
17	Waterchestnut	Pickled tea leaves	Die
18	Watermelon	Duck egg	Die
19	Frog	Mushroom	Die
20	Chocolate/Milo	Edible tuber of winged bean	Die
21	Chinese Potato	Ice lolly	Asthma
22	Jelly	Coffeemix	Die
23	Peacock	Tapioca	Die
24	Sour Bamboo shoots	Tapioca	Vomit

25	Let Pan Pwint (လက်ပံပွင့်)	Horse Meat	Vomit
26	Chinese potato	Candy/sweets	Vomit
27	Indian Trumpet	Canned fish	Stiffness
28	Bittergourd	Mushsoom	Stiffness
29	Shar Saung (Castus)	Honey	Stiffness
30	Lime	Arsenic	Die
31	Star fruit	Beef	Die
32	Bael (Oat Shit)	Honey	Die
33	Lemon	Milk	Die
34	Honey	Custard apple	Die
35	Plum	Green peas	Diarrhoea
36	Pork	Toddy (Palm juice)	Die
37	Potato	Bitter gourd	vomit/die
38	Chicken	Indian trumpet	Stiffness
39	Euginia fruit	Palm sugar (jaggery)	Die
40	Mushroom	Rabbit	Die
41	Honey	Jackfruit	Vomit
42	Candy (sweet)	Soya bean	Vomit
43	Durian	Djenkol bean (Danyinthee)	Vomit

* If someone suffers from food poisoning,

1) Try to take out those food by vomitting or discharge to loosen the affect of the poison first.
2) Pound the watercress and drink the liquid.
3) Eat a lot of palm sugar (jaggery). To cure quickly, take the liquid jaggery.

Danyinthee

⇢⊷ 🚂 ⊷⇠

Myanmar Traditional Medicines

One day, at the end of the Traditional Medicine course, the teacher of 'Ziwaka' (later he became the royal master of the traditional medicines in Lord Buddha's live time) asked him to bring any kind of plant which was not medicinal or useless. 'Ziwaka' went to the forest with the necessary tools to dig and in the evening, he came back to his teacher with bare hands. He found out that each and every plant had its own qualities and no plant nor leaf was useless. The teacher was very satisfied with Ziwaka's answer and he gladly exclaimed, "You have passed the examination!".

According to the Myanmar traditional physicians, there are 96 diseases which afflict human kind and Myanmar indigenous medicine is able to heal and cure all 96 maladies. They say that human body is composed of four elements: earth, water, air and fire. If we can keep it in balance, no disease will appear. If we suffer from a disease means that one element or other is deficient. So some cure it with food instead of medicine as 'Food is medicine and medicine is food' (အစာလည်းဆေး၊ ဆေးလည်းအစာ). The followings are days and their influencing elements so that we can know which food we should take.

Days		Elements
Sunday	-	Earth
Monday	-	Water
Tuesday	-	Fire
Wednesday	-	Air
Thursday	-	Bile
Friday	-	Nutrition
Saturday	-	Akasha

Diet for the Earth Element

Beef, Pork, Mutton, chicken, Rabbit, lobster, Hilsa, Gourd, Golden pumpkin, corn, coconut, Jaggery, Butter

Diet for the water element

Duck, turtle egg, water melon, lady finger, banana, fig, cucumber, watercress, spinach

Diet for the fire element

Lime, chilly, Marion, tamarind, tomato, ripe tamarind and salt, garlic, liquor, country spirit, sour prawn, sour beef, sour mushroom, sour bamboo shoot.

Diet for the air element

Bitter gourd leaves, neem leaves, Indian trumpet, Asparagus leaves, drum stick, papaya leaves

Diet for the Bile element

Custard apple, ripe papaya, ripe banana, jaggery, plum jam, molasses, sugar

Diet for the nutrition element

Ripe mango, ripe papaya, sugar cane juice, marrow, beans, pumpkin, dates, honey, sugar, jaggery, coconut juice, banana, guava.

Diet for the Akasha element

Chilly, lime, ginger, pepper, animals with furs, onion, garlic

Medicines for babies

1. **Coughing with mucas**: Mix with Kyaik hman leaves (*Eclipta alba*) and Kway-thay-pan leaves (ဒွေးသေးပန်းရွက်) and grind it. Add the Shein kho (Asafoetida, *Ferula foetida*) powder a little bit and apply the liquid at the top part of the head. (or) Give the baby the liquid of betel leaves mix with Thanakhar (paste by grinding from the bark of the Thanakhar tree) .

2. **Measles, chicken pox**: Give a little bit heat to the above three (Kyaik hman leaves (*Eclipta alba*), kway-thay-pan and Shein kho

(ရှိန်းခို) (Asafoetida, *Ferula foetida*) and take it. (Or) Put it over the mother's breast while she is breastfeeding that baby.

3. **Oliguria (poor urination):** Heat the onion. Cut from the middle and then put over the baby's suprapubic region while the onion is warm (or) Take the fresh pineapple liquid with sugar.

4. **Asthma:** Apply the white balm or sesame oil over the betel leave and then put it on the baby's chest.

5. **Constipation:** Please do not give the pills to babies for constipation. Bite the betel leave stem a little bit and apply the oil on stem and tickle the baby's anus a few times.

6. **To deworm** (သခ္ခရစ်လျှင်): Squeeze the pineapple to get the liquid and drink it together with honey. (or) Boil the bamboo leaves a long time and let the baby drink it. (or) Liquid from Mezali *(Cassia siamea)* leaves and mix with lime and let the baby take it.

7. **Gas Pain:** Bake three pieces of garlic and take three times a day for 3 days.

8. **Exposed smell of frying:** Give the real Thanakhar (paste by grinding from the bark of the Thanakhar tree) a little bit.

9. **Abscess:** Crush the Kway-thay-pan leaves and put over it.

10. **Catching cold and Bronchitis:** Take one tea spoonful liquid of horse Shoe leaves (*Hydrocotyle asiatica*).

11. **Vomit, sneezing and dysentery :** Give the baby the liquid of horse Shoe leaves (*Hydrocotyle asiatica*) mix with honey or sugar for about one tea spoon.

12. **Sneezing:** Sometimes, you may see the hanging dead spider on the wall. Those are very medicinal. Make it into powder and apply with the coconut oil to the top of the baby's head to cure the sneezing.

13. **Catch cold:** Give the baby one tea spoonful of horse Shoe leaves (*Hydrocotyle asiatica*) liquid.

14. **Having fit or tense:** Find the bitter-gourd leaves, fresh turmeric,

Shein kho (Asafoetida, *Ferula foetida*) and Pan-nyo leaves (ပန်းညို့ရွက်). Grind all those things and mix with oil and then rub two ears and nostrils. Also apply that oil from top of the head to buttom by hand 7 times without breathing.

The followings are some quick and simple remedies for common diseases:

1) **Toothache**: Grind some ginger and put on that tooth.

2) **Dysentery**: Eat jaggery (palm candy) with grinded salt.

3) **Heat Dysentery**: Put some white sugar in a glass of boiled water. Squeeze in half of lime and drink it.

4) **Retention of gas**: Take the whole plant of horse Shoe (*Myin khwar* in Myanmar Language) (*Hydrocotyle asiatica*) by making soup or salad or whatever.

Myin khwar plant
(Horse Shoe)

5) **Burnt Cases**: Squeeze the tomato and apply on the burnt area. (Or) Put the ripe banana over it. Both are very cool and recovery is very fast. (Or) Apply butter lavishly on the required parts.

6) **Insomnia**: If you suffer from insomnia, take rice cooked with butter.

7) **Spider bite**: Chew the seven grains of rice and put over it.

8) **Nettle rash** (အဏ်ဖြင်း): Grind the teak and apply on it.

9) **Heart disease**: After taking bath in the morning, put the betel leaves on the left side of chest where the heart lies. The betel leaf will slowly absorb the heat and can melt down the fat which blocks the arteries to the heart. When the betel leaf drops itself from your chest, you will find that the leaf is warm.

10) **Stiffness or weak nerves**: Drink the liquid of Kyaung pan *(Vitex trifolia)* leaves (or) Take the fried Kyaung Pan leaves.

11) **Malaria (or) fever**: Boil the Kyaung Pan *(Vitex trifolia)* leaves and take bath with it. And drink it regularly, too.

12) **Constipation, Headache, purify the blood**: Take the lettuce leaves (or) take the cabbage salad

13) **Belly pain**: Take the Phan Khar fruit (ဖန်ခါးသီး). (Myrobalan, *Terminalia chebula*) with rice.

14) **To stop Bleeding**: Put the flour/wheat over it.

15) **For eyes and blood**: Take tomato juice everyday.

16) **Diabetes**: Boil the neem bark and drink the liquid every morning.

17) **For longer life and youth**: Put the whole plant of horse Shoe *(Hydrocotyle asiatica)* under the shade until it is well dried and make it into powder. Mix with honey and take one tea spoonful every morning.

18) **Urine, High blood, blocked arteries**: Take one piece of garlic after every meal.

19) **Sore throat/lost voice**: Grind the drum stick leaves and drink the liquid a tea spoonful.

20) **Toothache, swelling, pus**: Boil the leaves or bark of guava and keep inside the mouth.

21) **Scorpion, bee, red ant or insect bite**: Grind the mango leaves or Mezali *(Cassia siamea)* leaves and put over the bitten area.

22) **Seasonal cough and sore throat**: During the intervening period between one season to another, some people get cough and sore throat. To cure it, pick up the small coconuts (it drop itself under the coconut tree) and boil it. And then gargle with it (keep the liquid in the mouth for a while before you spit it out).

23) **Loss conscious/epilepsy** (ဝက်ရူးပြန်): Smell the onion (or) put about two or three drops of onion liquid in the nose.

24) Nose bleeding: Mix the pepper powder and Shein kho (Asafoetida, *Ferula foetida*) powder (2:1, by weight) and drink the liquid.

25) For the gastric diseases: Peel the green banana. Put under the sun until it becomes dry and make it into powder and take it every day.

Drum stick and leaves

26) High blood pressure: Take the bitter turmeric with honey every day. (or) Chew the two or three seeds of lime. (or) Put the lime fruit in the hot water. When the water become cool, squeeze the lime in it and drink it every morning. Drum stick and its leaves can be taken, too.

27) Asthma cough: Take one table spoonful of onion liquid three times a day (or) Take the onion with rice. (Or) Take roasted grass- lizzard.

28) Internal injury (အတွင်းရခိုက်): Pound the betel leaves and put over it.

29) Dysentery/diarrhoea: Dry the mango flowers, make it into powder and drink three times a day (each time, one tea spoonful).

30) Urine stone/kidney stone: Take the Oak-shit (Bael) fruit juice every day. It can crush the stones of kidney and urinary bladder.

Stones from Nga Poke Thin's head

31) Gall stone, Urine stone, kidney stone: There are two small white stones inside the head of the Nga Poke Thin (Croaker fish). Burn it into powder and put into the coconut juice and add a little bit of Alum (Kyauk chin) and drink it.

32) To crush gall stone: Drink four cups of apple juice (or eat four or five apples) each day for 5 days. On the 6th day, about 6 pm, take one tablespoonful of Epsom salt (sa-khar) with warm water. You have to take one tablespoonful amount again at 8 pm. At 10 pm, you have to take half of a small bowl amount of olive oil (or sesame oil) and a half of a small bowl amount of lime juice together. Before you drink, you have to stir well the oil and the lime juice. (Please do not take dinner on the 6th day). On 7th day morning, you will see some small stones when you discharge.

33) **Dry cough**: Take the soup of Kim-pun-chim *(Acacia concinna)* leaves for about two or three days.

34) **Urine problems**: Wash the Myin khwar *(Hydrocotyle asiatica)* leaves thoroughly and pound it. Take that liquid with jaggery (palm candy).

35) **Stiffness on upper neck**: Slice the ginger, heat a little bit and then put it over the area.

36) **Exhaustion, loss of appetite**: Fry the fresh Hin Nu Nel (Spinach) with prawn or dry prawn and take a lot.

37) **Oedema** (ဖောရောင်ခြင်း): Grind the whole plant of sensitive plant (Hti-ka-yone). Mix with water and apply on the area with a chicken feather.

38) **Swollen gum**: Heat Ye Yo fruit *(Morinda angustifolia)* and take it with a little bit of salt.

39) **Dry cough after the fever**: Heat the sugarcane on fire and then peel it and take it. If it is not easy to get the fresh sugarcane, buy the sugarcane juice, heat it and drink it.

40) **Diabetes**: Place the Thagyar manine leaves (သကြားမနိုင်ရွက်) under the shadow. When it is dry, put it in the hot water and take it like Chinese tea.

41) **For liver weakness or swelling**: Drink the liquid from boiled Kyaik hman leaves *(Eclipta alba)* often.

42) **Appendix**: Swallow the bitter turmeric a lot.

43) **Swollen bones and pain**: Pour the boiled water over Roselle (Chin paung) leaves and put over the area.

44) **Male urine disease**: Grind the pure Thanakha (paste from the bark of Thanakhar tree) and take it with sugar.

45) **Bad breath**: Eat the cauliflower or white pumpkin (either fresh or jam). In the village funerals, people put white pumpkin under the bed of the corpse so as to absorb the foul smell if they want to keep the corpse longer.

46) **Earache**: Bake the onion and then pour the onion juice in the ear

47) **Eye disease**: You should eat banana or neem leaves.

48) **Headache**: Eat ripe plum. (Or) Take butter rice with either beef or mutton curry

49) **Cold, Cough/Asthma**: Take often the mixture of raw ginger juice and honey

50) **Constipation**: To get relieve from constipation, make a mixture of jaggery, ripe tamarind and salt and drink it.

51) **Urine disease**: Eat neem seeds everyday. (Or) Drink the boiled liquid of Thanmanine Kyaukmanine leaves.

52) **Apoplexy** (လေသင်တုန်း): If one suffers from apoplexy, let one eat plenty of coconut for ten days.

53) **Physical pain**: To cure the physical pain, apply the red earth.

54) **Herpes** (ရေယုန်): Let one applies the liquid that one gets after grinding a rabbit bone with water.

55) **Poisonous snake bite**: Poke the wound with a lighted wooden stick.

56) **Food poison**: Take stirred chicken egg or watercress or jaggery.

57) **Jaundice**: Take the liquid of Oat Shit (Bael) fruit (12 pae thar) (၁၂ ပဲသားခန့်) (12 pae thar = 0.432 ounce). Put a little bit of pepper and drink regularly.

58) **Pyorrhoea** (သွားအမြစ်ပုပ်ဆွေးနာ): Make the neem leaves dry and put that powder inside.

59) **All the teeth and gum problems**: Boil both mango leaves and bark and put in the mouth. (Or) You can use the guava leaves and bark too.

60) **Sinusitis** (ထိပ်ကပ်နာ): Crush the Pauk-pan-phyu (*Sesbania grandiflora*) leaves and smell it.

61) **Angular Stomatics** (ကရိုးပါးစပ်): This is the affect of Vitamin B2 deficiency. So please take a lot of gourd leaves or fruit either cook or fry.

62) **Sweet fungi (Hnyin /skin disease)**: Squeeze the orange skin and rub over it.

63) **Skin disease**: To cure skin disease you should apply the neem leaves extract.

64) **Fair complexion**: Take fresh (not cooked) tomatoes at least once a day and it will balance the four elements too.

65) **To reduce the body heat in summer**: Take jam made of dried plum and jaggery.

66) **Alzyma**: Steam the beef with the ginger (4:1 ratio). Take the steamed liquid. It will cleanse the impurities of the arteries to the brain.

Women Diseases

1) **To prevent the miscarriage**: Take a lot of sweet potatoes in early pregnancy. If you can take it raw, it will be better.

2) **White discharge**: Take the liquid of boiled Sintone Manwe (Moonseed vine). (Or) Grind the root of Thanakhar and pollen from Kantkaw flower (evergreen hardwood) and then drink with sugar.

Kyaik hman

3) **Slimming, hard body and clear complexion**: Mix the Turmeric

and bitter turmeric powder in equal amount and take one tea spoonful a day regularly.

4) **For blood purification and nice appearance**: Boil the Mezali (*Cassia siamea*) leaves and drink the liquid with honey (Or) Make the Mezali (*Cassia siamea*) leaves dry and take that powder with honey.

5) **Menstrual disorder**: Buy just-ripe tomatoes (not over or fully ripe). Cut those tomatoes and onions. Make it a salad with dry prawn and eat. (Please do not put chilli). (Or) Take a lot of Kyaik hman leaves (*Eclipta alba*) soup.

6) **Vomitting during pregnancy**: Take the jam of Kyaik-hman leaves (*Eclipta alba*) (Kyaik hman and jaggery 3:1 by weight and put a little bit of salt and boil it to make jam. Take three times a day.

7) **Post-natal diarrhoea**: It is terrible for women. If it happens, grind the kyaik hman leaves (*Eclipta alba*), Bael fruit (Oak-shit), Samone net (black cumin seeds) and garlic in equal amounts. Take it together with sesame oil at night.

8) **To cure Pimple, Freckles and spots**: Grind the Thanakhar with lemon and apply on your face before you go to sleep at night. Once a week is enough and it will slowly disappear.

9) **To get thick and black hair**: Dry Zeephyuthee (Eastern gooseberry), dry Kyaik hman leaves (*Eclipta alba*) and Myin khwar (*Hydrocotyle asiatica*) leaves) in equal amounts and put those powder in the bottle and pour the coconut oil and keep long enough under the shade before you apply your hair. When you wash your hair, you should use Myanmar traditional shampoo made from Kim pon fruit (soap acacia). (The oil can be applied to the eye brow too, if you want thick eye brow.)

10) **Smooth and soft complexion**: To get a smooth and soft complexion, take butter or avocado every day.

11) **Tin-Tate (Freckles)**: If women enter in their forties, some freckles appear on the faces and it causes them a lot of annoyances whenever they see in the mirror. Please grind the dried Thit-Phwe-Thee (သစ်ဖွေးသီး) on flat stone (Kyauk Pyin - ကျောက်ပြင်) with a little bit of rice water (san say yay) and apply it on that area every day.

Diet for the Brain

Nowadays, the world is very competitive. Brain works are more demanding. As a result, we suffer from stress and strain. That's why we have the nervous breakdown disease, Parkinson disease or other similar diseases. There is a saying 'Physical tiredness cannot beat the mind, but the mental tiredness can beat the body' (ကိုယ်ထောင်းလို့စိတ်မကြေ၊ စိတ်ထောင်းလို့ကိုယ်ကြေ). As prevention is better than cure, the followings are the foods for the brain:

- Milk
- Salmon and Tuna
- Blueberry, Strawberry
- Garlic,
- Spinach, Soya bean
- Oranges
- Plum (red color)
- Grape
- Cherry
- Walnut
- Take less oil and salt

To improve your brain power, you should take –

1) Yoga or meditation or light exercise

2) Breathe the sea breeze (or whatever wind which pass over the water)

Part (II)
BELIEFS and SUPERSTITIONS

BELIEFS and SUPERSTITIONS

Myanmar is composed of eight main races and more than one hundred minority groups. Geographically, it can be divided into seven states and seven regions with each region and tribe having their own traditional superstitions. Therefore, my private collection of Myanmar's beliefs and superstitions is like a few fishes swimming on the surface of an ocean of superstition which is full of fishes of many different colours and sizes.

Pregnancy, Childbirth, Baby Boy or Girl

In Myanmar custom and tradition, many beliefs and superstitions loom and influence our attitudes towards pregnancy, childbirth, and predicting the sex of a baby. Pregnancy is the most important matter for a family and they have to listen to the elders' words of advice.

Pregnancy – A pregnant woman and her spouse should not buy clothing for the baby until the last stage of pregnancy or bad luck will fall upon the baby. Pregnant woman will face a difficult delivery if she sews any torn-pieces or holes in the clothes. And, if she wears yellow coloured clothing, there is the possibility that the newborn may have jaundice.

Some say, woman in pregnancy should not participate in weddings, novitiations, funerals and pagoda or monastery construction. She should not walk over the timber to build a monastery or house and no other pregnant woman should be allowed to stay at her house. Otherwise, it may harm the baby.

People believe that a woman who bullies her husband too much will have to face a difficult delivery. At such a risky time, she can be saved from it by giving her the water after soaking with her husband's feet.

Some pregnant women avoid taking dark colour food out of fear that their baby's skin will be dark. Some of my friends believe this and they do not take even coffee or chocolate while pregnant. On the contrary, they take milk and eggs with the expectation that they will get a fair baby. Also, they say that if you take too much chilli, your baby will be born with only a little bit of hair.

For twins – some twins are born in same placenta and some are in different placenta. Twins from the same placenta will have very similar feature, character, likes and dislikes. They will get sick together even though they are staying in different places. So it is not good in practical life.

According to ancient people, to avoid that dual suffering, as soon as they are born, cut the placenta into two pieces and bury one on each side of the river. It should be done at the same river. Some say that you should often eat twin fruits, such as twin-bananas or others, to have twins.

If you want your babies to love each other, keep their chords together. I kept chords of my two sons together by tying them with a red string and put them in a small bottle to keep them united all the time. I got this knowledge from a part-time nurse who took care of my baby. I keep it in a safe box to show them when they grow up.

Baby boy or girl? It sounds interesting! Nowadays the medical science is very sophisticated and we can choose the baby's gender by scientific methods like IVF (In Vitro Fertilization) or PGD (Pre-implantation Genetic Diagnosis), but it is expensive.

There are some traditionally effective ways which are simple and inexpensive but you need to have great faith. First of all, it is common knowledge among married couples that there is a statue of Brahma (higher celestial being) at Shwedagon pagoda which is holding a baby boy. It is known as 'Thar Pike Kodaw'. The married couple can go and pray there to get a baby boy. Near that Brahma, there is also another standing statue of a Brahma who is holding flowers. If they pray from the baby's side, she will get a baby boy and if on the flower side, a baby girl.

If they want twins, they can pray in the middle of the two Brahmas. Most of the people including my sister-in-law say that it is quite accurate. According to some people, if you want twin babies, you have to eat the twin fruits as much as you can before pregnancy.

One astrologer says that if you want a baby boy, you should offer fruits to the Buddha or monks and if a girl, offer flowers and pray as often as you can. It is quite similar to what Ma Aeko said to me. When I was pregnant, she asked me, "What did you dream?" I told her that I dreamed different kinds of fruit every two or three nights. She confidently said, "The baby inside will be a boy. If you dream flowers, it will be a girl."

Some experienced people know that it will be a boy or a girl after looking at the mother's womb. If the womb is round and in a pyramid shape, it will be a boy. If the womb is flat and fully occupied on both sides, it will be a girl.

Some can say the next one will be a boy or a girl after looking at the first baby. After delivering my first son, my helper (who has three children) told me, "Don't take the second baby so fast, it will be a boy, too." I did not believe her until I got my second boy. So one day I asked her, "How do you know that my second baby will be a boy?" At that time, she smiled like a winner and explained to me that she could say by looking at the testicles of my first son.

To prove her right, while I was carrying my second pregnancy, one of my friends who visited me said that my second baby would be a boy too. At that time, my son was playing by himself near us. Why? Because when my first son made a fist, he put the thumb outside. According to her, if he hides his thumb inside of the other four fingers, the next baby will be a girl. After experiencing all those things, I dared not ignore the traditional beliefs and I started to take interest in traditional beliefs and superstitions.

One day, I visited my sister's apartment together with my 1st son. It is on the 9th fl. We met with a woman inside the elevator.

She say, "Oh, the baby is very cute, is it your son?

"Yes" I replied.

"How old is he? "

"Nearly 3 years"

"How many children do you have"

"Two"

"Is the second one a boy or a girl?"

In my mind, I was thinking how come I met with such a curious lady in the lift.

"Second one is a boy, too". I continued, "He is too young, just over a year old". Before she asked another question, I let her know. I thought that the lift was too slow at that moment. We had to drop at the 2nd floor and she would drop at the ground floor. The lift was arriving at the 2nd floor and we prepared to drop. At that time, unexpectedly, she said,

"If you want a baby girl..."

The lift door opened. We landed. But her last words aroused my interest. The lift door closed. I quickly pressed the button to reopen. I was very busy within a few seconds. Luckily, the lift door opened. She continued, "If you want a baby girl...". "Please say quickly before the lift doors shut!" I shouted in my mind. The lift (very slow, I thought before) was very quick now.

"You change your longyi (sarong) with that of a mother who have only daughters and wear it."

"Oh, thank you so much. I will tell about it to my friends, too. Bye Bye!"

Now I understand that she asked me questions because she wanted to share me her knowledge.

Some reliable astrologers can be consulted. They can predict whether you will get a baby boy or girl by checking your zodiac for a particular year. One of my friends told me that when she was single, an astrologer predicted that she would be the mother of six boys. She took it as a joke until she got three boys consecutively and noted that it had become practically true.

Infancy – If the baby does not talk even though he reaches the age to talk, feed him some chicken anus. They say that eating chicken anus makes the baby talkative.

Sometimes, the infants smile to themselves while they are sleeping inside the cradle. People usually say, "Ma Hne Lay is coaxing him." Ma Hne Lay is the nat (Please see under the chapter of "37 Nats") who died as a baby. Some people offer food (including boiled duck egg), small clothing, and very small slippers to her when their babies are not feeling well and pray to take care of their babies. Some babies often wake up or get frightened while they are sleeping. At such a time, white ginger should be tied to their bodies.

If an infant hiccups, chew a few threads from the white cloth which wraps the infant and put it on his forehead. After a few minutes, there will be no more hiccups.

They say that if we swing the empty cradle, the baby will get a stomach pain. If a baby looks back between his two legs while he is crawling means that he is looking back at the next child and his mother will get pregnant soon. If a baby is born with its feet first, he will possess healing power. If the baby ears are big, he will become wise and generous adult.

Some couples cannot get babies. They miscarry or lose their baby soon after the delivery. Every problem has a solution and if they are facing that kind of problem, once the baby is born, they must sell the baby to someone with a little amount of money to pretend that the baby is no longer theirs. After that, the baby will survive and they will not have to face with the same problem.

Suppose in a family of five children, there are four boys and a girl or four girls and a boy. The sole boy or a girl is considered unlucky as he or she may be either handicapped or experience poor health. The superstition is that it is taken as a bad omen meaning that the individual boy's or girl's coffin will be borne by the remaining four siblings. In order to avoid such misfortune, the parents may sell him/her to a monk or to a close relative for a small amount of money as if he/she no longer belongs to that family although he/she remains with the family all the time.

Baby Ogre – Some people believe that if a newborn comes into the world with teeth, he or she could be an ogre. In a village, a woman delivered twin babies with teeth. One day, the mother put them to sleep, went to the toilet and then tiptoed back to their bed. To her surprise, she found that her two infants were playing like adults and jumping over their bed. She asked a learned person about this and he advised her to destroy them quickly because they were ogres, otherwise the whole family would be in trouble. At first, she did not listen. One month later, her sister in law at their house passed away with a sudden illness. Although the mother did not want to do it, other people helped her. A few days later, she got a dream, and in which those ogre babies told her, "You kept one step ahead. We were going to eat your whole family!"

Man-eating Rivers, Bridges and Railways

People believe that there are guardian spirits on some railways, rivers, and bridges. Every year, they are waiting for their replacement.

My village house is very near to the railway, only about 100 yards away. The village is situated between the highway and railway road of Yangon-Mandalay. The railway is in the west part of the village and the highway is in the east quarter. So, the layout of the village is like an aeroplane. The highway is like the front of the two wings and the railway is like the back of the two wings. Our house is situated in a market quarter which is in the heart of the village. So, whenever we go to school or to the monastery to take the Sabbath, we have to pass the railway. Some people say that there is a guardian spirit in this railway, too, and that every year it needs a replacement to take a turn of duty. There is a family who live beside the railway and the wife sell gourd fritters, fried beans, fried potatoes, etc. She has to get up early to prepare her produce for business. Every year, she usually hears a grinding sound from the railway when it is time to handover the duty. Sooner or later, you may hear of a tragic thing happening after that sound.

One evening, my mother ran into the house calling out our names. She looked very excited so I asked my mother,

"Mom, what's the matter with you?"

"Oh, I just heard that the train had hit a child. So I was so worried and I wanted to check if all of you are at home and safe."

My mother is a very worrisome person and sometimes I feel pity for her over-worrying nature. At that time, I was only about 10 years old. I was so moved by that bad news. At the same time, I wanted to see the victim who was about the same age as me. So, my mother and I went there. The scene was so touching and we found the ankle of the child, which the train had cut, and I saw some white nerves coming out. Many people were watching and they explained that the child was from a nearby village and that his mother had asked him to buy cooking oil from our village market. I saw the cracked pieces of an oil bottle, too. He was still alive at that time and was brought to the nearest hospital by car. About 4 or 5 days later, we heard that the child passed away at the hospital. At the funeral, people heard his mother's loud crying, "What bad luck for my son! I cannot console myself. Even when my parents passed away, I did not feel as painful as now!"

That's why older people warn young people not to cross over the railway after sunset or in the evening whenever possible. A railway story from another place which my mother told us when we were young was this:

One evening, two friends, 'Ko Myint' and 'Ko Cho' went back home from work to their village by passing over the railway. While they were crossing the railway, suddenly, Ko Cho could not move his legs from the railway. Ko Myint had already reached the other side.

The victim shouted, "Hey, I cannot move my legs from this place." At that time, the train was slowly coming towards them.

So Ko Myint shouted, "Come very quickly. The train is coming."

"I can't move my legs anymore. The railway is gripping my legs." He shouted with great fear. "Please help me, I am going to die!"

Ko Myint became very irritated and, suddenly, he rushed to his friend and pushed him away from that place with all his strength. Ko Cho escaped from that place. But unfortunately, Ko Myint, in his turn, could not move his legs. He lost his life instead of his friend. Ko Cho was so moved because the accident took place right in front of him and he felt sad for the friend who had sacrificed his life for him.

Most of the people believe that it is a true story. Every year, the replacement of duty takes place at such kinds of railways. If the guardian spirit cannot find a suitable human victim, it has to be satisfied with the lives of some animals, like cows or buffaloes. Once, the train hit a cow and I asked the cow's owner whether he got any compensation or not. He replied that far from getting compensation, the railway authorities charged him to pay some money as a punishment for leaving the animals in a dangerous area so that the owners would be more careful in the future.

Another story about the man-eating river

There is a village called 'Pa De' which lies near the 'Pa De creek'. If you walk about two hours to the east from our village, you can reach there. Pa De is famous for its notorious people. They are always fighting, stabbing, and raping cases occur especially during the pagoda festivals. So, there is a saying:

"If you visit Pa De, don't stay overnight;

If you stay overnight, don't sleep;

If you sleep, don't close your eyes;

If you close your eyes, don't dream." (scary?)

In Myanmar language, there is rhyme and rhythm in the below verse.

(ပတဲ့၊ ပတဲ့၊ မတည်းလေနှင့်
တည်းလေ၊ တည်းလေ၊ မအိပ်လေနှင့်
အိပ်လေ၊ အိပ်လေ၊ မမှိတ်လေနှင့်
မှိတ်လေ၊ မှိတ်လေ မပျော်လေနှင့်)

One day, U Hla Sein, from another village came to Pa De to stay overnight to attend the Shinbyu ceremony of his relative. He knew Pa De was notorious so he brought along a 'Hnget-kyi-taung' (ငှက်ကြီးတောင်) (it is a sword with a broad blade) with him. He always carried it across his shoulder. He announced, "I got this from my grandpa and nobody can dare touch me when they see this." In the evening, he drank a lot of toddy (palm juice) and his voice became louder than normal. "I am not scared of the people here however daring you may be! That's why I have come here alone." "Anybody who wants to fight me will get a taste of this Hngetkyitaung!" He repeatedly said this. In the village, people can easily get toddy. In the evening, after taking the toddy, U Hla Sein was feeling hot and he left for the creek to take a bath alone. By night time, he had still not come back. Two days later, in the lower part of the creek, people saw the lifeless body of U Hla Sein. He died, not because of the Pa De people, but by the man-eating creek. One strange thing was that when people saw his dead body, it was totally naked, but his favourite 'Hngetkyitaung' was still firmly attached to his body.

My brother in law's (my eldest sister's husband) small town lies on the bank of Sittaung River. When I was young, after the final exam was over, sometimes I visited their town. I was happy to play in the water when I took bath there. As a curious teenager, seeing all the floating things and the working people at the river bank gave me enjoyment. Whenever I told them that I was going to take bath in the river, I saw a wave of worries pass over their faces. They asked someone to accompany me and also asked me not to play too long in the water. Later on, I came to know that this area of the river usually changed duty every year and for that year, the river had not yet handed over the duty. According to them, the time of handing over the duty was after the state school exam because the students usually were very happy and relaxed at that time and came to take a bath. According to the people who live near the river, they usually get a foul smell from the river if the timing is getting nearer. At such a time, they anticipate that the victim is coming soon.

Dear reader, do you notice that all those rivers, bridges, and railways' victims are from other places? No one is a native person. Although they are spiritual beings, they have a discipline of their own. (ရွာခံလူများကို စားလေ့မရှိဟု သိရပါသည်။)

Trips and Travelling

'To travel hopefully is better than arriving.' That saying is quite similar with the belief of Myanmar people, too. Myanmar people enjoy going out on pilgrimage. When we go out, we should not ask "What time will we arrive there?" or "What time will we be back home?" or "How much longer, brother?", as this is only tempting fate. The drivers don't like such questions because it can delay the trip more than it should. Also, they say that if we see a snake along our way, the trip will be lengthened. While travelling, if a pregnant woman delivers a baby in your car, it will bring good luck to you.

People should not wear totally red or totally black colored clothing when we go to nat worshipping areas like 'Taungpyone' or 'Mt. Popa', and eating pork is forbidden or the local nats will give you trouble.

People say that the Northern part of Shan State is occupied by 'Koe Myoh Shin' nat (ကိုးမြို့ရှင်နတ်) (a spiritual god). 'Koe' means number 'nine' in Myanmar language. If you want to go there, the number of travellers should not be nine. If you cannot find one more person to join, you should invite a stone by saying, "Mr. Stone, please be our travel partner." and bring it along on the trip so that the total number will be ten or else your group will be in trouble. Please be careful that if you do some trading business with trucks, you should not send nine at the same time to go there. If it is not avoidable, please bring a toy car to make it 'ten'.

Some Myanmar people believe that they should not start travelling on Saturday and Monday or the trip will be delayed and meet with some inconveniences on the way.

Three years ago, I went to Maymyo (Pyin Oo Lwin) for a 2-night-trip with my family to see the coffee plantations. A couple, who were friends of my husband, accompanied us. On our way back from Maymyo,

Koe Myoh Shin nat shrine

Mr. Koh and my husband proceeded to Kyaukse on business and, left three of us (me, Myat, and my eight months old boy) at Mandalay airport. After waiting for about 45 minutes, the airline abruptly announced that our flight was cancelled due to bad weather.

The other flights were not sure, too, due to weather condition. To be honest, we did not have enough money left to hire a car to go back to Yangon. It looked like we might have to stay overnight at the airport by waiting for the unsure flights. It was so miserable to sleep at the airport with the little baby. Finally, we tried to see the airline manager and she kindly arranged a flight with a different airline (without buying a new ticket) to come back to Yangon after having anxiously waited for nearly the whole day at the airport. That trip was not a pleasant one for me.

I rechecked an old calendar before I wrote about this topic and I found out that the day we went to Maymyo was Saturday (5th Jan, 2008) and the day we came back was Monday (7th Jan, 2008). What a coincidence!

Don't you think that your return trip is faster than the going trip? When I was about 10 years old, we went to Kyaikhtiyoe pagoda with my family and some relatives. We all felt that the return trip was faster than going up. So, my aunty explained the difference to us, "If we go on a pilgrimage, a female angel accompanies us, but on return, a male angel takes a turn to send us home." We were so amused by what she revealed.

Shwe Nyaung Pin (Golden Banyan Tree)

One year, on our school holidays, we went back to our home town of Toungoo with my aunties. Half way through our journey, our car tyre punctured. My aunty said "That is because we did not pay respects to 'Shwe Nyaung Pin' when we left from Yangon". In my mind, I was thinking that my aunty was too superstitious. This might be a coincidence. If nothing happened to our car tyre, she would not say this.

Shwe Nyaung Pin lies on left side of the road on the Yangon to Bago highway (near Htauk Kyant). After buying new cars, the owners bring their cars and pay respects there in order to avoid any future danger or accident. Every year, car owners, especially those who are earning money from the car business such as highway express cars, truck cars, and pilgrimage cars, etc., come to pay respects at Shwe Nyaung Pin. The car has to be parked towards the shrine and driven to and forth three times. Prayers

Shwe Nyaung Pin Shrine

are offered while spraying the car with perfumes. They will tie a red ribbon and put flowers in front of the car. At the same time, they recite the incantations for the car to be blessed. Remember to ask the price first before you let them recite the blessings or do the usual things to your car.

Thamyinnya trip (The vegetarian saint)

There was a very famous saint who lived in Thamyinnya mountain (he passed away in 2005) so people called Him 'Thamyinnya Sayadaw'. He was a vegetarian. Because of his power, all the people living around this area do not take any meat out of respect to the Sayadaw. If we want to go there, we should not consume any meat during the trip until we arrive back home or else the pilgrimage will not be successful. Some people don't take any meat once they have decided to go and see the saint. They also avoid drinking alcohol, using nasty words, and making dirty jokes because the guardian spirits of that area do not like it.

Plant Guardian

A toilet problem can be sometimes a hindrance during a highway trip, especially in the jungle or on trekking tours. There is no choice that you may have to urinate somewhere along the way. At that time, please do not forget to ask permission from lords of the forest, or mountain, or tree.

I still remember, one day, a man from our village urinated to the root of a big tree outside of our compound. In the evening, the nat or guardian of that tree possessed him. His tongue came out long and angrily rebuked, "You are very rude. You insulted me by urinating on my head". So people around him suddenly realized what had happened and they apologised and promised to bring a meal with chicken curry for that tree nat the next morning. If they don't do like that, the spirit may take away that man's life.

When I was young, my family ran a logging car business. The government hired the cars from us to carry the logs to allocated areas. Each year the allocated areas were different. It took the whole summer from late winter to finish the assignment. We had to make tents and store food for the drivers there. In one particular year, our drivers were told by the villagers that they could not take pork because that was a nat-worship area.

They say that a person should not go on a voyage on a Friday. The sailors usually pay respect to 'U Shin Gyi' nat (ဦးရှင်ကြီး နတ်ရှင်ကြီး) to be safe along their voyage. Not only sailors but also those who earn for their living by sea or water (such as fishermen, shipping agents and so on) pay respect to U Shin Gyi nat before and after Thadingyut so that he will help them out of danger or disturbances in their business. Moreover, such people should not disrespect the water by urinating into the river for example. U Shin Gyi nat is well known in delta areas.

Pagodas and Monasteries and Heavenly-beings

Myanmar is well known as 'The Golden Land'. It means it is full of golden pagodas. When we go to pagodas or monasteries, we have to take off our slippers and the youngest person has to carry all the slippers of his elders. It is a Myanmar cultural tradition and they believe it meritorious. When we walk on the pagoda platform, we should walk with the pagoda to the left side first. It means to circulate it in a clockwise direction. Once we enter into the pagoda or monastery compound, we feel secure and peaceful.

In every village, whether big or small, they have at least one pagoda and one monastery. They enjoy going to pagodas and monasteries for moral refuge and encouragement. There is a saying between Myanmar couples 'Walking to pagodas and stepping on the monastery staircase together.' (ဘုရားသွား၊ ကျောင်းတက်ဖော်). But not all the pagodas are for couples. There are some exceptions.

There are two pagodas to which unmarried couples should not go. If they go there together, the marriage will never take place. They will separate. Why and which pagodas? There was a tragic story between the Mae La Mu Pagoda and Thanlyin Kyauk Tan Pagoda (Pagoda in the middle of a creek).

Thanlyin Kyauk Tan Pagoda

The Princess 'Shin Mway Nunn' was the daughter of the Thanlyin (formerly known as Syriam) King. Minn Nanda was the son of King Okkalapa. They fell in love at first sight but they secretly met only at night because King Okkalapa did not want to accept the princess, who lived outside of the town. What happened was that Shin Mway Nunn's mother passed away during a mature pregnancy. When she was brought to the cemetery, people found out that the baby inside was still alive and moving. Shin Mway Nunn was taken out from her mother's womb at the cemetery but the king was advised by the wise men that the baby from the cemetery should not be taken to the royal palace. The king dared not go against that wise advice even though he deeply loved the daughter. He showed his love by giving her the same status as a princess of the palace and keeping her outside of the royal city with many maids.

Minn Nandar went to the lonely princess on the other side of Yangon river by riding a big and powerful crocodile, Nga Moe Yeik (not an ordinary crocodile). Nga Moe Yeik played a vital role in this story.

One day, a jealous maid advised the princess to test her lover's devotion. If Minn Nandar did not allow her to sleep on his right arm, his love was not deep. The innocent princess decided to test him without thinking twice. Minn Nandar was amazed by his lover's request to let her sleep on his right arm. When he was young, the astrologer told him that, as his talisman was on his right arm, he must not allow anybody to sleep on it to preserve his power. So he refused. The princess was broken hearted by his refusal and claimed that his love was not real. Finally, the prince allowed her to sleep on his right arm to prove his love. Once she slept on his right arm, he felt that he was falling down into a deep gorge. He realized that he had lost all his powers. (The superstition 'Man should not allow the woman to sleep on his right arm, or he will lose his power' originated from this story).

On his way back to the shore where Nga Moe Yeik was waiting to carry him as usual, the prince was feeling weak and knew this night was not the same as the other nights. Unfortunately, the weather was very cloudy as well. The prince noticed that a little bit of worry entered into his mind that he had never felt before but he had to return to the palace before dawn or else his father would get very angry. He rode on the back of Nga Moe Yeik. Unfortunately, in the middle of the river, a storm arose and the prince nearly lost his balance. At this critical moment, 'Ma Lat To' a female crocodile, an old enemy of Nga MoeYeik fiercely attacked him. Nga Moe Yeik sympathized with the prince and advised him to take refuge inside his mouth. It was the only way out. The prince was so confused by this advice and pondered whether he should accept it or not. Finally, he agreed to do so as he was in such a helpless situation.

The faithful crocodile tried to carry his master to the palace in time following the battle with his enemy. The prince was so tired that he could not survive the ordeal. When they arrived at the other side, people found the lifeless body of the love hero in the mouth of Nga Moe Yeik.

When love-sick princess heard the sad news, she felt guilty and immediately died of a broken heart. The cruel destiny was so unkind to these two lovers as the saying goes, 'True love never runs smooth'. Both of their bodies were cremated at the same time on the two banks of the river. People mourned this double tragedy and they saw that the smoke of Minn Nandar's cremation curled over the river towards the Thanlyin side where his lover was waiting for him and the two columns of smoke combined in the sky.

Up to this day, their tragic story is still popular and people believe that there are still influences in those two pagodas; 'Mae La mu' and 'Thanlyin Kyauktan'.

Taung Kwe Zedi

Another forbidden pagoda for the lovers is 'Taung Kwe Zedi' which is situated in Loikaw, Kayah State. 'Taung' means 'mountain', 'Kwe' means 'broken or separate' and Zedi means 'pagoda or stupa'. Some say that if the lovers go to that zedi together, the marriage will never take

Taung Kwe Zedi

place between them. Please refer the photo and you will see that the pagoda is built on the two mountains and it looks like a broken one.

Nagar yon Phayar (Buddha, on the lap of Dragon)

While Lord Buddha was dwelling in *Phala*-consciousness near the 'Mu Salainda' Lake, untimely rain fell heavily. In order to provide a shelter from rain and the insects, the Mu Salainda Dragon coiled its body as a throne and let Lord Buddha sit on it. At the same time, its head covered Him like an umbrella and Lord Buddha dwelled in *Phala*-consciousness meditated in that position for one week. That is why you may see that statue in some pagodas. People cannot help praising the dragon for its cleverness despite being an animal and that scene makes people feel serene. Although that statue is very peaceful, one must be

Nagar Yon Phayar

very careful when one builds it. When one builds the dragon, the important thing is that the dragon's head and tail should be on the same side. It means that if the head of the dragon faces the east, his tail must be at the east side (နဂါးအမြီးနှင့် အမောက် တည့်ရမည်။). Do not put the dragon's tail at the back like other animals. If the head and tail are on different side, the donor and the people involving in this statue will have to face with many problems. According to the old people, there are a lot of rules and regulations in building pagodas, Buddha's statues, and such holy things. One must learn them before he makes such kinds of donation or his merit may become demerit instead.

Do you notice that every reclining Buddha statues are lying on the right side? It is the correct position. When Lord Buddha passed away, He lay to the right side. According to this, you can check human beings, too. They say that when a person dies, if his head lies to the right side, he will go to higher existence; if left, he will go to lower existence.

Amazing Kyaikhtiyoe

Kyaikhtiyoe Pagoda as well as Golden Rock is situated in Mon State, 125 miles far away from Yangon. It is very famous for its defying the Law of Gravity as a huge golden rock is standing on the edge of the hill. In olden days, before the cars were not accessible, pilgrims had to walk up about four to five hours to reach up to the pagoda from base which is about 3,600 ft above sea level. It was a tough journey and one needed a lot of strength and diligence.

According to an old saying at that time, the merit gained from going to Kyaikhtiyoe Pagoda three times is equivalent to repaying back half of your mother's gratitude for breast feeding. (ကျိုက်ထီးရိုးဘုရား သုံးခေါက်ဖူးလျှင် အမေ့နို့တစ်လုံးဖိုး ကျေသည်ဟု ရှေးအခါက ပြောကြပါသည်။) I think, at that time, they were trying to encourage to the pilgrims to walk up to Golden Rock with that saying. Or they are trying to praise with that hyperbole how great Kyaikhtiyoe Pagoda is.

Another saying is that if a person visits Kyaikhtiyoe Pagoda for three times within a year, he will be wealthy.

Heavenly beings

We have heard from our great grandparents that every morning our 'ko-saunt-nat' (Angels who guard each of us) has to attend the 'Nat Tha Bin a-si-a-way' (နတ်သဘင် အစည်းအဝေး) (Angels' Conference) at 8 am. Our spiritual guard cannot go to the conference until we get up from bed and wash our face. They are punished if they are late to attend the conference. So, when we are in bed till late morning, our parents will wake us by saying, "Get up, lazybones, your ko-saunt-nats will get angry and curse you. They won't guard you anymore!" At such a time, we are very scared and get up quickly worrying that the angel guardians won't take care of us anymore.

In the morning, do not eat the food without washing your face first. The angel guardian will get angry. My grandma said that we should not take anything even a small flower from pagoda or monastery compound without getting permission. If you do, it is a sin because the properties of pagoda and monasteries are forbidden things and things from pagoda are like 'hell fire' and things from monasteries are like 'poison fruits' (ဘုရားပစ္စည်း ငရဲမီး၊ ဘုန်းကြီးပစ္စည်း အဆိပ်သီး). If you keep it at home, the angels cannot pass over your house when they go to the angel's conference or somewhere because those celestial beings can feel that the house is very hot and burning with fire and so they avoid your house from far away.

They also say that the silk velvet of Thagyarmin (Chief of the celestial beings) is very soft and whenever a good person (who keeps his morality and doing merit) is in trouble, the soft velvet becomes very hard like a rock. At that time, Thagyarmin checks the human world, comes down and helps him practically.

In rainy season, we hear the thunder striking, and see flashes of lighting because there is a war between two layers of celestial beings. There is a story about the war of the two heavenly layers.

Grandpa said that if we tell the stories at night, the angels are listening too. I did not ask my grandpa at that time why they did not listen in day time. May be they are too busy in the day time to listen to the stories.

Old people said that children should not play 'Hide and Seek' games at night or in the late evening. The heavenly gods do not like playing it at night and they will hide one of them. I think it is a warning to the children not to play too much at night.

According to old people, every year, during Water Festival, Thagyarmin personally comes down to the human world to take a list who are doing good deeds and who are not. He brings two folds of paper - one is made of gold leaf and another from the dog's skin. He writes down the good people's names on the gold sheets and bad persons on the dog's skin.

Oat Sar Saunt (Guardian Spirit to the pagoda's hidden treasures)

Those are the spiritual guards to take care of the jewellery inside the pagodas. They say that every pagoda has Oat Sar Saunt (ဥစ္စာစောင့်). Most of them are in beautiful women forms with long hairs. Oat Sar means 'valuable things or jewellery' and Saunt means 'guards'.

When a pagoda is built, people donate their gems and jewellery to be placed inside the pagoda. Oat Sar Saunts are assigned to take care of those as a special duty. They never die and their assignment last until the next Buddha appears. There are some popular stories that these Oat Sar Saunts sometimes become very bored in their monotonous duty and ask permission from their leader to let them go to the human world. When they are allowed, they have to promise to come back from the human world (for example they will have to come back after getting a baby or in a limited number of years). Once a person knows that his/her spouse (mostly women) is Oat Sar Saunt, he has to invite a magician to help her cut the relationship with her former world and continue living as a human being. It is called 'Theik Kyo Phyat' in Myanmar meaning (သိုက်ကြိုးဖြတ်ခြင်း). We can see some Oat Sar Saunt stories in some dramas which are presented at pagoda festivals. Most of the stories are tragic because after the Oat Sar Saunt returns back to her world, the spouse is left broken hearted.

That's why, if a close friend has deep attachment to his properties or if he does not want to donate or spend money even for his own good, he is usually given a friendly warning, "Don't be too attached to your properties or you will be Oat Sar Saunt after you die!"

Hidden Treasure – In our great grandparents' time, there were no banks or safes yet so the only way for them to secure their wealth was to bury the jewellery under the earth for safe keeping. When I visited my brother in law's small town named (Htan-ta-pin), I was told that the jewellery buried underground in that area were very slowly moving (a few inches in every year) towards the 'Myat Saw Nyi Naung' pagoda (a famous pagoda around that area) due to the power of that pagoda.

A wise man explained to us about it, "Due to the Law of Gravity and geographical movement, the things under the ground including the buried jewellery are very slowly moving from the original place. To solve this problem, when the old people buried the jewellery pot, they should have put the charcoal or burnt paddy husk (မီးသွေး (သို့မဟုတ်) အိုးတိုက်ဖွဲ့ပြာ) under the pot so that they can trace the way where the treasure pot has moved."

Reincarnated Persons

Nga Nyo's small measure of rice (ငညို့ဆန်တစ်စလယ်)

In Myanmar Calendar year 1270-1280, the two friends named 'Nga Nyo' and 'Ba Saing' lived in the village of 'Chaung Sone' which was situated ten miles away to the north-east of Taung Twin Gyi. They earned their living by selling betel leaves and betel nuts from one village to another. One evening, on their way back home, Ba Saing borrowed 'ta sa lei' of rice from Nga Nyo ('Ta sa lei' in Myanmar measurement is equivalent to two tins of condensed milk) to cook for dinner due to a shortage of rice at his home. After the dinner, he went around the village for an evening walk. Unfortunately, Ba Saing passed away on that night due to a snake bite.

Nobody knew what was in Ba Saing's mind about Nga Nyo's 'san ta sa lei' ('San' means rice in Myanmar language) before he died. Ba Saing became a fighting cock at Nga Nyo's house. Nga Nyo trained him very well. He won three times in fighting the rival cocks. On the fourth time, he failed because the opponent was stronger and more experienced. Nga Nyo was so angry that he hit the cock's head on the ground and put it near the water pot stand. While Ba Saing was half dead, a cow came to him and kissed him.

Poor Ba Saing was reincarnated again as a calf inside the cow who showed her sympathy to the cock in NgaNyo's house. When the calf was four years old, Nga Nyo sold him to his friends who wanted to eat him and the cow was killed. When the wife of the superintendent from Taung Twin Gyi saw the dead cow, she said "Why did they kill such a pitiful calf? If the calf were mine, I would never be so cruel as this. Even if he dies, I will bury him."

Ba Saing was reincarnated again inside that kind-hearted woman's womb and born as her son. But he did not say a word until the age of seven. So the parents became very worried. One day, the father spoke to him "My dear son, today is pay day. This evening, on my way back from office, I will buy nice clothing for you. Please say something for we really want to hear your voice."

As he promised, the father bought some nice clothing and toys for his silent son. "Look, all these are for you my son, please talk."

Ba Saing's first words were; "Nga Nyo's san ta sa lei". First they did not understand. But the smart father encouraged him by saying "My son, it is a very small thing for us. Not only 'ta sa lei', even a whole bag of rice, we are ready to pay for you". The boy suddenly said "Are you sure, my father? If so, please bring a bag of rice to the bullock cart and we will go to that place right now."

By the direction of the little boy (Ba Saing), they reached in front of Nga Nyo's house. U Nyo was old already. As soon as the boy saw U Nyo, he greeted, "Hey, Nga Nyo, do you remember me?" U Nyo was very angry by the tone of a young boy calling his name like a friend of same age. So the parents apologised to him. "Forgive him, U Nyo, this boy has some unusual circumstances and please let him explain."

After hearing the boy's long story, U Nyo felt very sad and cried for his ill treatments to his dear friend when he was his cock and cattle at his home. Ba Saing said, "Because my mind was pending to pay back your small measure of rice, I could not escape from you."

▸▸ *This is a real story retold by U Nyo. From this story, we can take out the lesson that unless the attachment has been rooted out, repeated rebirths in similar existences are unavoidable.*

Ma Tin Hla's story

One evening, a young man was killed near the farms of a village in Toungoo township. Nobody knew who the culprit was and they could not find any clue. People slowly forgot about the case.

About five or six years later, a little girl from that village was very frightened whenever Ko Thar Aye who lived in a nearby village, passed over her house. Ma Tin Hla's house was beside the main road and people from other villages had to pass in front of her house whenever they wanted to go to town. Whenever she saw Ko Thar Aye, she ran inside the house and hid herself and she said, "I am so scared of him. He is a killer. He killed me." She repeatedly said this and her parents were surprised to hear that. When they asked her, she said, "He killed me about 6 years ago near the farm. At that time, I was a man and people did not take my death seriously, as I was drunk. He cut my fingers, too." So they brought her to the head of the village and the little girl explained in detail what she remembered of her previous life. The village head informed the head of the Ko Thar Aye's village and asked them to come. The little girl proved herself by showing her hands. "Do you remember that you cut my fingers at that time after killing me? Now, this life, I was born without some fingers". Ko Thar Aye was so surprised upon hearing all those things and could not argue. He admitted that he killed that young man at that time. At that time, nobody suspected that Ko Thar Aye killed that young man because he was a quiet person and had no criminal record. That's why 'There is no escape for criminals'.

►► *This is a true story, too, and by the time I am writing this book, Ma Tin Hla is married and already has her own children.*

Earth-Swallowing, Thunder-Striking and Taking an Oath

"**Y**ou will be swallowed by earth." (မြေမျိုခံရလိမ့်မည်။) "The thunder will strike you." (မိုးကြိုးပစ်တတ်သည်။) These warnings are given by older people when they want to teach the young generations not to be rude or insult the parents or teachers or other older people. This is not merely a threat because there are real stories behind the warnings.

When Lord Buddha was alive, there was a woman named 'Cinca Manavika' who took refuge in a wrong belief. One day, she put a pillow around her womb and covered it with some blankets, pretending to be a pregnant lady. While Lord Buddha was preaching

Cinca Manavika accused Lord Buddha

to the congregation at 'Zetawun' Monastery in the city of 'Thawahti', she accused of Lord Buddha in front of the congregation that she was impregnated by Him. Lord Buddha was calm and he kept on preaching to the people.

But four nearby angels disguised themselves as four mice and bit the rope which she had tied around her womb. The pillow and the blankets dropped to the floor and she was ashamed. She ran away from the monastery as the people wanted to punish her for insulting the Lord Buddha. When she arrived to a safe place from the people, unexpectedly, the earth cracked open, swallowed her into the hell, which was full of flames. Nobody could help her.

Thunder striking story

Kyaik Pi village is situated in Ayeyarwady region near Kyaik Latt. Villagers earn their living by fishing or farming. There was a widow named Daw Htwe Tin and Mg Chit Phe was her only son. The father had died when Mg Chit Phe was young. Daw Htwe Tin loved him very much and she tried to fulfil her only son's wishes. Mg Chit Phe left the school early, on his own accord, regardless of his mother's pleas. She wanted to see him become an educated person. Most of the time, he usually drank toddy with his friends and gambled on cock-fighting. Every night, he came back home very late. The old mother could not sleep until he arrived back home. She waited for him by praying and reciting holy verses so that her son would be free from dangers. After he arrived back home, he gave trouble to his mother. He complained to her for not cooking very well. Sometimes, he even kicked the dinner table. The whole village knew that Mg Chit Phe was a rude son but Daw Htwe Tin's love for Mg Chit Phe never faded.

"Since your father died, we have to spend money sparingly. How can I afford to cook delicious curry every day?", Mother told him.

Mg Chit Pe replied very rudely, "Are you saying that I am a useless son? Tomorrow I will go out for fishing."

The next morning, he left to go fishing. When he returned home, the mother asked "How was your day, my son?"

"Today was an unlucky day. I could not get fish the whole day. I will try again tomorrow." But Mg Chit Phe could not get any fish for a few days.

He was very angry and blamed his mother, "It is because of you!"

"Why, son?"

"Because you are praying all the time, reciting those useless mantras, and wishing for the animals to be safe from danger. So how can I get any fish? You must not do this in the future."

"You are talking nonsense. It is my daily work and I enjoy doing that."

Mg Chit Phe kicked his mother. Daw Htwe Tin tried to run away and she fell down from the stair case but Mg Chit Phe did not stop his cruelty. He pulled out a wooden stick and tried to beat his mother. Already, the power of liquor had overwhelmed him. He saw his own mother as an enemy so the neighbours came and tried to beat him off.

They said, "Mg Chit Phe, this is your mother, aren't you afraid of 'Nga Ye Kyi' (suffering in hell)? What he replied was "I don't care! If I am 'Nga Ye Kyi', I will win the 'Nga Ye Lay.' (ငရဲကြီးရင် ငရဲလေးကို နိုင်တာပေါ့။) The neighbours were very angry with his sarcastic reply and tried to beat him. ('Nga Ye' means 'suffering in hell' and 'kyi' mean 'big' and 'Lay' means 'small'.)

As 'Mother nature is always right', she quickly apologised to them, "Please, do not hurt my son. He is innocent and too young to understand everything. It is only my fault that I did the things he doesn't like."

One night, it was rainy. About 10 pm, people heard a terrible thunder sound after a big lightning. After that they heard Daw Htwe Tin's loud cry, "Oh my son, what a poor fate! How can I console myself!". Mg Chit Phe was struck by the thunder-bolt. The neighbours saw that a ray of lightning was going in and out of the windows of a few houses before it stroke Mg Chit Phe, as if it were searching for the sinner.

Taking an oath

When people take an oath, they usually say, "May the thunder strike on me if I break this promise.", "May I be swallowed up by the earth if...", "If I said something not true, may I vomit blood or may I die by snake bite." etc. But the wise warning from old Myanmar people is :

> "Don't take an oath unnecessarily. If a person breaks an oath or takes a wrong oath, his/her younger generation has to pay for it."

So one must be very careful before taking or breaking an oath. Let your future generations be innocent!

Love, Romance and Marriage

Thanakhar from cemetery (သချႋုင်းေျမမ္ သနပ္ခါး)

One popular ancient story is about the 'Pi Ya Sey' (ပိယေသး) (love potion). A few men and the black magician (necromancer) who want the love potion have to go to the cemetery late in the night. They dig out a coffin which was sent to the cemetery on the same day. The corpse must be a female who die violently or accidentally and must be buried on that day. So they must wait until there is any funeral for a female who die of that kind in the village. On that night, the magician and a few followers (who want Pi-ya-sey) secretly go to the cemetery while other people are asleep. It is very important that all the persons who go to the cemetery must be very brave. If there is a coward, they cannot succeed and it is very dangerous for their lives, too, because it is like playing a game with the spirit world and the cemetery is their territory. After digging out the corpse, the magician orders the corpse to sit down, by showing his magic cane. If his order is ignored, he has to repeat his order very sharply a few times until the corpse listens. (It is better to learn at the funeral, whether the dead woman is stubborn or obedient person).

Secondly, they put the 'Thanakhar' (a bark of Thanakhar tree) and a 'Kyaukpyin' (a circular slab of stone) in front of the sitting corpse. The magician orders her to grind thanakha on the kyaukpyin with a little bit of water. While she is grinding, the magician has to chant some mantras for it to be effective. After that, he commands her to apply it on her face. When the thanakhar is dried, he orders her to scrape the thanakha from her face. The next order is to hand over the dry thanakhar to him, that is the love potion. According to magicians, it is difficult to get the thanakhar from the corpse. Although most of them listen to previous orders, they may refuse to give the thanakhar from their face. The final stage is very exciting, too. The magician has to order the corpse to get back to her coffin. Some do not listen easily. As soon as the female corpse is back in the coffin, they must quickly run away from the cemetery. You have to be very careful not to fall down. While running, if you fall down, you will be the loser. It means that the spirits from that cemetery may take away your life. Sometimes, the corpse chases them to ask back her thanakhar.

If a person keeps these magic thanakhar, he can win the hearts of women.

Another method I heard is to put a white handkerchief under two snakes while they are mating. Then put that handkerchief on your pillow and sleep on it and everybody will love you.

One method I heard when I was young is that while male elephants are in musth (uncontrollable passion), they try to attack anything in front of them. Even their master cannot control them at that time. If they see a tree, they attack by putting their tusk into the tree. When they pull back their tusk, some pieces of the tusk are left in the tree. If a person keeps that piece (ဆင်မာန်စွယ်), he/or she definitely can charm the opposite sex. According to someone, "As it sometimes is too effective, unrequited love may occur and it may lead to an elopement without one's agreement."

Among the above three methods, the first method is very dangerous and risky and no longer used nowadays. All these methods are actually ways to influence the opposite sex but please do not forget that "Love 'sought' is good but 'unsought' is better."

Sometimes, you may see that a lizard with a forked tale. It is not an ordinary one. If you keep it, you will get money especially from a sales business. It is very useful for magicians to create the 'Pi Ya Sey' too.

Some say that if you put a wedding card or wedding flower under your pillow, you will see your prince charming in a dream that very night. You should not give a red flower to your lover or the romance will break off. Also, you should not put a red flower in your hair (for women) or you will miss your first love (ပန်းနီနီပန်ရင် ချစ်ဦးသူနဲ့လွဲတတ်သည်။).

The couple who in their first marriage can prepare the wedding bed for a newly-wed couple. It means that divorcees or the widows/ widowers should not prepare the wedding bed. The wife must sleep on the left side of the husband because they believe that a man's power lies in his right arm. A man should not allow a woman to sleep on his right arm or he will lose his power. Couples should not sleep in the shrine room because the gods do not like it. On the wedding day, the plates and bowls should not be broken or the marriage will not last long.

The four heavenly kings who are responsible for religious affairs usually come down and wander around the human world during 4:30 to 6 am every morning. They spread loving kindness and blessing to people and they personally see who get up early and doing meritorious deeds. So making love during that period should be avoided by couples.

During the Buddhist Lent period, couples cannot get married as weddings are forbidden.

Old people warn that the husband and wife should not go out trips separately to opposite directions at a same time (လင်မယား:နှစ်ယောက် ဆန့်ကျင်ဘက်အရပ်သို့ တစ်နေ့တည်း၊ တစ်ချိန်တည်း ခရီးမထွက်ကောင်းပါ). The couple may get divorced. Also, one brother and one sister from a family and one sister and one brother from another family should not get married. If they get married, among two couples, one couple will end up in divorced or by death. (မောင်လှယ် နှမလှယ် ယူလျှင် မကောင်းပါ။ တစ်တွဲမှာ သေကွဲ သို့မဟုတ် ရှင်ကွဲ ကွဲတတ်ပါသည်။)

All I have to do is dream

It is not the title of the song by 'the Everly Brothers'. Do you want to see your lover in your dream or do you want to let him/her dream about you? If yes, at night, before you sleep, you have to offer one candle light and an incense stick to Lord Buddha (at your home or pagoda) and call the name of 'Ba Li Yaza' seven times (in your mind). Ba Li Yaza is a celestial being and who can influence all dreams. Then you have to chant the 'Gon Taw' (the attributes of the Buddha) nine times and pray.

Secret Admirer (တိတ်တခိုးချစ်သူ)

If you are a secret admirer, you should get small photo of the one you love first, and then put the photo together with your photo face to face and keep in a safe place or inside your bag. If you keep it in a stationary place, the man's photo should be on top and tied with a string. Then, you must think about him/her from a positive point of view most of the time and pray for the well-being of that person in your mind. Sooner or later, that person's attention will slowly sway towards you and the rest depends upon you.

The followings are the different degree of effectiveness of marriage in each Myanmar month:

If you get married in ~

Tagu	-	You will go crazy.
Kasone	-	Will get money
Nayone	-	Safe from danger
Waso	-	Separation by death or while alive
Wakaung	-	No harmony, no baby
Tawthalin	-	Get ashamed
Thadingyut	-	Short life-span
Tasaungmone	-	Get diseases
Nattaw	-	Get properties
Pyatho	-	Short married life-span
Tapotwe	-	Will be wealthy
Tabaung	-	Separation by death or while alive

1500 and 528 in Love

There are two types of love according to Myanmar people's belief.

- '1500' represents the love between opposite sex such as husband and wife or lovers. They say it is love mixed with sexual desire.

- '528' represents the love between parents and children or grandparents and grandchildren, brother and sister, between friends, etc. So they say '528' is pure love.

That's why some express to their lovers, "I love you with both 1500 and 528".

Othello's handkerchief

"If you give a handkerchief to your lover, the relationship will be split off." Myanmar people believe that, too. At that time, I remembered Shakespeare's drama "Othello", which I studied in my University days. According to the drama, Othello was a fighting hero and he gave a handkerchief (which he received from his mother) to his beloved Desdemona as a token of his love. The handkerchief was not an ordinary one. As long as a wife keeps it, the husband's love will be flowing to her unconditionally. But that drama ended in tragedy!

In the drama, Iago played as a clever villain and he plotted a misunderstanding between the couple because he resented Othello for ignoring the promotion he expected. To cut a long story short, finally Othello killed his wife out of jealousy because he misunderstood that his wife was involved with another man. Although physical pain was nothing for a professional soldier like Othello, he could not tolerate the heartache. Anyway, my personal thinking is whether the couple separated in tragedy because of the handkerchief?

I still remember what my English lecturer commented of the drama, "Jealousy is not a monster but a nature". "The more the love, the more the jealousy; if there is no love, there will be no jealousy..."

Housing, Accommodation and Kitchen

Housing

If you go into a forest to chop a tree to build a house, please do not chop the tree in which the eagle or Khin-poke bird (brown hawk-owl) are making a nest or resting. But if you see an egret, crane, peacock, chicken, or koel on that tree, you can chop it quickly. When you chop a tree to build a house or a monastery, if that tree does not fall down directly to the ground and hangs or leans onto another, you should not use that tree because the house owner or the Abbot of the monastery will not live for long. That log is called 'hanging wood' (သစ်ဆွဲ). You should cut a little bit of the top part of the log or bamboo (which you bring from the forest) with a sharp knife so that the spirit from the forest cannot be attached to the log or bamboo anymore.

You should not start building a house on Sunday and a monastery on Monday (Eain Galon Kyar Kyaung Ma Saut Kaung) (အိမ်ဂဠုန် ကျားကျောင်း၊ မဆောက်ကောင်း). When we consider building a house in a large empty compound, we should build the house at the head part (in the directing of the head when sleeping and considered to be a place of honour) of the plot so that the younger generation can build the house on the remaining part of the land in the future. Myanmar people believe that the young people should not live at the head of the parents. But when we build a monastery in a big empty plot, a monastery should be built at the foot part (in the direction of the feet when sleeping and considered to be inferior to the head part) of the plot so that the pagoda, stupa, well or the Thein Kyaung (Buddhist monk's Ordination Hall) can be built on the head part. (အိမ်ဆိုလျင်ဆန်၊ ကျောင်းဆိုလျင်စုန်).

Lan Oo Tite House

Do not live in a house which is directly opposite of the direction of the lane or road. If you do, you will have to face a lot of accidents. Myanmar people call

Lan Oo Tite House

it 'Lan Oo Tite Eain' (လမ်းဦးတိုက်အိမ်). *Please see the picture.* If you have no choice, you should build a drinking water pot stand for public use (ရေအိုးစင်) in front of your house. Or you can put a small mirror facing the lane in front of your house.

You may have seen that some branches of a big tree are hanging on to the roof of the house. When the wind blows, the branches are moved and look like sweeping the roof. If you see this, you should chop the branches without delay because those branches will sweep off not only your roof but also all your money, too.

Sometimes you may find that your house is situated between two houses in which the people from both sides are relatives such as brothers or sisters or in-laws. For example, there are three houses named A, B and C. Your house is B and A and C are your neighbours. The people from A and C are relatives to each other but not with B. Myanmar people call the house B 'Eain Kyar Hnyat' (အိမ်ကြားညှပ်). According to Myanmar's superstitions, it is not auspicious. To remedy this, you can build a small pigeon house or bird house and put it one side of your house (do not put on both sides).

You should not make only one door for going into the house and going out for some sound reasons. That house is called 'one hole cave' (ဂူတစ်ပေါက်အိမ်တွင် မနေကောင်း) and you will have to face health and financial problems. Normally a house should have an entrance as well as an exit even in a very small hut. A one-hole house is not appropriate for human lodging.

When you build a house, you should not build the entrance door from which you can see straight through to the backyard door. Otherwise, you will not be able to save money and all your money will go straight outside for one reason or the other. If you have already built in that style, block the backyard door and make a door in another place instead.

In some wooden houses, you may see a beam which is supporting the roof and it is wet without raining or pouring water down on it. Sometimes water is dropping from that place like tears. If so, you should quickly change that beam and give donation or you may have to cry due to financial and health problems.

If there is a beehive on top of the right side of a roof, it is a sign of fortune to the person who lives in it and if it is on the left side, it will be a sign of misfortune.

Do not allow the children to walk down or walk up in backward position or some children to slide down from the hand rail of the stair case instead of walking down in an ordinary way. The guardian spirit of the stair case does not like it.

You may notice that a small mirror is hung in front of some houses or shops. It means that if someone uses black magic with jealousy to the occupants of that house, it will reflect to the original person.

You should not allow young persons (including your children) to stay at the head of your room in the same house or head of your house inside the same compound. It will bring bad luck.

Some people tie a rope between the house and a tree in their compound in order to hang their clothing. Old people do not like it as it may block your prosperity. (အိမ်နှင့်သစ်ပင်တန်း၍ ကြိုးတန်း မလုပ်ကောင်းပါ။)

Thit Min (King of wood)

Thit Min

When I was young, a guest visited our house. He was an old friend of my father and they worked together while my father was running the logging cars business. There was a stem of wood in his hand and he gave it to my father as a present. At that time, I was beside my father and I heard what they were talking. He explained to my parents that the wood stem was not an ordinary one. It was the King of all woods (သစ်မင်း). Its design was very attractive and quite different from other woods.

After building a house, a man in their village noticed that, at night, he always heard the sound of 'tauk..tauk..tauk'. Although the sound was not loud in the day time, it annoyed them very much at night. So one night, he carefully checked the whole house. He found out that the sound could be heard from a corner of his house. When he came nearer, there was no sound. When he walked far, it appeared again. So he asked a learned person about it. The old wise man advised him to keep the king of wood at his house because when he built his house, he used a log which was alive with spirits and that it was now haunting him. They called it 'Thit-chaut' (ghost wood). Surprisingly, once he kept the king of wood he did not hear any sound in his house. Some people insert a sharp piece of Thit Min into the Thit-chauk (သစ်ခြောက်) with a hammer (if it is not convenient to change it with a new one). That's why they say 'Thit Min' can solve all wood problems. If 'Thit-chauk' is built in a staircase of a house, you will hear the haunting sound like someone is coming up or going down along the staircase without seeing anything. At that time, you can keep Thit Min or insert it in the stair case.

'Thit Min' or 'Lord of the woods' usually grows only in the deep forest and is difficult to find. Some people (who usually run the wood business like furniture or handicraft) keep it at home or shop as a talisman. (Please see the photo. The older the tree, the larger and deeper is the design on the bark.)

How to choose the first pillar of the house?
(မြန်မာ့ရိုးရာ ပထမဦးဆုံး အိမ်တိုင်ထူနည်း)

Do you want to know how to choose which log is suitable to be the first pillar before building a house? This method is used by ancient Myanmar people and they carefully choose the first pillar for the auspicious house. On the morning of the day when you are going to start building a house, you must prepare two small bundles. You have to put some gold in one bundle and some silver in another. And then give these 2 bundles to a baby and let him/her put it onto the group of logs which you gather to build your house. The log which the baby put the gold bundle on it, is the first pillar for your house.

Each and every Myanmar month has its own impact in building a house:

🏠	If you build a house in Tagu, the house owner will be wealthy.	
🏠	Kasone	-	abundant of crops
🏠	Nayone	-	in danger
🏠	Waso	-	will get ill-luck
🏠	Wakhaung	-	Prosperity
🏠	Tawthalin	-	ill health

🕮	Thadingyut	-	in trouble
🕮	Tasaungmone	-	Unhappiness
🕮	Nattaw	-	will be famous
🕮	Pyatho	-	Peace and will be praised by others
🕮	Tapotwe	-	Loss in materials
🕮	Tabaung	-	get rich

From the Kitchen

There are so many things to observe from the kitchen too:

In the village, children are warned by the elders that a tiger will bite them if they clap earthen pot covers. If you eat food clean out of a plate it is a bad omen of poverty.

You should not put the stone pestle (ငရုတ်ကျည်ပွေ့) (Ngayoke Kyipway) in the stone mortar (ငရုတ်ဆုံ) (Ngayokesone) if you are not pounding anything. You should keep them separately. They say that a thief won't come if you put the ladle in an upside down position at the roof of the kitchen.

Sometimes you may notice a purple mark on your body without hurting or hitting with anything. In villages, they believe that it is a sign that you have been bitten by a witch. If the purple mark is in the lower body, it is a love-bite; if in the upper, it is a hatred-bite. Do you want to know who is the witch or sorcerer? Apply the turmeric powder from the kitchen on that place without letting other people know. The next morning, the culprit will come to your house and ask, "Please give me a little bit of turmeric powder".

Sometimes, I think, I am very lucky that I had a chance to stay together with my grandma (my father's mom) in my young age because although she is a Sino-Myanmar, she knows a lot of Myanmar superstitions and I learnt a lot from her. Although her other daughters and sons asked her to stay with them in town, she never left her eldest son (my father) until her leg was broken due to an accidental fall. So my cousins only had a chance to meet her when they visited our village house on their holidays. She is like a queen bee to our family and I notice that among the younger generation, there is no one who can follow in her footsteps. I admire her for her strength of heart. Now she is in town with her eldest daughter. Although she is in bed most of the time and can move only with the help of a wheel-chair, she is still very strong mentally and her old age cannot beat her strength of heart. (*My 100 year old grandma already passed away in May, 2012, after I finished writing this book.)

When I started to learn cooking, after stirring the curry, I would hit the ladle on the upper corner of the pot to drop the curry paste which was still sticking on the ladle. When my grandma observed this, she warned me not to because it was like hitting my parents' head. At the same time, she taught me not to scrape the pot until it made a gritty sound. If you have cows or buffaloes in your house and they hear that sound, they will cry tears because they will think that their master still does not have enough food even though they are working hard for him.

Growing up together with our beloved grandma was not always an easy matter. Sometimes she pretended to beat our legs with a cane when she saw us playing with the chair while we were eating (such as leaning the chair forward and backward). Later I learned that it is a sign of poverty.

One must be careful not to step on rice or curry if it drops on the floor or ground. Old Myanmar people say 'HtaminNgaye, HInnNgayekyi tat thi' (ထမင်းငရဲ၊ ဟင်းငရဲကြီးတတ်သည်) (it means we will go to hell if we pay disrespect to the food). Similarly, if we sometimes accidentally step on rice and go to sleep without washing it, you will have a nightmare. It was one of my experiences.

They say that it will bring you poverty if you eat food out of a cooking pot instead of using a plate.

You should not eat the food that had been offered to the spirits on an altar. The spirits concerned can give you trouble. If you want to eat, you must ask permission from the spirit concerned.

When someone gives you eatables in a plate, you should not clean the plate with water and soap with a view to receive similar presents in the future.

According to ancient people, drinking soup by making sound, putting your elbow on the dining table while you are taking meal, and licking your hand, the spoon, or plates should be avoided. Such behaviours are the signs of poverty.

At the dining table, when two persons are going to pick up the same curry at the same time, a guest will come. If the tea stem is standing in the tea cup, a visitor will come to your house.

Sometimes, if an unwanted guest is staying long at your house and you want him to leave, throw some salt on a stove in a backward position and say, "Go back to your house". He will leave from your house soon.

If you take the last piece of curry when eating with others, you will become a spinster/old bachelor. It means you will remain unmarried. Some of my friends believe it and they never take the last piece of food whenever we eat together.

They say that only one chicken foot should not be eaten. You should eat both feet.

By eating rice or curry directly from the cooking pot, you will be accused by others that you are the culprit when their things disappear.

If you are thinking of taking more rice, do not eat all the rice in the plate, a fistful amount should be left. Or it will lead to poverty.

Some people put the bones on the table (near the plate) while they are eating. After taking meal, you should not put those bones back into your plate from the table in order to clean the table. Why do you put that rubbish in your plate instead of throwing them into the rubbish bin? Please do not do it because it will lead to poverty.

You should not sing while you are cooking or you will get married with a widow/widower. Only the beggars sing while they are eating.

When you stir the pot with a ladle, you should stir in a clock-wise direction if you cook before noon. But you can stir anti-clockwise if you cook in the afternoon.

They say that you should avoid cooking late at night because night time is the cooking time of the ghosts. At the same time, it is advisable to bring raw meat along with pieces of coal if you bring it at night or in the late evening, or else the hungry or evil spirits will follow you and give you trouble.

Pets, Animals and Plants

Before Lord Buddha's mother (Maya) was pregnant, she got a strange dream that a white elephant entered and stayed inside her womb. Very soon, she got pregnant. The wise men predicted that the baby inside will be a holy person or a ruler. So Myanmar people take the white elephant as a royal animal. If the white elephant appears in the Kingdom, the king will bring it to the palace and keep it because that king will live a long life and will be powerful.

Cats and Dogs

They say that 'Dog south and cat north' (ခွေးအိမ်တောင်၊ ကြောင်အိမ်မြောက်). It means that you should not bring a dog from the south of your house and the cat from the north area of the house. If you do, those pets may not stay long in your house.

They also say that dogs can take the misfortunes of their master while cats cannot. If the dog dies while someone at home is sick, that person will be free from death. It means that the dog takes the misfortune on behalf of his master. If the mother cat (from another house) brings her kittens to your house, it is a sign of prosperity. On the contrary, if the cat leaves your house without any reason means your business or health will decline.

Normally, people are not too willing to bring a totally black cat from another house as there is a saying, 'The total black cat and total blue chicken should not keep at home'. (ကြောင်အနက်၊ ကြက်အပြာ) But, if black kittens are delivered at home or they come and stay at your house without your invitation, please do not send them away. They will bring prosperity to you.

If kittens are delivered, do not say "They are like small mice." When the mother cat hears that, she will eat her children thinking that these are mice because mice are a delicious food of cats. If a mother cat eats her own kitten, you should not keep her at home. We call her 'ogre cat' (ကြောင်ဘီလူး) and you should send her to the monastery or to other places.

If the dog or cat delivers 4 babies at home, they say it is the dog bed or cat bed (ခွေးခုတင်၊ ကြောင်ခုတင်) as the bed has four legs. It will bring prosperity to that house. If a cat delivers 7 kittens, it is very good. How poor the house owner may be, he will surely get rich one day.

If the female cat or dog delivers babies in a barn or basket, it means that you will get abundant of food with the full amount of barn or baskets. If the kittens are delivered among the clothing, you will get a lot of new clothing.

If a cat is cleaning his face or ears with his hand, rain is coming soon. In drought area, they give a bath to a cat expecting that the rain will fall.

Sometimes, the male cats run away from your house as they do not want to stick at home anymore. To avoid that, cut the moustache of the male cats when they grow up.

If the puppies are delivered under the house or staircase, you will be wealthy. If a mother dog delivers four female puppies and one male puppy, the owner will be in danger. If a dog delivers puppies in bed, dog owner will be in trouble. (Of course, you do not know where to sleep after they occupy your bed!)

If you are bitten by a dog, it means that you are unfortunate and your servant will be rebellious to you.

If you want a dog to be aggressive, give him a little bit of tiger bone and it will become very fierce. If a dog drags his anus on the ground, a guest will come.

Sometimes, naughty dogs climb over the roof of the house. If a dog climbs over the roof from the west and down to east or from north to south, it is good and you will get properties. But if it climbs up from east and down to the west or from south to north, you will be separated from your spouse. To remedy this, please put some gold and silver ornaments in water and you should wash your hair with that water and pray.

Take Me Home, Country Roads

They say that cat's memory is very sharp and if you want to send them away, you should cover their eyes first not to remember the way or they will come back to your house.

Ta Kwet Ma

My mother kept a lot of cats and some people asked her to share cats due to mouse problem. A female cat named 'Ta Kwet Ma' from my mother's house returned back home for three times after we sent her to other places. The last place was a monestery from another village, about ten miles far from our house. Also the journey was very tough. We were very surprised for her intelligence and attachment to our house. Finally we decided not to give her away.

Notice! for eaters of cat and dog

There is a single pin among the furs on the cat's body that causes the eater into deep poverty. (ကြောင်၏ ကိုယ်ထဲတွင် ဆင်းရဲမွေးတစ်မွေးရှိပါသည်။)။

So cat eaters must be very careful not to eat any fur of the cat.

According to animal's instinct, dogs can sense those who ate dog's meat. So they bark at only dog eater even he is among other people.

Plants

They believe that the Eugenia tree (Thapyay) should not be planted in front of the house because if someone pours blood on it, an evil spirit can dwell in it. Similarly, some magicians invite the devil by pouring blood on a lemon grass (စပါးလင်ပင်) bush every day. They say that the banana tree should not be planted in the south part of a house and sugarcane in the north. The banyan tree should not be planted at home.

The papaya tree has two types - male and female. Only the female papaya tree can bear fruits. If you want the male papaya tree to bear fruits, wrap around it with a woman's longyi (sarong). Sooner or later, it will bear fruits. Actually, you can choose the fertile female seeds before you plant the papaya tree. When you cut the papaya fruit, you will see that some seeds are black and some are not. Black ones are the fertile seeds. Take all those black seeds and put them in water. Some will sink down to the bottom while some will go up to the surface. All the seeds at the bottom are female and those will surely bear fruits after you plant them.

If you point with your index finger to a gourd fruit, it will get rotten. If you want to chop a coconut tree inside your yard, consult with a monk or an astrologer because chopping a coconut tree in your compound may cause health problem to someone at home.

Myanmar people believe that if the banana fruit or bud is bearing towards the house, someone of that house will get sick. *(Please see the photo)*. To avoid this, before you plant the banana tree, you can choose the direction of the sprout. If you plant the bending side of the sprout towards the house, the fruit will bear towards the opposite side (means outside of the house). It is the correct position. But sometimes, new sprouts may grow itself from the root and the banana may bear towards the house. At that time, you can pull the root with a rope to change the direction slowly while the bud is very young.

Banana bud

Do not plant chilli in front of the house or you will often have to face hot problems in your house. However you can plant it in the backyard of the house. They say that if you want the plant to grow well, ask a Friday-born person to plant it.

Some people say that if you intend to plant the seed, do not suck the remaining flesh on that seed after cutting the flesh, or it will never germinate.

Daung Gamone (ဒေါင်းဂမုန်း) One day, U San Yin from Ywa Thit village, a trusted person of my father brought a plant called Daung Gamone (a kind of *kaempferia*) to my mother as my mother is fond of gardening. It is not an ordinary plant. In the evening, leaves of Daung Gamone usually gather into the middle as if it were asleep. If the leaves do not gather, thief will come on that night. According to their experience, one night, it did not sleep so they waited the whole night with a curiosity as to what would happen. After midnight, a thief really approached their cowshed to steal their cows. As they were watchful, the thief's intention was not successful on that night. Please see in the photo. The design on its leaf is like a design of peacock's feather.

Daung Gamone

U San Yin told us that if Daung Gamone is still awake until the evening, you can recite 'Mawra Sutta' (Oo Daung Min' Mantra) 'မောရသုတ်' (ဦးဒေါင်းမင်းဂါထာ) seven times to make it sleep and you must be alert on that night.

Mouse

When you visit the countryside, you may see notices on the wall of some houses, "Mice are for sale at ten pyas each." (ကြွက်ရောင်းရန်ရှိသည်၊ တစ်ကောင်ဆယ်ပြား). By doing this, mice will run away. They say that you should not be aggressive to rats or mice as they are very sensitive animals. If you are aggressive to them, you will never win. They will be more rebellious than before. According to ancient people, mice will destroy your things more if you curse them. So a tactful and gentle way should be employed with regard to mice problems, especially those people who are doing business with rice, beans, crops and other foods which mice like to eat.

If a mouse runs over your foot, you will get money but if a mouse runs in front of you, the money you lend to others will never be returned. When you see a group of rats or mice in a long queue, go and buy the lottery. You will surely win the lottery. If the mice are making noise, you will hear bad news.

When we were young, if our tooth was broken, we put it in a rat hole hoping that the new tooth would appear as strong and sharp as those of the rat. When my son's tooth was broken, I could not find a rat hole in town. So I dropped it into a hole below a tree in our compound assuming that it was a rat hole.

Birds, Crow, Eagles, Owls

If you see two little birds on your way, it is a sign of good luck. For example, if you see two little birds on your way to the examination hall, you will answer very well on that exam.

There is a bird named 'Hnget Soe' (ငှက်ဆိုး) which is regarded as bird of ill-omen. If that bird flies over the house by chanting "Ghit... ghit...", a funeral or ill health will come to that house sooner or later. So people are very scared to hear the chanting of Hnget Soe. Its sound is really an unpleasant one!

Indian grackle (Thar Li kar) knows who the witch is. Parrot and Thar Li Kar are clever birds and they can imitate human speech, too.

If the crow carries away some things from your shop, you will get disease. If a crow unusually caws from the nearest part of the house, a special guest or the lover will come that day.

If an eagle takes a rest on the roof, the parents of that house owner will be in danger.

Owls are night birds. If an owl takes a rest on the roof of your house, it is a sign of good health and freedom from disease. If an owl makes nest at a house, that house will be prosperous. If an owl enters the kitchen, it means food will be abundant in that house.

If an owl takes a rest at the water pot, the house owner should do a business concerned with water such as beverages, or fishing, or shipping and so on.

If an owl touches a pregnant lady while it is flying, that woman will deliver a baby boy. But if it is just flying near her without touching, she will deliver a baby girl. Some Myanmar people put a couple of big paper/plastic owl dolls in the guest room as lucky symbols.

> ►► *(If vulture, owl, egret or eagle takes rest on the roof of a house, most of the people do not like it because they think that it is not a good sign although it can be either a good or a bad omen. If you are not sure, you can pour the holy water on that place and pray not to have any misfortune.)*

Goat, Cow, Horse

If you see a goat eating grass, things which you are doing at the time will be accomplished. If the calf is bleating and looking for its mother, your romance will not last.

If you see a running horse, you will receive an emergency message from afar. If you hear the neighing of a horse, you will win the legal case or you will take a temporary trip.

Swan, Egret, Duck, Rooster

If you see swans walking in front of you, you will meet with a good teacher or a saint.

If an egret enters the house, it is not a good sign.

If ducks pass in front of you, you will eat a delicious curry or you will meet with a good friend. If a duck passes through between your two feet, you will meet with a good teacher. If you see ducks are swimming, the trip you are taking will be a smooth one.

If you see two cocks fighting seriously, you will be attacked unexpectedly or you will win a legal case. If a hen eats her own eggs or she crows like a rooster, it should not be kept at home. Some people send it to a monastery. If a hen lays two eggs a day, the owner will get prosperity.

Bees

People generally say that if the bees make their hive in front of the house or at the upper part of the house such as in a roof, walls, it is unlucky; but in the lower part such as under a bed or a mat, it is a good sign.

If a bee-hive is at the south-west of the house, your things will be stolen. If in the south-east, there will be fire alarm.

If the bees make nest on clothing, it is the sign of prosperity. If you see the bee hive in the water pot, you will become a rich man.

▶▶ *(If you are not sure whether that bee hive is good or not ; or if you do not want them on that place, please do not destroy it. You should spray some water or holy water on the bee hive with your hand gently and tell them "This place is not suitable for you to make a hive and please move to other place." Sooner or later, they will stop dwelling on that place.)*

Gecko, House lizard, Monitor lizard, Grass lizard

If you hear a gecko making a sound 9 times, go and buy lottery ticket as fast as possible. You will win. Please do not delay.

But if you hear the house lizard's making sound, don't be in a hurry. Even thieves do not go out to steal if the lizard makes a sound before they go out, because they are scared that they will get caught.

There is a saying that if a monitor lizard enters the house, the house owner will be extremely poor with nothing to pick up (ဖွတ်တက်လျှင် ကုန်း ကောက်စရာမရှိအောင် မွဲတတ်သည်). Please do not be in a panic if it enters into your house. To remedy this, you have to say "A very wealthy person visits our house and it is a sign of prosperity." And then donate gold to others.

If a person is bitten by a grass lizard (ကင်းလိပ်ချော) he should quickly drink water first. If a grass lizard takes water before he takes it, he will die.

When you go to a deep forest or jungle with friends, do not call their names because Pangolin (သင်းခွေချပ်) will hear the names and call them. Also, do not answer if someone calls your name. May be pangolin is calling your name. If you answer back, you will die.

Frog/toad, Snake

If a frog enters your house, you will get money. If the frogs come up to the shore, it is the symbol of drought.

In rainy season, if snakes climb up trees, heavy rain and wind will come soon.

Seagulls

If seagulls come up to the shore without any reason, the earthquake will occur soon.

Rabbit

If a rabbit passes in front of you, it is a sign of good luck. But if it passes from behind, it is a bad omen.

Some people do not take the rabbit meat because rabbits are very gentle and timid by nature. Some people are afraid that if they take it, they might become cowards.

Spider

If you see a spider spinning its web, you will get presents soon. If it is done in the morning, it is a sign of good luck. If it is noon time, you will have to go out on a temporary trip.

If you see a spider going up along its string, you will hear good news. But if you see the spider hanging down along its string, it is a bad luck.

Others

By carrying a hair of an elephant's tail, you can avoid evil.

If birds and bees are making their nests and hives lower than the previous years, there will be heavy rain in the coming year.

If beasts enter the town or village, it is a sign of great change.

If animals are eating their own species, scarcity of food will occur.

If snakes, crows, dragonflies, mouse or rats, cats become abundant, it is a sign of scarcity.

Sun, Moon, Stars, Clouds and Planets

When I was very young, and under the moon light, the old people would point to the moon and say, "Look at the moon carefully. You will see an old man pounding rice and a rabbit is sitting near him" (ရွှေလမှာ ယုန်ဝပ်လို့ ဆန်ဖွပ်သည့်အဖိုးအို). I looked at the moon and I slowly saw the vague figure of an old man and a rabbit. The old man is about 80 years old and his back is bent due to his old age and slowly pounding rice all the time. The rabbit is looking at him. Also, there is a saying that if we politely ask, 'Mr. Moon, please give me oily rice in a gold plate' (ဖိုးလမင်းကြီးရေ ထမင်းဆီဆမ်း ရွှေလင်ပန်းနဲ့ပေးပါ) repeatedly to the moon on a full moon night, we will get it. So according to my childhood thinking, I connected those two sayings and imagined that when we ask for the oily rice, the old man on the moon has to cook his rice for us and ask the rabbit to send it to me. When babies cry at night, people talk about it in order to arouse the baby's

The Old Man and The Rabbit inside the Moon

interest and to divert the baby's attention. Up till now, whenever I see the full moon, I still remember that saying and see the old man's figure and rabbit on the moon. I did not complain to the old people at that time although I did not receive the oily rice practically. But when I applied the same method to my son, I was asked, "Mom, why does the oily rice take so long?". I replied, "The old man forgets where he has kept the oil bottle and he is still looking for it."

I spent my childhood in my home town and when I reached the teen years, my father sent us to Yangon to get our higher education. When I was in the village, after school was over at 3:30 pm, we ran back home. (Of course, we were very happy when the school was over although I was not an active person to enthusiastically go to school in the mornings). Once we arrived back home, I threw down the school bag which was heavy with books, changed from the school uniform into comfortable clothing, took the food which my mother had prepared for us (my mother never failed to prepare for us something to eat after school, such as snacks or light foods) and then, I (sometimes my elder sister joined me) would rush to our friends to play. Sometimes, we would play very late until my mother followed to the playground with a worried look. At sunset, we looked at the sky and sometimes we could see a rainbow.

In the village, there were no high buildings and we could see the open sky, the mountains, and forests very clearly. Sometimes, we saw clouds at sunset which were in different shapes, colours, and forms. Some were like animals, vegetables, angels, and some like soldiers. Slowly, slowly, those clouds changed from one shape to another. We gazed at those clouds with surprise and pleasure. Not only that, but I felt that the sky was very near and sheltering us. I thought, if I were a little bit stronger, my hand could touch the sky within one utmost jump. I saw that the sky was kissing the mountains on the other side of the horizon. We watched the rainbow and clouds together until it slowly faded away. Also, I imagined using the sky as a canvas and I wanted to paint it with those colourful clouds and make a mess of the whole sky as if the artist's palette was falling down to the horizon. When I was tired, I imagined using a rainbow as a swing to take rest! Now that I have grown up and I realize that those were just childhood fantasies. Sometimes I want such kind of ignorant bliss again!

Although I did not know the meaning of those clouds at that time, now I have a little knowledge about their meanings.

- They say that if the cloud is like a buffalo's head, prosperity will come soon.

- If the cloud is white and in the shape of a flower, there will be trouble.

- If you see elephant, tiger, buffalo, deer, eagle, crocodile and vulture in the clouds, the animals will be in trouble.

- White and blue clouds mixing together in the form of waves or tides means that relative from distant place will arrive.

- If you see a penguin in the cloud, the leaders will be faced with difficulties.

- If you see a crocodile, you will have some difficulties.

- If you see a peacock, you will win over all other competitors.

- If you see a Hamilton's carp fish (ngagyin) in the cloud, food will be abundant.

- If you see a military uniform, do not be in a hurry to do things. Observe first and you will win by patience.

- If you see a dragon, you will surely win and do not hesitate to do things which you have to do.

- If you see a lion in the cloud, you will be the winner.

- If you see a woman's figure wearing a scarf, you will win over the enemy.

- If you see a cow/ox in the clouds, you will lose.

- If you see a man in a red cloud who is holding a weapon, you will win on the battle field.

- If rainbows appear from four directions (East, west, south, north), a new virtuous king will appear.

In the late afternoon, around the sunset, the sky sometimes is very beautiful and the whole sky is brightened up with prawn-fat colored (Pazun Si yaung in Myanmar language) clouds. When I observed this extraordinary spectacle unlike other evenings, a happy mood came into my mind. My mother explained to me that it was called 'Yoke Soe Hla Chain' (ရုပ်ဆိုးလှချိန်၊ ကျည်းတန်လှချိန်). It means 'the period when even the ugly ones look beautiful'. Everybody will be very good looking if they go out at that time due to the reflection from the sky's color. Even the ugly ones (who dare not go out in day time) will be beautiful at that time. So those who are very ugly will not refuse to go out at that time because they may secretly hope to meet their prince charming under such a favourable weather condition.

There is a saying that if the evening star (which usually can be seen near the moon) comes very much nearer the moon or across the moon, a war will come soon. (သောကြာကြယ်ကြီး လနဲ့ နီး စစ်ကြီး ဖြစ်လတဲ့).

The star comet - If a comet comes from the east, the king will be plotted against by someone. If a comet comes from the south, the kingdom will not last long. If a comet appears from the west, the ministers will be rebellious. If a comet appears from the north, the ministers will live long. If a red comet appears, the country will be prosperous.

The earthquake

- ☉ If the earthquake appears in Tagu (Myanmar month) - The enemy will disappear. There will be abundant fertile soil.
- ☉ In Kasone   -   The fruits and vegetables will be damaged. The religion will be tarnished.
- ☉ In Nayone   -   The pregnant women will be harmed.
- ☉ In Waso   -   The king will pass away.
- ☉ In Wakhaung   -   The diseases due to poverty will come.
- ☉ In Tawthalin   -   The monks and hermits will be harmed.
- ☉ In Thadingyut   -   The ministers and the military leaders will be in danger.
- ☉ In Tasaungmone   -   The people will get diseases.
- ☉ In Nattaw   -   There will be war.
- ☉ In Pyatho   -   The country will be unsafe.
- ☉ In Tapotwe   -   The rural areas will be harmed.
- ☉ In Tabaung   -   There will be rebellions.

The cloud comet

- If you see a cloud comet on Sunday, there will be war in north-east area.
- On Monday   -   The rain will fall heavily in the beginning and in the middle of the rainy season. There will be war in north-west area.
- On Tuesday   -   The rain will fall very little. There will be war in south-west area.
- On Wednesday   -   There will be war in the western part of the country.
- On Thursday   -   A gift will come from other country.
- On Friday   -   The wild people will make war. Heavy rain.
- On Saturday   -   Heavy rain. Country affairs will be peaceful.

The Sun Comet

- If you see a sun comet on Sunday, there will be war in the eastern part of country.
- On Monday   -   There will be war in the western part of the country.
- On Tuesday   -   There will be danger in north areas.
- On Wednesday   -   Elephants and horses will be sent to the king.
- On Saturday   -   There will be a very heavy rain and an earthquake.

About the Sun wearing a halo
(နေအိမ်ဖွဲ့)

If you see the sun wearing halo on Sunday, there will be drought followed by scarcity of food. There may be many fire alarms in town.

Sun halo

- ✳ On Monday   -   The crops will get damaged due to the heavy rain.
- ✳ On Tuesday   -   Very windy without the rain.
- ✳ On Wednesday -   Regular rain and the crops will be abundant.
- ✳ On Thursday -   A treasure will be obtained. The ministers will be awarded.
- ✳ On Friday   -   The country will be rich and the king will receive treasures.
- ✳ On Saturday -   There will be dangers in urban and rural areas.

If the Sun is wearing halo in the morning, women will die more than men. At noon, there will be war and a lot of deaths. In the evening, the king will die and the war will come. If you see half of the sun wearing halo, people in the country will be frightened. If it is from the east, there will be war between leaders.

About the moon wearing halo (လအိမ်ဖွဲ့.)

Moon halo

If you see a moon wearing a halo on Sunday, there will be heavy rain and the country will be rich.

- o On Monday   -   Little rain and worries in town.
- o On Tuesday   -   Windy and rainy weather. Paddies will be abundant.
- o On Wednesday -   Heavy rain. The country will be rich. The white elephant will appear.
- o On Friday   -   Wealthy persons will appear.
- o On Saturday -   Not good. The country will be in trouble.

According to old people, if the sky is white while raining, the rain will fall longer than we expected. Although the sky is cloudy and dark, the rain may not come. (မိုးဖြူမဲ၊ မိုးမဲမရွာ)

During rainy season, if you see the prawn's fat color sky after sunset time (please refer on page 214), the next very early morning, the rain will come before dawn time. (နေဝင်တိမ်တောက်၊ မိုးသောက်မလင်း)

From Farmers and Villagers

Being an agro-based country, there are a lot of belief and superstitions among Myanmar farmers and villagers. The following is some knowledge which we have obtained from them and some of their beliefs and superstitions may surprise you.

For the farmers, crops are like their brood. They will be happy if they see the successful crops but they feel very disheartened whenever the crops are eaten by insects. There is a traditional way to prevent it by avoiding certain planting days. The saying is 'Eate-chin-maw-swa-nay-yit-ha, Eain-ka-so-lain-myi' (အိပ်ချင်မောစွ နေရစ်ဟ အိမ်က ဆိုလိမ့်မည်). These twelve words represent Myanmar twelve months as follows:

* Tagu   -   Sunday (Do not plant the crops on Sunday in Tagu (roughly April)
* Kasone   -   Monday
* Nayone   -   Thursday
* Waso   -   Tuesday
* Wakhaung   -   Saturday
* Tawthalin   -   Wednesday
* Thadingyut   -   Friday
* Tasaungmone   -   Sunday
* Nattaw   -   Monday
* Pyatho   -   Tuesday
* Tapotwe   -   Wednesday
* Tabaung   -   Thursday

Every year, on 3rd waxing day of Tabaung, the farmers pay respect with proper offerings to 'Pone-Kyi-Ma' nat (a harvest deity worshipped by cultivators) to take care of their crops. They put steamed sticky rice, coconut, banana, traditional snacks, jaggery, a glass of water and some woman's appliances such as Thanakhar, perfumes, or flowers, on a nice bullock cart and pray; "O, our goddess Pone-Kyi-Ma, please have mercy on us by helping our plants to grow as tall as palm trees and the vegetables as big as the bamboo baskets until we do not know where to keep those excess foods after putting it in our barns. Not only that, please take care that our plants will not to be eaten by insects and not to be disturbed by natural disasters such as rain, storms, etc....." Sometimes a traditional music troupe is accompanied by the village dancers while they are offering food.

Sometimes, a group of little birds like sparrows flock into the field and eat the paddy. You may see the scare crow (စာခြောက်ရုပ်) standing in the middle of their farms. Another way is that if two halves of onions (by cutting from the middle of an onion) are hanged in the middle of the farm, the sparrows won't come.

How to predict the crop market for next year?

Do you want to know how to predict which kind of crops (besides rice) will be a good sale for the next year? Each year, the hot market is not the same. For example, although the sesame price is very high in this year, the bean price may be high next year. You do not need to go and ask the astrologer or the market expert. The method is very simple:

Normally the farmers start their plantation in the rainy season. In Tagu, in the evening of Thingyan A-kya day (1st day of Water festival), you take a fistful of a few types of seeds which you are interested to plant for the next year. They must be of the same weight and put in small separate bundles. On the Myanmar New Year day (it means 3 days later), open those small bundles and weigh each one again, one by one. You will know the difference in weight. If the white sesame bundle is heavier than the black sesame one, the price of white sesame will be higher than that of black sesame the next year. Its production will be very good and you can make more profit by planting white sesame. (My personal thinking is that during Thingyan (Water festival), the chief of the celestial beings comes down to earth to take record of the human beings who is good, who is bad and that he may be practically helping the farmers to know that).

By checking the Thingyan A-tet day (4th day of Water festival and final day of Myanmar year), farmers can predict what kind of products will be scarce the next year as follows:

If Thingyan A-tet day is:

- ♔ Sunday — the fruits and vegetables, etc will be scarce and expensive in the next year.
- ♔ Monday — Dry fishes/prawns, Fish paste, Fish/prawn sauce, etc...
- ♔ Tuesday — Betel leaves, green tea leaves, etc...
- ♔ Wednesday — Paddy, crops, etc...
- ♔ Thursday — Betel nuts, coconuts, etc...
- ♔ Friday — Chilli, onion, garlic, etc...
- ♔ Saturday — Gold, Jewelleries, etc...

➤ *(The above traditional belief is derived from the Mon tribe.)*

Nowadays, a pregnant woman knows if the baby inside is a boy or girl by taking an ultrasound but how about for the animals? A farmer says that he knows whether the calf inside the pregnant cow is male or female by checking the way she stands. Normally, cows and oxen stand with the front two legs on the same level. But if the cow stands on her right leg ahead of the left leg, she will deliver a male calf and if her left leg is forward, a female calf is inside.

Do you have difficulties putting the farm animals like cows or buffalos on to the platform scale? You can know their weight by this formula:

{(Girth)^2 x Length} divided by 300 = Its measurement (in lbs).

➤ *(When you measure the girth and length, you have to measure in inches.)*

The farmers can forecast the weather by looking at natural things.

The farmers love the rainy season. All their works such as planting, cultivation, and ploughing depends on the mercy of the rain. Heavy rain and flooding can destroy the crops and scarce rain prevents the crops from growing properly.

1) If little birds build their nest in a strong condition, there will be heavy rain for that year. If they build it too loose, there will be drought.

2) If the mango trees bear fruits earlier than its usual season, the rain will come early. If late, the rain will be late, too.

3) If you see many flowers on the mango trees, jackfruits, or tamarind, heavy rain will come. (Before bearing the fruits, the flowers come first).

To avoid foot and mouth disease in farm animals
(နှာနာလျှာနာ)

Some farm animals such as cows, buffaloes, and oxen usually suffer from foot and mouth disease during the change of the season and it is an infectious disease. As 'Prevention is better than cure', there is a Myanmar traditional way to prevent it. It is not a medicine but just 16 grain of roasted lablab beans (Pe Kyee Hlaw) (ပဲကြီးလှော်). You dig a hole at the four corners of the stall and then bury the four beans in each hole and pray, "May my cows and buffaloes be free from suffering until these beans sprout." It will be safe for one year.

To avoid thieves

In the middle of the night of Myanmar New Year while people are sleeping, you dig holes in eight directions starting from the east. After digging a hole, you bury an onion in an inverted position. It means, the root is up and the sprout is down. So you need eight onions to put in the eight holes. The thief will never come in that year. This method is quite similar with the foot and mouth disease method.

How to check pure honey or not?

There are so many ways to check whether honey is pure or not because some honey is mixed with Tin-le-yay (တင်လဲရည်) (molasses) which can be obtained by boiling the sugar cane juice for a long time. The colour and the taste of honey and Tin-le-yay are quite similar. The only difference is that if you keep Tin-le-yay for long, it slowly changes to a dark colour and only then you will know that you have been cheated. So, you can check in the following ways:

1) Dip a match stick in the honey and scratch it on a match box. If it burns, it is pure.

2) Dip cotton (ဝါဂွမ်း) in the honey and burn it. If it makes fire, it is pure.

3) Put a little bit of lime (Htone-ထုံး) and honey on your hand and rub your two hands. If you feel hot like fire, it is pure.

4) Put a tamarind seed in the honey bottle and hold the bottle up-side down. If tamarind seed is floating, it is pure.

5) Some say that dogs do not eat the pure honey.

6) Mix a spoonful of honey and a spoonful of pure sesame oil and stir well. Then put it in a spoon and if you find that you get only a spoonful amount instead of two, then that honey is pure.

7) Put a bee in that honey. If the bee does not die, it is pure. If the bee dies, it is not pure honey. Bees are never drowned in pure honey.

8) Drop some honey on paper. If the paper absorbs it, it is not pure.

Real boa bile or not?
(စပါးကြီးသည်းခြေ စစ်၊ မစစ်)

Bile of the boa snake (Sabagyi The-chay) is very medicinal and it can cure a lot of diseases such as asthma, stroke, even HIV (according to some). Nowadays it is very difficult to get the real one. 'Boa snakes' usually stay in the deep forest and if a villager gets a real one, they keep it for their family use instead of selling it. Only when they are in a very difficult financial situation, they sell only a portion of boa bile. So if you want to know whether it is real or not before you buy -

Gall bladder of Boa

☑ You can rub it on your palm. If some golden colour remains on your palm, it is real.

☑ Dip a little bit of boa bile at the corner of a little leaf and put it into the water. The leaf will be swimming on the surface of water. *(It is true because I have experiment it.)*

Malaria

Malaria is a disease which usually happens among villagers and farmers who work in the forest. It can relapse at anytime, especially if the weather is cold or if a person becomes weak. One symptom of Malaria is that the victim feels very cold and shivering inside until nothing can make him warm and sometimes he loses his consciousness. There are a few simple ways used by the villagers to cure it:

1) Dig the root of a jasmine plant and boiled in a small, new pot until one third of the boiled water is left. Drink that warm jasmine root water for 3 days continuously.

2) Mix an equal amount of pepper powder and Sheinkho (Asafoetida) powder to get the amount of a half tea spoonful. Take it morning and evening.

3) Put a small packet of Masalar (spicy powder) in the village-alcohol (country spirit), stir well, and drink it.

4) If a person is severely suffering from Malaria, you can let him drink the urine of his mother or father 'as a medicine' as an urgent treatment. (It is better not to let him know before he drinks it.)

▸▸ *(The above all methods should not be tested at the same time. It means that you can test it only one method at a time.)*

Traditional way for women menopause problem

Women usually will face some health problems as they enter menopause. To overcome this, they must take 'six boiled chicken eggs' within 3 days every year when they approach the age of menopause as follows:

- One egg in the morning of 1st waxing day of Nattaw (Myanmar month),

- Two eggs in the morning of 2nd waxing day of Nattaw,

- Three eggs in the morning of 3rd waxing day of Nattaw.

➤➤ *(When you eat the eggs, you need to eat continuously. It means that you should not leave some portion of it for the evening.)*

To bear more coconut and gourd

Put green tea leaves and jaggery (palm sugar) (which you get from a wedding) inside the leaves of the coconut trees so as to infuse the tree with the things from the auspicious occasion. (ထုံကူးသည်ဟုခေါ်ကြသည်)

To bear a big gourd, thrust a bone of Sturgeon fish (Ngagyin) into its stem.

How to cleanse the wild virgin land

A virgin land may have some guardian spirits. The farmers should not stay or plough after extending into some wild land without any proper preparation. They should pay respect to the guardian spirit of that land. Put the Three kinds of jam, some paddy and rice, a glass of water, and Eugenia leaves on a tray and pray, "The guardian spirit of this land, we are going to stay or work on this land and please allow us to do so. If there is any living or non living thing in this land which can be harmful to us, please remove them for us."

Hallucination in the jungle (တောခြောက်ခြင်း)

A villager said that while he was about to sleep on a tree as it was too late to go back home after a hunting trip, he suddenly saw his wife following him not far away. At that time he was about to go down from the tree to call his wife who was looking for him. His friend strongly warned him not to go down as it was a very dangerous zone. When they arrived back home the next day, he asked his wife whether she followed him last night to the jungle or not. She said 'No'. At that time his friend explained that they had killed a big snake and that the partner of that snake disguised itself as his wife and followed them. According to him, if a person kills a big snake in the jungle, he must bury the head of the snake because the eyes of the snake can photograph the killer and the partner can know who the killer is by seeing the eyes of the dead snake.

Mat guardian 'Ma Aung Phyu' (Phyar-Late-Nat)
(ဖျာလိပ်နတ်မအောင်ဖြူ)

In village, when the women are free in the afternoon, sometimes, they ask the mat guardian 'Ma Aung Phyu' who is a nat (spirit) and who dislikes men. The procedure is that a group of women secretly gather in a room. The room must be safe enough so that anyone especially men cannot peep in. So they usually ask that nat while the men are not at home. They find a new or a clean mat and roll up it properly. And then they apply it with Thanakhar (Myanmar traditional make up) and lipstick and put on some flowers just like a woman. Wrapping it up with a new or clean blouse and longyi and perfume is preferred. If a wig is available, they can put it on the top of the mat as if it is alive. First, they invite the nat and pay respects. Three or four women are needed to hold the mat in a vertical position and the rest can watch with curiosity. After inviting Ma Aung Phyu, the mat becomes lively and they must hold it firmly so as not to let the mat fall down to the floor. Then, they ask the questions to the nat according to what they want to know. For example, if a woman asks, "Our goddess, Ma Aung Phyu, if Ko Kyaw Win will be the future husband of Ma Aye Thit, who is sitting near me, please strike her head three times". They all know both persons and they are curious if Ko Kyaw Win and Ma Aye Thit will get married or not. According to them, it really works and the mat slowly bends down to that person and gently strikes her head if the answer is 'yes'. They take turn holding the mat to ask questions and sometimes there is laughter after asking funny questions about their romance and marriage. But they dare not laugh too loud because other people may come and peep in on them. If a man peeps and sees that show, the mat nat gets very angry and she will not answer their questions anymore. The show will come to an end.

Why does Ma Aung Phyu dislike men? A village woman explained to me that while Ma Aung Phyu was a human being, her husband became a prisoner. One day, she carried a pot in her hand and a mat on her head to see her husband and cook for him. When she passed near the unfinished dam, she was killed by the security guards of that dam. Construction of that dam was unsuccessful a few times before and astrologers calculated and advised the chief that a Sunday-born woman carrying a mat on her head, and whose name included 'Aung' ('Aung' means 'successful' or 'win' in Myanmar language), would come to that place one day and, if they sacrificed her life, the construction of the dam would be accomplished.

The spirit of Ma Aung Phyu became an ogress in the forest as she was very angry with them since she was killed without any fault or sin. However, her love for her husband never died. With her innate power, she brought her husband from the prison to her place and they stayed together until they got a baby boy. One day, when the boy knew that his mother was an ogress, he asked his father to run away to the human world. Both of them run away and the ogress died with a broken heart. After dying twice, the poor Ma Aung Phyu became a nat with her attachment to the mat she carried before she was sacrificed. At the same time, she hated men due to her resentment towards the husband and son who were so cruel to her.

Not to be eaten by the book worms

Bite the bottom parts of cloves (lay Nyin) and at the same time, you have to say, "Before the worms bite the books, I bite the clove" ('ပိုးမကိုက်ခင် ငါကိုက်သည်' ဟုပြောပါ). Then, put those in the book cupboard.

Not to be eaten by rice worms

First, put *eucalyptus* leaves at the bottom of a basket or container before the rice is put in. After putting some rice, put some of the leaves again in the middle and then finally, put some leaves on the top.

Not to be bitten by the chicken louse

Put an iron nail in the nest where the hen is laying eggs.

Kyauk Letwar (Magic stone hand) (ကျောက်လက်ဝါး)

Magic Stone Hand

Kyauk Letwar is rarely found in the deep forest as they are usually attached to a rock mountain. It is like a human skeleton hand but very hard like a fossil. People seldom recognize it and only a very few people and magicians who are interested in mysterious things know about it. Someone said, "Kyauk Letwar is alive and it can be used in doing business or making money. If you want something, it can bring it to you with its power. You have to feed it as if it were alive. If you put it together with a chicken in a basket, later, when you check, you cannot see the chicken because the chicken has already been eaten up by Kyauklat war. It likes blood, too. Sometimes you need to feed it with blood." "But there are some Kyauk Letwar which are not alive."

But it is a dangerous thing to keep it. If you cannot handle it properly, it will be harmful to you although it is very powerful and worth a lot of money. Some people waste many years in their life time in finding Kyauk Letwar with a great hope of selling it to the wealthy people for a large amount of money or they can use it for their own prosperity.

▸▸ *I made a drawing of one Kyauk Letwar which I saw in the Bayint Nyi cave in Mon State about ten years ago along my pilgrimage trip. Although I wanted to go there and take a photograph of it while I was writing this book, I did not have a chance to do so. (Please see the picture)*

Lu Chauk Lay (Little dried baby)

Have you ever heard about Lu Chauk Lay (လူခြောက်လေး) stories before? I have heard a few stories about Lu Chauk Lay from the villagers. Lu Chauk Lay means very little dried baby. Some give dreams to their mother before they come. Before it is delivered, the mother endures 9 months of pregnancy like other women. But, when she delivers, they find that the baby is very, very small and her womb is full of fluid. The baby is only a few inches long. It is put in a bottle and should be treated like an adult by providing a good mattress, food and clothing of his own. When they reach the marriageable age, some of them give dreams to their mother that there is a female 'Lu Chauk Lay' giving her full address and asking the mother to make a marriage proposal for him. Although some are ordinary, some have power to some extent. Some give lucky lottery numbers to their parents in their dreams.

On 1953, July 19, one 'Lu Chauk Lay' was born in Thanphyu street of Kyone Ma Ngay township in Ayeyarwady division. His parents were U Mg Tun and Daw Thein Shwe. Mg Kyaw Zaw was his name and he usually gave dreams to his mother what he wanted to do and so on. He possessed healing power. He came to the human world to cure diseases. In the dream, he insisted that his mother cure patients on his behalf. At first, his mother refused but when he gave her these dreams again and again, she agreed. Also, he asked his mother to promise not to take money from patients and not to tell any lie to the people.

As medicine, he instructed the mother to collect 32 kinds of

Lu Chauk Lay

fruits and vegetables such as rose, shell of orange, pomelo, dawna flower, etc. She was asked to make those herbs dry and pound it into powder. According to Daw Thein Shwe, his medicine was very strange. He asked her to give only this same medicine for all kinds of diseases and it could cure well. It was like a panacea. As his mother often vomited blood due to eczema (Hninkhu) and stiffness, after taking that medicine, she had no more suffering.

After curing for 18 years without charge, he instructed his mother to take very small amount of money from the patients because he wanted to repay his gratitude to her. With that money, Daw Thein Shwe made a lot of donations for him, too.

He told his history to his mother. In one of his previous lives, he was a vegetarian saint in India in Lord Buddha's life time. At that time, he had a wrong belief that only the vegetarians were holy persons and he looked down and blamed other people, including monks who were not vegetarians. Because of his ego, he still could not escape from being in Lu Chaunk Lay. He said that if his body became dry, he would be liberated. Daw Thein Shwe put her son Lu Chauk Lay in a wide bottle and covered him with small robe coloured cloth.

⇥●◆● ◆◆◆ ●◆◈⇤

Prosperity and Poverty

Nail-cutting at night will bring bad luck. If toe nails drop in the house, the house owner will become poor. There is a story. In ancient times, the great thief 'NgaTetPyar' (ငတက်ပြား) went back to the palace again to remove his toe nail which was left behind. He was worried that the whole country would get poor if the palace was poor. The king awarded him with the post of treasurer because, although he was a thief, he was faithful to his country.

The windows and doors of houses should be opened in the morning otherwise it will hinder prosperity. When you sweep the house in the morning, you should clean from the front to the back. If you sweep in the evening, you should clean from back to the front.

There is a Myanmar saying 'Nay win mee let, See pwar tet' (နေဝင်မီးလက်၊ စီးပွားတက်). It means that, in the evening, you should switch on the light in the house so that you will be prosperous.

It is unlucky to wear clothes that are either torn or stained. You should not do stitching or ironing the clothing while wearing it because it will lead you to poverty. Only the beggars who have no extra clothing do such thing.

It is unlucky to use a cracked or broken mirror at home. Hanging women's longyi (sarong) in a higher place or in front of the house is to be avoided because it will block the prosperity.

On New Year's Day, people close their business and stay at home happily or they go for picnic with the intention to be happy the whole year. Some people do not spend money on that day so that the money won't go out unnecessarily during the whole year. On the contrary, some people think that if they happily spend money on that day, they will get enough money to spend for the whole year.

Myanmar people believe that the Eugenia plant (Tha-pye) is the symbol of luck, peace, and victory. So by offering the Eugenia to Lord Buddha at home or pagodas, they expect that it will bring them good luck, peace and that all their wishes will be fulfilled.

If your hand is itchy, you will get money in the near future.

Avoid cursing, using rude words, or shouting, or quarrelling with each other or bearing a sour face in the morning. Those will hinder the prosperity.

You should not wash clothing at night (after 9 pm) or prosperity will not come to you. You should not patch up the hole while wearing it or it will adversely affect the prosperity.

You should not stand an umbrella on slippers. While some people are talking, they absentmindedly put their umbrellas on one side of their slippers by holding the shaft of umbrella in their hands. It is a sign of poverty.

A person should not bring lamp, or bulb, or fire from another's house to his own. It means, he accepts the heat from others and their hot problems will be infectious to him.

Some say that three Saturday-borns should not stay in the same house or that house will be full of worries and problems.

To bring good luck, one should dispose of old umbrellas or slippers, etc. Similarly, you should not keep a broken mirror, umbrella, or clock at home.

You should place things in proper places. For example, shoes should not be kept in a high places or an umbrella should not be put on the floor. Not only that, if you take off your slippers/shoes in an up-side-down way, your life will be in disorder.

You should not keep the altar in a place which is directly facing to the main door of a house.

At the altar for Lord Buddha, the flowers should not be withered and the water should not get dried. If you are negligent, it will bring you unhappiness without any sound reason. Try to refresh all those things as best as you can.

You should not dispose off withered flowers and water of the altar by throwing it into the backyard of your house together with other rubbish.

At home, restaurants, and offices, one should not hang the posters or photos of scary pictures such as the skeleton, ghosts (as a style or for any other reason). Anyway, it will hinder prosperity.

Witchcraft, Ghosts and Other Spirit Guardians

Witchcraft

There is a saying that every village has a witch and a village cannot be built without the existence of a witch ('စုန်း'မရှိဘဲ ရွာတည်လို့မရ). Witch means 'Sone' in Myanmar language, 'Sone Htee' is a wizard and 'Sone Ma' is a witch. Most are witches. Some witches are very powerful. When we were young, we were told the story of a witch who usually ate the cloud on every waning moon night. Only the head flied and she left the body on her bed by covering it with blanket as if she were asleep. When her husband noticed one waning night, he applied TayawKinpun (Myanmar traditional shampoo) at her neck. When she came back after eating the cloud, she could not fix her head to her body as it was very slippery. She apologised to her husband and her husband helped her after getting her promise not to do so again in the future. She abandoned witchcraft and they lived happily together as an ordinary couple. Such kinds of witch are called 'Tainnyuntsarsone' (တိမ်ညွန့်စားစုန်း) (cloud eating witch). There are some lower class witches who eat excrement. At night time, their heads go to the toilets and consume the excrement.

On waning night, you may see some multi-coloured fire balls flying around the top of the big trees not too far away from the village. I do not know how the modern scientists will explain this but the villagers will say that those fire balls are witches and they are very active in waning nights.

We cannot know who the witch is as they are just ordinary human beings with innate negative power because of their bad karma. Some witches do not notice their own power until other people accused them of being witches. If a woman is evil- minded, poor, old, ugly and who usually uses rude words or cursing all the time, they may guess that "She might be a witch". But they say that 'Tharlikar' (Indian grackle) birds know who the witch is. When I was young, I read a story about an old witch who secretly kept her life in a Thalikar (သာလိကာငှက်). So nothing could kill her until the bird was killed. Some say that if you carefully look at the pupil of a witch's eyes, your image will appear in an up-side-down position. Anyway, people are scared of the witch because if she gets angry and makes a curse, that curse will come true. It is not like 'Voodoo' in Haiti Island in the Caribbean. The inborn power of a witch is neither created nor learnt like other techniques. If a person wants to obtain the same power like a witch, that person has to swallow the saliva of the witch.

People believe that witches can cast a spell on people and babies whom they do not like. To the babies, she may annoy them by making them cry the whole night without any reason, and to the adults, she may do something malicious such as causing one leg to be painful without any reason, or an abdominal pain, or eye sore, or a hand stuck to the body which cannot be moved. Those are just mild disturbances and some witches can curse until a person die due to their resentment. For example, a witch may cause suffering to a village girl if she does not accept her son's proposal or if a person refuses to lend money to her. So people avoid them and do not want to get involved with them.

If they doubt that they are victims of black magic by a sorcerer, they arrange to 'ywa cha' (means feeding foods to a witch) in time to heal it. Rice and chicken curry are put on a tray and left outside of the village. Either cooked meat or raw meat is acceptable. The witch will disguise as an animal such as a black dog or a cat or a crow and take the foods. If the food is eaten by an animal, it is well done. But if some foods remain uneaten, they need to prepare the food again until she eats in such a disguised form. If a person is bewitched for a long time, they will have to ask help from the 'hmawsaya' (ဟမော်ဆရာ) (a kind of magician) who can cure all witchcraft. Once in a village, a woman was feeling an abdominal pain and after meeting with the saya, she vomited out a lot of long hair and she was cured. Some people say that if a witch covers her head with a longyi (sarong), she can turn into a vulture (Linnta) and flies to find food.

The witches can harm by putting something in the food which they feed to others, or if they look at the food with negative intention while other people are going to take their own food. They can change things from one form to another with their power. For example, they may change a slipper into a fat fried fish or worms into delicious fried noodles etc.

Ghost

Ghost stories are many. Some cannot be seen and they just haunt with sounds or horrible smell. Some can be seen in scary or vague forms. Besides ghosts, there are some beings like Phoke, Peta (hungry spirit), Hminsar (elf), Kyatt (a kind of elf which can be seen in a group form), etc.

Lat Pan Pin Ghost near Wan Be Sar village

I visited Ma Than Swe's village for her village novitiation ceremony. On our way back home, she sent me back in a bullock cart. I enjoyed riding in the bullock cart, listening to those simple villagers, and talking about their life style. My mind was quite open to them because they have no pretence or secrets. I have a sincere love for rural people because of their simple nature and frankness. There is a saying 'If you want to escape from stress and strains, pay a visit to the countryside.' When we passed by a tree near Wan Be Sar village, she pointed out that tree and told me. "That tree has a story"...

One late afternoon, Pho Thauk Kyar (means 'Mr. Friday') sent the guests back to town. It was already evening when he came back after dropping off the visitors so he was in a hurry to reach home. On the way, he saw a woman and two babies waiting for his cart. "Could you please let us ride your cart? We have been waiting for so long here and no cart has passed by. I will give you the cart fare." Actually, Pho Thauk Kyar did not want to allow them because it would delay his arrival home but he felt bad (Arr Nar Tae) to refuse. She said, "I will let you know when our place is near".

They rode in the bullock cart together without saying a word. Pho Thauk Kyar noticed that the woman was good looking, in her middle age, with long hair. However, their eyes looked very strange and lifeless. There was no blinking of their eyes. They passed by Wan Be Sar village. "We will drop near that tree". When he looked at the tree she pointed to, he could not find any house or lodging near that tree. He pulled the bullocks' nose-ring to stop the cart. Once they dropped, Pho Thauk Kyar rushed the cart by hitting the oxen hard with a cane without looking back. The woman shouted from behind, "Hey, boy, why didn't you take the cart fee? Here is the cart fee, please take it!" When he looked back at that woman to say that no cart fare was needed, he found that although the woman's body was far away, her hand stretched out and reached his shoulder to give him the cart fare.

In another story, a man saw that a ghost was sleeping on one of his own ears and he used the other ear as a blanket. You can imagine how big the ghost's ears and how shocked the man would be. We should not be scared of all those things and we should take them as beings in different existences in this Universe (Please see the chart of 31 Planes of Existences). According to a monk, actually they are not haunting the people, they are begging merit from you or they are trying to let you know their presence in some ways. So if you think that you are haunted by a ghost or a spirit, it is better to share merits to them instead of being frightened or cursing them. Some spirits can be liberated if they receive shared merits from their relatives or someone. The main reason of being in such a kind of lower existence is due to their lack of merit or bad karma in their previous lives. That's why they still cannot escape.

Like human beings, ghosts or spirits have different characters. Although some are gentle, some are very rough. I heard a story about a brave man who encountered a ghost. They wrestled and when the ghost lost, the man brought him home as his servant. The ghost accepted his slavery for a few years and provided duties such as taking care of the house and farm with his power so that nothing was stolen.

One night, a man was sitting on the railway and smoking a cigar. A stranger from behind touched his back and asked, "Please give me a light" (မီးတစ်တို့လောက်ပေးပါ). When he turned, he saw that the stranger had no head and only the body was seen. As far as I know, ghosts are scared of human urine, light (including sun light), thorns from trees, and Buddhist mantras. If you encounter a ghost, you can use one of them as a weapon to protect yourself. You should not bring raw meat in at night time from outside of your house as a ghost is likely to follow you.

My uncle's experience

While one of my uncles was in government service, he was promoted and transferred to a small town near the Thai border. Let me relate his experience in his own words:

"There was a haunted house near my residence. It was occupied by the Chairman of the Township Council, who dared not sleep alone as the ghost would often interrupt his sleep by making a lot of noise by stamping loudly on the floor, opening and closing doors and windows, or taking a bath at a nearby well in the middle of the night. The story was that there was once a customs officer who stayed there and he committed suicide because of failed love affair. A year or so later, my landlord who owned both the houses asked me to shift my residence to the haunted house. It was a big house with many windows."

"Naturally, I was waiting in great suspense as to whether the ghost would appear to me or not. One early morning, I was lying in bed leisurely, listening to the birds singing and the bullock carts going outside my residence without opening my eyes. Suddenly, someone appeared standing across my legs, his arms akimbo in a defiant posture. I realized it must be the ghost and at the same time I was indignant at his rude behaviour and I rebuked him soundly. The ghost quickly changed his position and sat docilely at the foot of my bed and he informed me his desire to apply for pension. I told him to see the pension clerk concerned at my office and to fill up the necessary forms and that I would do the needful. The ghost thanked me and disappeared. He never appeared again."

"In our country, every government servant is entitled to get pension when either he has completed his 30 years of service or when he reaches the mandatory retirement age of 60 years. As this ghost in the story was still in the government service when he chose to commit suicide, the idea of getting the government pension must have embedded deeply in his mind even though he was no longer in the human world and he seemed to be much relieved now that I, as a government official, have promised him to grant the pension he craved for."

Believe it or not

Nowadays as the population is increasing rapidly, it is duty of the governments to arrange proper lodgings for its people. Yangon is no exception. They removed the old buildings and a few cemeteries which were near the downtown area to the outskirts of the town.

In a big cemetery in Yangon, there was a plan to build a market. So the old cemetery was moved to an allocated area. There are some procedures in moving a cemetery. 'The spirit world should not be neglected' is one of the procedures. According to the advice from the 'Sayadaws' (very senior monks), the officers from City Development Committee arranged a big truck and informed the spirits, "According to the government's order, you all have to move from this place and we have arranged this truck for you all to move to another place. So please get on the car with your belongings". As soon as they announced, a noisy sound of carrying kitchen accessories was heard and there seemed to be a big crowd. What they found was that the truck became very heavy after giving the order although nothing could be seen. The driver drove to another place carrying them. When they arrived at the destination, "This is your new place. You all go down with your belongings." On his way back, the driver noticed again that the truck was not as heavy as before.

On that night, the senior officer who was responsible for the assignment got a dream. In his dream, a woman with a vague figure, whose face he could not see, told him, "Sir, one of my children is left at the old place and he does not know how to come to the new place. Could you please arrange to bring him to us?". First, the officer was not sure if it was a hallucination or real. So the next morning, he went to the old place with a car. He heard a low cry of a child. He walked nearer to that voice and whispered, "Get into the car." He drove back to the new place. Strangely enough, on that night, that woman appeared in his dream again and said "Thank you" for helping her.

Kyaw Pauk Gyi Ghost from the University compound
(တက္ကသိုလ်ပရဝုဏ်အတွင်းမှ ကျောပေါက်ကြီးသရဲ)

Kyaw Pauk Gyi means 'big hole on back'. It is one of the scary University stories. After the crisis between the University students and the government a long time ago, it is said that spirits of some students are still wandering in the Yangon University compound.

One day, a girl went to the University. The University compound was very quiet as it was a holiday after the exam but she wanted to inquire about some information. She walked alone and at one corner of the corridor, she saw a young man who looked like a University student. He smiled at her and when he slowly turned his body, she saw a very big bloody hole on his back. It looked like he was shot with a gun in his chest. She was so frightened that she ran away. At another corner she bumped with a man who looked like a security guard.

The girl : "Please help me. I....I was just haunted by Kyaw Pauk Gyi ghost."

The man : "Are you kidding? I have been working here for so many years. I never heard about Kyaw Pauk Gyi ghost".

The girl : "I am not joking. I just saw Kyaw Pauk Gyi with my own eyes".

The man : "So, tell me how Kyaw Pauk Gyi looks like."

The girl was very exhausted after describing to that man how big was the hole on his back with blood flowing. After listening to the girl, that man by turning his body and asked her, "Hey girl, look at my back. Did the hole you saw on Kyaw Pauk Gyi's back looked like mine?". Oh my God! He was another Kyaw Pauk Gyi ghost, too.

Although I have heard ghost stories in different forms and different styles, I have never been haunted by a ghost up to this day. Sometimes, due to delusion, we think that we are haunted by a ghost. I still remember a short story I have read about "A Haunted House" (Thayechauk thaw EainGyi) by 'Dr. Tin Shwe'. In this short story, a big old house was famous for the ghosts and nobody dared to approach or sleep in that house. One night, the writer went and slept there. Finally, he found out that all the gossip about that big house was an illusion and he found out that:

- 'Someone pulling the mosquito net while sleeping' was caused by the bats

- 'Terrible grumbling voice of a dying person' was caused by the cooing voice of the pigeons

- 'Someone knocking the door at night' was caused by the stray dogs

- 'A watching pair of red eyes' was by the wild cat

- 'Walking sound on the floor' was caused by the rats

Anyway, although old people do not like the children listening and talking about ghost and spirits stories, (they think that it will make the children frightened), young people are very curious to listen as one of the interesting topics among their bed time stories.

Other Spirit Guardians

Myay boke Bilu (Earth guardian): The earth has guardians too. They can be everywhere on this earth. If a person falls down on the ground and his pain is longer than it should be, they say, 'Myay Kaing Thi' (မြေကိုင်သည်). It means, he is disturbed by the Myay boke Bilu. At such a time, you can ask advice from experienced old people how to manage it. It is not too difficult. Like appeasing a witch, you should prepare seven pieces of raw meats like beef or chicken and seven mouthful of cooked rice and bury in the ground where you fell down or nearest to that place and pray, "Please release my suffering from knee pain". Some bury a bone of beef or two chicken legs in a hole nearest to that place.

But dealing with the Earth guardian is not always scary as one supposes. There is a story of a man who buried his jewellery under the ground for safe keeping while the country was in turmoil and he migrated to another place. When the war was over, he came back to his native place and dug. He could not find his jewellery anymore. He approached a reliable monk and confided in him. He was advised

Small Lodging for Yokegasoe

to pray to the earth guardian with proper offerings. Finally, he discovered his jewellery as the earth guardian showed him the exact place in his dream.

Yokegasole (Plant guardian): It is the spirit guardian of big trees especially banyan trees. People say that every big and old banyan tree has a yoke ga sole. In the stories, they are seen as in higher forms. They do not give harm to people unless people insult them such as urinating under the tree, or cursing, or leaving rubbish, and so on. People come and pay respect to them for fulfilling their worldly wishes such as promoting their business, to get a baby, or to find a good husband or wife. Sometimes, you may notice, the small lodgings at some big trees are for yokegasole (Please see the photo). There is a story that after a father died, he became yoke ga sole and that yokegasoe gave lottery number to his poor son in the dream. The son bought that number and won the lottery.

If you want to chop a tree, you should ask permission first and give some time for them to move to other place or you will have to face with some mysterious problems. According to the old people, every living and non living thing has its guardian. Even a chair has a guardian spirit and we should not kick a chair to make the guardian get angry with you.

Death and Burial

They say that a Myanmar funeral is more complicated than the Western one. There are so many customs and traditions to observe which make the rest of the family busy when a person leaves this world.

There is a saying among Myanmar people 'Funeral one time; monastery ten times'. It means that the merit you gain from sending the dead person to the cemetery one time is equivalent to going to a monastery ten times to take the Sabbath.

A 25 pya coin is put inside the mouth of the corpse as a ferry fare (ကူးတို့ခ) to the next world. If 25 pya coin is not available nowadays, other available coins can be used instead.

In a house, if two persons die on the same day, the second corpse must be sent to cemetery first.

If a person dies in another place or outside of the village, the corpse is not allowed to bring into that village because it will bring bad luck to that village.

If a person dies on the day of the year end, the corpse should not be kept until the New Year. It should be buried at the cemetery on the same day or it will bring bad luck to that house.

After sending the corpse to the cemetery, some dust from the funeral ground or a leaf or flower near the corpse is to be brought back home with the intention of showing the spirit of the dead person the way to his home on the 7th day when the religious service will be held. After taking that piece, the carrier should not look back until he reaches home. According to the Buddhism, on the 7th day of his demise, the rest of the family makes a donation and shares their merit to the dead person so that he can reach higher level of rebirth by rejoicing in their donation. So it is important to invite him on the 7th day by calling his name. For the whole week, doors are unlocked and windows are opened at home so that the spirit can wonder inside the house. However, after the 7th day, they are not allowed to enter the house.

They say if a person commits suicide by hanging (ကြိုးဆွဲချသေခြင်း) or jumping down into water, he/she will die in the same way for the next 500 consecutive lives. It is like a curse made upon himself. We cannot know how many previous lives they have committed this sin but we can know whether he is going to be liberated or not by checking the distance between his feet and the ground/floor. If his feet are going to touch the floor, it means he is going to be liberated soon. If his feet are still far from the floor, he still has many lives in which he will commit this act repeatedly.

It is believed that by exchanging clothes of a revered elderly person who has just passed away, and by wearing them, it brings good luck.

You should not keep the corpse for an even number of days. It must be odd number of days, like 3 days or 5 days. All mirrors should be covered because the spirit can hide inside it.

In the village, before the preservative injection (formaldehyde) was invented, they put a white pumpkin (marrow) under the bed of the corpse to absorb the foul smell if the corpse were to be kept longer.

When the corpse is carried to the cemetery from the house, it should be carried feet first, we should not carry it head first in order to prevent the spirit from looking back into the house and beckoning another member of the family to follow him. After the corpse is carried out from the house, someone at home must break a water pot, to change with fresh water to the flower pot dedicated to Lord Buddha, and extinguish all the fire in the kitchen.

In the village, the two big toes of the corpse are tied together with the hair of his children or thread fearing that other spirits may possess the body and walk.

What I learned from a monk's preaching is that we can know where a dead person will go (higher or lower level) by checking his head. If his head leans on the right side, he will go to a higher existence and if he leans on the left side, his next world will be a lower one.

If a Hnget Soe (bird of ill omen) flies by chanting "git...git...git" over a house where there is a sick person, it is an omen of a funeral. So people are afraid of that bird especially when they hear its unpleasant chant.

Myanmar people believe that old bedridden people usually pass away on their birthday. So the patient's family is very worried whenever his/her birthday is drawing near and they sigh with relief when the birthday is over.

If a dead person talks to you in your dream, he/she is liberated to another world. If he is silent in your dream, he is still a spirit which cannot find a place yet to rebirth. Sometimes, they give dreams to their relatives to donate on their behalf so that they can be liberated.

If a person did a lot of unwholesome actions in life and, when he is dying, he sees terrible scenes of hell. He will take rebirth there. At that moment, some people shout with fear on the bed. In that situation, the people near him should allow him to listen to the Buddha's teachings and pray for him. By doing this, his rebirth may change to a better condition.

The concepts of time between the human world and other worlds (heaven and hell) are quite different. There are some true stories about it. A person was brought mistakenly by the messenger of death before his time. When he came back to the human world after his trip to the hell for a while, it was his funeral day already.

If a stillborn baby is born, an iron stick should be wrapped around him before he is buried. It means that he will never come back to the mother womb as a stillborn again until that iron becomes soft. If a spinster dies, put a banana stem beside her corpse in the coffin to prevent her becoming a spinster in the next life.

If a woman dies during a mature pregnancy, the baby inside her womb must be taken out and buried separately in a secret place because if the magicians know, they will take the corpse of the baby and use it for black magic purposes.

When you come back from a cemetery or from somewhere at night, you must spit and step over it by saying 3 times 'phat...phat...

phat' at the gate before you enter the house. It is to prevent the spirit accompanying you to enter your house. You must do it, especially, if you have small babies at home.

Leitbyakwe (လိပ်ပြာခွဲခြင်း) – It means separating the two spirits. 'LeitBya' means 'spirit' here as well as 'butterfly' in Myanmar language. Spirit is compared as butterfly which can gently fly away from the human body. 'Kwe' means 'seperate'. This especially happens when a mother dies leaving a little infant. Fearing that the deceased mother might take back her baby's life, or the infant may follow her mother, the rest of the family have to do 'Leitbyakwe' before the funeral day. We can observe this practise in villages.

An old wise woman should be invited. She recites some mantras and her chanting becomes faster and a little bit louder. She puts some cotton on both sides of the scale pans and orders with sharp words not to take the baby's life and let the baby survive in the human world. After that, the old woman asks, "To whom are you giving away your baby?" by calling a few people's name such as infant's father, aunties, grandparents and relatives. She is holding that scale while she is calling each name. If the deceased agrees a name to take care of her infant, one side of the scale will go down. Although the cotton is weightless, surprisingly, it really works. Similar happening can also be seen when one of the couple passes away who are very much attached to each other like, 'Romeo and Juliet'.

'Phoke Thet Win' people (ဖုတ်သက်ဝင်ခြင်း)

'Phoke' means 'a kind of spirit' 'Thet' means 'life' and 'Win' means 'enter'. 'Phoke Thet Win' means when a dying person loses his consciousness and dies, during that very short period, a certain spirit suddenly enters that body and nobody will notice it. The spirit pretends as if the dying person gets back his consciousness and stay as usual in bed. This happens mostly to those who are ill for a long time.

Although 'Phoke Thet Win' people are lying in bed in the day time, they are very active at night. Sometimes, they quietly go to the kitchen and take all the meat curry while the family members are asleep. They like meats, especially beef. They want someone to take care of them regularly by giving massage or holding them tenderly so that they can absorb the blood and energy from that person by touching the body. The person who is touched slowly declines in health.

Later, when people at home begin to doubt his strange behaviours. A monk or magician who knows how to take the 'Phoke' out is invited in such a case. Some say that if the Aw-zar (custard apple) leaves or an old slipper is placed under the mattress of the 'Phoke Thet Win' patient, the spirit cannot stay anymore. Actually, it is not easy to drive them out. Sometimes the magician has to be aggressive in order to do so.

There was a real story from Upper Myanmar I heard when I was young. The 'Phoke' spirit entered a man's body and he survived for some years until he got married and had 2 babies. Nobody noticed and he earned his living by climbing palm trees to collect toddy. How strange? One day, a magician from another village came to that village and he saw that man on the palm tree. Magician knew at once that he was a 'Phoke'. So he asked "Hello, Mr. Phoke, are you climbing the palm tree?" Once the Phoke heard this greeting so unexpectedly, he was shocked, dropped down from the tree, and died (meaning the spirit ran away from the body). At the same time, his two children at home died, too. His wife, however, survived as she was a human being. You can imagine how shocked and sorrowful she would have been!

Miscellaneous Superstitions

1. If in a family, there are two maidens, the elder must marry first, otherwise, it would be hard for the elder one to get a husband.

2. In some parts of Myanmar, raw pork or beef is not allowed on the public transport in order not to invoke the anger of the local spirit.

3. In upper Myanmar, some local people are afraid of pronouncing the 'Mway' (snake) by its name due to the tradition of 'Amay-Yayyin' nat worship. So they call the Snake Gourd (ပဲလင်းမြွေသီး (သို့) ဖုံလုံသီး ကို ပဲတောင့်ရှည်ဟု ခေါ်ကြသည်) the 'Long Bean' instead.

4. It is believed that by keeping a piece of mother's sarong gives protection from danger especially in a battlefield.

5. If the twins born are either boys or girls, it is lucky; if a boy and a girl, it is unlucky to the parents.

6. If a child cries early in the morning, it is unlucky.

7. Don't say nasty or dirty words in the forest, the spirit tiger will chase you.

8. Thieves won't come if you stand a broom in up-side-down position during the night.

9. When a star falls, make a wish and your wish will be fulfilled. Some say that it is the demise of a heavenly being.

10. Men should not go under a place or rope where women hang their longyis (sarong) to get dry. He will lose his will power (ဘုန်းနိမ့်တတ်သည်) because they believe that a man (husband) is the god of a house or family.

    (When I was young, I hung my longyi to make it dry over my father's bed. When my mother saw it, she was shocked.)

11. A woman should not take off her longyi over her head. Her angel guardian does not like it.

12. Don't take kids to dark places or don't go out with the kids in the late evening. Ghosts may possess them.

13. You should not step on/over a paper with printed words like newspapers or magazines because Myanmar people believe that 'one word is one stupa' (စာတစ်လုံး၊ ဘုရားတစ်ဆူ). If you do, you will become stupid and you will have low IQ.

14. If you are watching a drama or stage show in your dream, you will here the news of funeral from relatives.

15. You should not be disappointed if a crow or a bird discharges on you. It is a good omen.

16. Sometimes you suddenly feel sleepy; you accidentally bite your tongue; or stumbles while you are walking. If one of those things happens, someone is talking or gossiping about you.

17. If a person appears while other people are talking or gossiping about him, people usually tell him, "You will have a long life; we are just now talking about you!" *(Actually, they are gossiping...)*

18. Delicious curry will be waiting for you if you choke with spittle.

19. If you feel itchy in your sole, you will have to go out on a temporary trip without any plan.

20. Do not allow the children to play with the scissor; the couple at home will quarrel.

21. During water festival, don't allow the children to splash water on pregnant woman, or drought will come.

22. If a person likes to eat the crust which is stuck at the bottom of the pot after cooking, he will become lazybones. (ထမင်းချိုး၊ ကောက်ညှင်းချိုး၊ တို့ဟူးချိုး စသည်၊ ချိုးကြိုက်သောသူများသည် အပျင်းကြီးသည်ဟု ပြောကြပါသည်။)

23. In the morning, when you go to the office or somewhere, you must put on the right (not left) shoe/slipper first to avoid unnecessary problems for that day. (You should check yourself which side you usually wear first.)

24. You should not leave a shoe or a slipper up-side-down or your parents will get divorced.

25. According to the old people, a family should not celebrate two auspicious occasions (two weddings or two novitiations or one wedding and one novitiation) *within a year.* (တစ်နှစ်ထဲမှာ မင်္ဂလာနှစ်ခု မပြုလုပ်အပ်) If it happens, they must make a small donation at home such as Swun Kyway (ဆွမ်းကျွေး) (offering meal to the monks) to make it three celebrations in a year.

26. If you see a hearse (funeral car) coming from the opposite direction, it is good luck and you will get money. Some people tap their bags with their hands in order to get money sooner. But if the hearse is following your car, or leading your car, it is not good.

27. If there are two cowlicks on a person's head, he will be rich and he will be very successful in the sales business. It looks like a scale and they call it 'Bway Chain Kwin' (ဗွေချိန်ခွင်) in Myanmar language.

28. Ancient people believe that men should not enter the chamber where a woman is giving birth or their glory will be decreased. (I wonder what will happen to the male OGs nowadays.)

29. You should not whistle at night because it will invite the ghosts.

30. Wednesday is a day off for the nats. So the astrologers close business on that day and the offering to nats is not done on Wednesday.

31. Some Myanmar people avoid making appointment on Monday (Ta-nin-lar) because 'lar' means 'come' and they are superstitious that they may have to come again for the same purpose if it is not yet done. For example, going to ask their

money back or similar things which they do not want to do again and again.

32. When people give medicines in tablet form to the babies, they usually make it into powder first and then they stir it in a spoon with water to dissolve it. Do not stir it with your forefinger; otherwise the medicine will become ineffective.

33. According to the traditional physicians, man is strong in his right side; and woman, in her left side. In other words, man's weakness lies in left side and woman's in right side. So old people said, if a man gets injury or stroke on his left side of the body, it will be difficult to heal. Similarly, if a woman suffers on her right side, it will take longer to recover than it happens on her left side. (ယောက်ျားဘယ်၊ မိန်းမညာ)

34. People pay respect and pray to 'Shin Upagutta' before they celebrate important occasions such as novitiation ceremony, wedding, drama, to deter the rain or other disturbances by Mara, the devil, who usually gives disturbances to one who is doing meritorious deeds. Shin Upagutta is the one whom Mara is scared of.

35. If the first baby is born on a Saturday, the father must walk over that baby three times by carrying a knife (Dha-ma) on his shoulder with a hope that the family will not be influenced by that baby. Most Myanmar people do not want to deliver their first baby on Saturday due to a saying (သားဦးစနေ၊ မီးလို့ဓွေ့) *"Saturday-born first baby will bring hot problems like fire to the family."*

36. If the second toe of a woman is longer than her big toe, she will have great influence over her husband. (Have you ever checked your wife's toes?)

Dream Interpretations

In ancient time, whenever the king had a dream, the wise men were consulted to interpret it and they noted it down. According to them, the effect of the dreams depends on the days and the effects are not the same. A dream which you have in the early morning after mid night is most likely to be true and will be effective soon.

If you dream:

- On Sunday   – it is for your husband or wife.
- On Monday   – for relatives
- On Tuesday   – for children
- On Wednesday   – for parents
- On Thursday   – for friends
- On Friday   – for servants, animals and properties
- Saturday   – for yourself

Dreams upon seeing

In your dream, if you see:

1. A tree falls down – means will be in danger
2. Attacked by a buffalo – harmful
3. Babies – happiness
4. Bamboo – will meet with advantages
5. Banana plant – your job will be transferred
6. Banyan leaves – very lucky
7. Banyan tree – long life
8. Bear/wolf – will be in danger
9. Bird eggs – business will be good
10. Bird in a cage – will be in a wed lock
11. Bottle – be successful
12. Bridge – worries and anxieties
13. Broom – will do auspicious deeds

14. Cabbage — have to work for others
15. Camphor balls — hear the good news
16. Candle light — the heavenly beings will help you
17. Cane stick (old people use as supporter) — will get help from others
18. Canyon — meet difficulties
19. Cave — get worries
20. Cemetery or tomb — will get inheritance
21. Cocks are fighting — face legal matter
22. Coconut or palm fruits — will get money
23. Coconut tree — happiness
24. Cotton wool — meet with very innocent lover
25. Dancing, concerts or stage shows — one of the relatives will die
26. Deer — you lover will rely on you
27. Delia flower — will get a lot of followers or servants
28. Dove — be peaceful
29. Duck egg — will be prosperous
30. Egret — get a good wife
31. Elephant, horse and army — get rich
32. Fire balloons — get rich
33. Fishing net — get a lot of money
34. Flag — free from dangers
35. Flour mill — will be wealthy
36. Flower garden — get suddenly rich
37. Frog — good weather
38. Fruits — can charm the people
39. Gamone plant — business will be very good
(some aromatic herbaceous
plants from the ginger, lily and orchid families)
40. Garden — will get money
41. Gold or Silver — get a good wife
42. Golf ball — smooth in business
43. Gray hair — get new friends

44. Guinea pig — you have to stay with the relatives
45. Guitar string is broken — bad luck
46. Guitar — fall in love with a sweet talker
47. Heart-shaped leaves (swal taw) — will get many lovers
48. Heart — get married with your lover
49. High tide — have to travel long journey
50. House is burning — will be in danger
51. Jade — be wealthy or win the lottery
52. Jasmine — get promotion
53. Key — will get baby
54. Knife — (Be careful) Someone is plotting you
55. Lake or stream — will get promotion
56. Late grandparents — have to talk about the inheritance matters
57. Map — have to travel
58. Mermaid — will meet with danger on a voyage
59. Monks or hermit — you will be respected by others
60. Monks who gained zen — very good
61. Nyaungyay pot — will get babies
    (vase holding offering of flowers)
62. New boots — meet a new good friend
63. New house — go out for a trip
64. Oak tree — hear the unexpected news
65. Oil — will be wealthy
66. Orchid — meet with strange happening
67. Oyster — will be prosperous
68. Paddy husk fire — you feel hot with anxieties
69. Paddy in the barn — the rain will be heavy
70. Peacock — will do good deeds
71. Pearl — get wealthy
72. Pear — be happy
73. Pendulum (of a clock) — have to travel
74. Pepper — will get anxieties

75.	Photograph	– very lucky
76.	Pigeon	– hear the news from afar
77.	Pole star	– realize your aims
78.	Postman	– will receive the reply letter/email
79.	Potatoes	– business is not good
80.	Pot seller	– not good
81.	Pot	– get advantages
82.	Prison	– unlucky
83.	Quail	– your love affair will be split off by a bad person
84.	Railway stations	– the trip will delay
85.	Rhinos	– your wish will be fulfilled
86.	Sacred lotus flower	– hear auspicious news
87.	Salt	– good health
88.	Sandalwood	– get rich
89.	Sapphire	– lucky omens
90.	Sesame farm	– successful in plantation
91.	Shark	– will get diseases
92.	Sheep	– will be prosperous
93.	Ship's mast	– go for an urgent trip
94.	Shrimps	– get anxieties
95.	Silver coins	– will get angry
96.	Snakes	– free from danger
97.	Snow flower	– a lot of lovers
98.	So many bells are hanging	– live long life
99.	Stamps	– have to cooperate with seniors
100.	Stars	– will be honoured above others
101.	Sun or moon eclipse	– you will get a powerful son
102.	Telephone	– you will be persuaded
103.	Dry prawns	– successful business
104.	Knots or the ropes are in a mess	– have to argue for money
105.	Pagodas or statue	– you will get prosperity and blessed by the holy beings.

106. Toad	– you have a lot of competitors
107. Tide rising	– So much worries
108. Tiger	– someone is plotting you to be in trouble. Or It is about nat worshipping concerned.
109. Torch	– you have to make a new roof
110. Tweezers	– get anxiety
111. Umbrella	– peaceful
112. Wall clock	– a lot of advantages
113. Water melon	– get a good son
114. Water well	– wealth
115. Whales	– voyage
116. White mouse	– your wish will be fulfilled
117. White paper	– wife will be loyal to you
118. Zayat	– have to go for a tiring trip

(Small wooden rest house along the highway road)

| 119. Zebra | – will get good advice from a friend |

Dreams upon eating and drinking

In your dream, if you are:

1. Drinking cow milk   means more popular than others
2. Drinking the blood   – get the properties
3. Drinking the custard oil – you will get disappointment.
4. Drinking water   – will be famous
5. Drinking whisky   – the money you borrowed will never be returned
6. Drinking yogurt   – will be famous
7. Eating almond   – heavy hearted or get high blood pressure
8. Eating a pear   – get rich
9. Eating banana   – the lover will be unfaithful to you

10. Eating bird meat — wish will be fulfilled
11. Eating butter rice — stay in luxuries
12. Eating cheese — will make a mistake
13. Eating chilli — will become a senior person
14. Eating fish curry — get sick, but eating the sardines (tinned fishes) — will be healthy
15. Eating gourd fritter — will be poor
16. Eating grape — get inheritance
17. Eating human meat — Extremely rich
18. Eating liver — be lucky
19. Eating pork curry — have to make donation
20. Eating tortoise and fishes — rice and crops will be abundant
21. Eating watermelon — relief from diseases
22. Eating with a gold plate — win the lottery
23. Having dinner — peace at home
24. Taking food with chopsticks — will meet a lover
25. Taking ice-cream — lucky in love affairs

Dreams upon actions and behaviors

In your dream, if you are:

1. A little elephant is born   means   will get wise children
2. A person is wearing new clothing and dress up very nicely — that person is sick or have health problem
3. Asking pardon by kneeling — you have a great hatred to that person
4. Attack by a goat — bad luck
5. Bitten by a bat — loss in materials or people
6. Bitten by a dog — you will be the victim of black magic.
7. Bomb blast — you have to talk unspoken words with relish
8. Breathing breeze — love affair will be smooth
9. Buy an umbrella — will be married

10. Catch a bird alive   – will get a lot of money
11. Catch and get an eagle– your income will grow slowly
12. Catching an oyster– business is blooming
13. Celebrate novitiation – will get luxury
14. Chopping with knife   – your marriage will be broken
15. Climbing a fence   – have to solve many problems
16. Climbing a staircase/ladder – get promotion
17. Climbing a steep mountain – escape from difficulties
18. Deliver twin babies   – hear good news
19. Digging the soil with a spade – you will get your long lost money
                          from others unexpectedly
20. Fail the exam or cannot answer well in exam – will get help from
                          an unexpected person
21. Fishing in a stream or creek and get fishes – will win the lottery
                          (please do not forget to buy the lottery)
22. Flying in the sky   – will become a senior or powerful person
23. Get a fish   – will be prosperous
24. Get a ruby   – will get a good son
25. Get pregnant   – auspicious thing will happen
26. Go crazy or mad   – get freedom and very happy
27. Going to pagoda or stupa – will meet with unexpected person
28. Golf playing   – your wish will be fulfilled
29. Holding an axe   – (control your anger) you are going to
                          kill a person
30. Holding the crops in your hand –   things are ok with you
31. Hosting with so many foods – have to go out on a pilgrimage
                          tour
32. Keeping a fox at home – will get married with a woman who
                          is very greedy
33. Kissing with your lover– means saying goodbye to your lover
34. Land sliding   – lose some things
35. Lighting incense sticks – your wishes will be fulfilled
36. Lighting the candles – famous

37. Moon or sun enter your belly – very good dream and will be blessed
38. Nose bleeding — other will rely on you
39. Planting jute — will get a happy family
40. Planting pumpkin — people will blame on your current action
41. Playing a harp — get rich
42. Playing billiard — will be successful after overcoming many difficulties
43. Playing cards — have to argue
44. Playing guitar — will be popular
45. Plucking vegetables — lover is unfaithful
46. Putting red lotus on your head – you will get a good spouse.
47. Riding a bicycle — have to take a long journey
48. Riding a boat — will live very peacefully
49. Riding a buffalo — you will get a servant
50. Riding an elephant/horse/cow – get rich
51. Riding a white elephant — will become a senior person
52. Riding the crocodile — victory
53. Shaft of the umbrella is broken – the spouse will die
54. Shaving the moustache — live happily
55. Sitting at an entrance of the cave alone – you are in dilemma, undecided, over thinking for an action
56. Sitting on a broken chair — will get married with a divorcee
57. Sleeping at a farm — people will love you
58. Sneezing — will be famous
59. Spinning — get worries
60. Stormy weather and dark sky – will be robbed
61. Swimming — have to work very hard
62. Taking a car — you have to help a good woman
63. Taking boat or ship — get rich
64. Taking photograph — a stranger will make a friend with you
65. Taking shower — in good health

66. Talking with the father who have already passed away
   – get inheritance
67. Buddha statue is preaching – will be famous
68. Glass fall down and broken – your secrets will be revealed
69. Tide rising   – will be in despair
70. Tooth is broken   – will get transfer to another place or get sick (Upper tooth is for the older relatives and lower tooth is for the younger)
71. Violin string is broken – misunderstanding with the spouse
72. Walking on the wheat farm – will get married with a superior person
73. Washing your hair   – escape from difficulties
74. Watching a circus   – will get a lot of friends
75. Watching the drama (Zatpwe) – one of the relatives will die
76. Watching the movie   – have to cry
77. Watering the banyan tree (Nyaungyethoon)
   – get married surely
78. Water pot is broken – will get cheated
79. Wear diamond   – face with difficulties
80. Wearing a garnet ring – other people will accept your words
81. Wearing an ear ring – will get promotion
82. Wearing a new belt   – get the glory
83. Wearing a robe   – full of glory
84. Wearing graduation dress – get promotion
85. Wearing shoes/slippers – glory
86. Wearing socks   – get inheritance
87. Wearing the gold ornaments – will get married
88. Win the lottery   – get babies
89. Wrestling with a pig – will meet with destruction
90. You are making a fence – to work hard first and then get rich
91. you are photographed by others – will get disease
92. You are ploughing the soil – get marriage proposal

93. You are robbed — you will lose money in gambling
94. You get a pen as present — will be very famous in the literary world
95. You get dysentery — long life
96. Your body is swelling– the followers will be unfaithful to you
97. Your friend/lover is wearing a jacket or wearing two clothing at the same time — he/she is unfaithful to you
98. Your hair are very long or growing – will be powerful, dreams will be realized
99. You urinate or discharge – your wealth will decline.

The remedies:

If you have a bad dream,

1. The next morning, wash your hair with traditional shampoo (tayaw-kimpoon thee) and take Sabbath. (OR)

2. The next morning, please donate something to holy persons such as monks, hermit or saint and pray not to be effected by a bad dream. Or you can donate flowers, water, candle light and incense sticks at your birthday corner of a pagoda. If you cannot go out, you can do the same to the Lord Buddha at your house. (OR)

3. Put a cup of water and a small plateful of cooked rice between two branches of a big tree and say, "I leave all my bad dreams here." And then you eat a good food you like and come back home.

4. In order not to be effected by a bad dream, you should tell someone about it while you are eating. However you should not tell good dreams while eating.

   ►► *(If you want to know in more detail about the dreams, please refe to the dreams interpretation books in Myanmar.)*

Moles

The moles on human body can be differentiated as seven types.

1. White mole   – The effectiveness is neither too good nor too bad, just medium.
2. Red mole   – The advantage is stronger than disadvantage.
3. Brown mole   – Kind hearted, strong morality.
4. Yellow mole   – Imaginative, love of arts
5. Black mole   – The disadvantage is stronger than the advantage. (The effectiveness of black mole is opposite to the red mole).
6. Green mole   – It is the best. You can see the green mole only in the holy persons.
7. Alive mole   – The color of this mole can be one of the above six moles. It can be very effective. This mole can be found only in the saints, notorious people and the magicians.

For men

If you have a mole:

- At the right centre of the forehead, other people will regard you as a wealthy person. People will think that you have a lot of money more than you actually own so that sometimes you may be disappointed for that.

- A mole between two eyebrows – will be famous at the same time, he has a cruel nature.

- Over the right eyebrow – wealthy, no need to worry about worldly matters

- Over the left eyebrow – will become a gambler or drunkard. He loves gambling more than his wife.

- At the end of the right eyebrow, nearer to the ear – you will become a senior person

- Right side of the nose – one of your children may die
- Middle at the top part of the nose – you will be famous with arts especially in drama or music
- Under the right lower eyelid – you can charm the opposite sex
- Right cheek – you will see life philosophically. In his old age, he will become a hermit or monk.
- Left cheek – you will get married with a beautiful woman or famous woman. You can attract the women. (Mole on the cheek is called 'sabei tin hme') (စံပယ်တင်မွဲ)
- Lower part of the left cheek – be wealthy and successful
- Left side of nose – your wife will be in danger
- Right side of the mouth or between mouth and cheek – you like to gossip about others and be popular
- Left side of the mouth – the same
- At the middle of the chin under the lower lip – you will get married again and again
- At the centre of the chin – will be successful in your own business
- At the right chin – the wife will die after getting married with you.
- Along the way which the tear drops – be poor, wife will die young
    - At the neck – will be rich. If you are poor now, one day you will surely get rich with unexpected things.
    - three moles on your chest (one on the top right side, one on the middle and one near the waist) is called 'hmesalwe' (မွဲဝင်လွဲ). – In his previous life, he was a king and he will never be poor and low in life. He will be respected by others and can influence his wife.

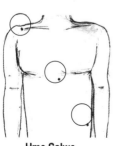

Hme Salwe

- Middle of the upper chest – will become a saint. See life from religious point of view.

- At the centre of the chest – will be very wealthy. That mole is called 'treasure pot'.

- At the right hand   – have to face legal case for money. Selfish.

- Mole at the male sex organ – Can attract the women easily. If you have more than one mole will be more effective. You will take more than one wife.

- On foot   – he will be a good traveller. (for male and female)

- At the centre of the palm of the leg – your life is not stable and you have to walk around for your living.

For women

If you have a mole:

- At the right side of the forehead – you will get married with a powerful husband and get rich and live a long life

- At the left side of the forehead – will get not only a good husband, you will also deliver many good children.

- Mole at the centre of the forehead is called 'yadanar sankyit'   (ရတနာဆံကျစ်မွဲ) (means treasure plait) – will get reliable husband and children. After getting married with her, even a bad person becomes a good husband.

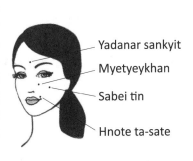

Yadanar sankyit

Myetyeykhan

Sabei tin

Hnote ta-sate

- If you have a distinct mole on the forehead, just above the eyebrow – you will get a husband who has wealth and fame. Your son will take a few wives.

- Inside your eye – you will be a widow in your young age.

- Between the right lower eyelid and right upper lip (it is the way which the tear drops) – the husband will die young. That mole is called 'myetyeykhan' (မျက်ရည်ခံမဲ့).

- If you have 'myetyey khan' mole on your left – it is worse. Not only your husband, you may die with a violent death

- At the right cheek near the mouth – you will love the husband. That mole is called 'yeypatonesut' (ရေပုတုန်းစပ်မဲ့).

- At the left cheek near the mouth – you are eloquent and very clever in talking. That mole is called 'hnote ta-sate' (နှုတ်တဆိတ်မဲ့).

- Near the upper and lower lips – Men will be fascinated by you. You are very emotional in love affairs, too.

- Mole on the cheek is called 'sabei tin'. If you have a sabei tin mole on left cheek – you are very soft and easily fall in love. You easily trust in men. (*Be careful!*)

- At the inner neck – will be wealthy

- Outer neck – you have to take burdens

- Between the two breasts – get rich and get a husband who is ready to fulfil your needs.

- At the left breast – you will get a good daughter and she will take care of you.

- Right side of the belly – not good, the children cannot survive. Husband has diseases. You may fall down from a high place.

- At your back – you will get cheated

- Above the naval   – your husband will die within a few months or years.

- Above or below the naval, under the belly – your husband will face a legal case and in troubles

- Right side above the female sex organ – you may plot the husband to die

- Mole above the female sex organ – you will get married three times and all husbands will die. You are bound to be a widow. But all the husbands will adore you. Not only the husbands die, finally, you may have to face with a woman disease.

- At the right thigh   – First husband will die. Only the second marriage will be stable.

- At the left thigh   – very wily. She knows how to win the men's heart and sometimes she will commit adultery.

- At the female sex organ – will be attractive to men and wily.

Nowadays, you can remove the mole easily at a clinic. But you should consult thoroughly with a learned person before you remove because some mole's effectiveness may vary upon a person's merit and morality. Please make sure the mole is not connected with the nerves and that the clinic is a reliable one so that you will not be infected.

Flesh Shaking and Its Meanings (အသားလှုပ်နှိမ်တ်)

Sometimes, you may feel a little shaking in some parts of your body. Do you think it is a coincidence? It has different meanings too.

Head

If you feel the shaking in your :

- head   – you will become a slave
- forehead   – awarded by the king
- right eyebrow   – get money
- left eyebrow   – your plans will be accomplished and meet a good friend
- right lower eyelid – will meet a lover
- left lower eyelid – have to cry
- left upper eyelid – will meet with a lover
- right upper eyelid – will have to cry
- lower eyelid – get the money or gold
- nose – get so many lovers
- upper lip – quarrel or argue
- lower lip – hear the good news from afar
- right cheek – meet a lover
- left cheek – get money or gold
- chin – argue
- right ear – get angry or plotted by a woman
- left ear – will get money

Upper Body

If you feel the shaking in your:

- Inner neck — will have to wear jewelleries
- upper back — get clothing
- right back near the armpit – you will be outstanding
- heart — a good husband will bring property
- naval — get the property you need
- body — argue with the wife
- right shoulder — will get a good wife or get the clothing
- left shoulder — abundant of foods
- right armpit — get rich
- left armpit — money will come to you
- right arm — meet a good husband
- right ribs — get prosperous
- right breast or chest –good and get money
- left chest — will get worries and win the legal case
- left breast — will meet a good friend
- palm of the right hand –will get the clothing
- palm of left hand — will win the legal case
- right waist — get the money from a friend
- left waist — lose money or material
- right stomach — get good food
- left stomach — get money
- right little finger — mother will get angry with you

Lower Body

If you feel the shaking in your:

- ✗ Right thigh — will fulfil wish or get good wife
- ✗ right buttock — get misunderstandings
- ✗ left buttock — will win over the enemy
- ✗ right knee — will meet a lover
- ✗ left knee — will be plotted by others
- ✗ right sole of foot — have to travel
- ✗ left sole of foot — will be rich (for women)
- ✗ male sex organ — argue with wife.

► *(The remedies for the flesh shaking with bad omens are the same with the dreams.)*

White spot on finger nails and their effects
(လက်သည်းပွင့်အဟော)

If there is a white spot on your:

- ◇ thumb nail — you will be separated from relatives or friends
- ◇ forefinger nail — Love affair will be broken.
- ◇ middlefinger nail — You will get a husband/wife.
- ◇ ringfinger nail — You will be worshipped by others.
- ◇ littlefinger nail — You will get servants.

► *(Men can check on right hand and women on the left.)*

References:

English Publications

- The Burman: 'His life and Notions' by Shwe Yoe
- 'Culture Shock' by Saw Myat Yin
- 'Myanmar (Burma)' by Lonely Planet
- 'The Art of Living' by William Hart
- Some Dhamma teachings from 'International Meditation Centre' by Sayagyi U Ba Khin and 'Dhamma Joti Meditation Centre' by Sayagyi U Goenka.
- Mahasi Dhamma Site
- 'Snow in the summer' by Sayadaw U Jotika
- 'The 31 Planes of Existence' by the Venerable AcaraSuvanno Mahathera
- 'From cradle to grave' by Dr. Hla Phe
- 'Myanmar Attractions and Delights' by Ba Than
- 'A wonderland of Burmese Legend' by Khin Myo Chit
- 'Letters from Burma' by Aung San Suu Kyi
- 'Myanmar In My Mind' by H.C. Matthew Sim
- 'Myanmar Yellow Pages' by IMEX (Myanmar) Co., Ltd.
- The New Light of Myanmar (Daily Newspapers)
- The Myanmar Times (Weekly Journals)
- What the Buddha taught by Wapola Rahula
- 'Myanmar Culture, Traditions and Scenery' by U Than Phe (Tour Guide)
- Matching of Myanmar English Proverbs by U Aye Chit (EEAC)
- A Father's Book of Wisdom by H. Jackson Brown, Jr.
- The Little Oxford Dictionary & Thesaurus
- Myanmar-English Dictionary by Ministry of Education (Myanmar)
- English-Myanmar Dictionary

Myanmar Publications

- ဗုဒ္ဓဘာသာလက်စွဲကျမ်း၊ (ပ)၊(ဒု)တွဲ၊ သာသနာရေးဦးစီးဌာန (A Buddhist way of life (1 & 2) by Ministry of Religious Affairs)

- မြန်မာ့မိရိုးဖလာဝေလေ့ နတ်သမိုင်း၊၊ ဘာသာပြန် ဦးထွေးဟန်နှင့် သုတေသီ ဦးဘညွန့် (Myanma Traditional Nat Worshipping and How to pay respect to them by Translator U Htwe Han and Reseacher U Ba Nyunt)

- လောကဟိတရာသီကျမ်း၊၊ ဆရာကြီး ဦးဖိုးမြစ် (Compilation of Worldly Matters by Sayagyi U Pho Myit)

- နိမိတ်တစ်ထောင် အကောက်ကျမ်းကြီးနှင့် နိမိတ်များ၊၊ သုတေသီဆရာငြိမ်း (1000 Dreams & Preludes by Reseacher Saya Nyein)

- လက်ယာတောင်ကျွန်းမှာ ထွန်းတဲ့ နိမိတ်များ၊၊ ဇင်ယော်နီ (Appearance of omens in the Right island by Zin Yaw Ni)

- မြစေတီမွန်ကျောက်စာ၊၊ ဦးနိုင်ပန်းလှ (Myazedi Mon Stone Inscription by U Naing Pan Hla)

- လောကီပဒေသာည္ဉ်ပေါင်းကျမ်း၊၊ ဆရာမင်းသော်တာ (Compilation of Worldly Knowledge by Saya Minn Thawta)

- စူလာနဖာနှင့် ဆေးနည်းဆေးပင်များ၊၊ ဦးသာဂဒိုး (Sularnaphar & Herbal Medicines by U Thagadoe)

- ၃၇ မင်း၊၊ အမျိုးသားပညာဝန် ဦးဖိုးကျား (37 Nats by National Inspector of Education U Po Kyar)

- မြန်မာ့မိရိုးဖလာ ယုံကြည်မှုနှင့် အကျိုးအပြစ်များ၊၊ ကျော်ဇောဟိန်း (နံ့သာ) [Myanmar Traditional Beliefs & its Benefits' by Kyaw Zaw Hein (Nanttha)]

- ရွှေတိဂုံအောင်မြေမှ အံ့ဖွယ်ကိုးပါး၊၊ မင်းသော်တာ (Nine Wonders from Shwedagon Aung Myay by Min Thaw Tar)

- တိုင်းရင်းမြန်မာ ဆေးနည်းကျော်များနှင့် အခြေပြုဒွိဒသိမ်ကျမ်း၊၊ ဦးသိန်းလွင် (Famous Myanmar Medicines by U Thein Lwin)

- ၃၈ဖြာ မင်္ဂလာ၊၊ ပန်းတောင်းအေမောင် (38 Auspicious Deeds by Pan Taung Aye Maung)

- ပိတ္တာလောကမှ ဖြစ်ရပ်ဆန်းများ၊၊ တက္ကသိုလ်ရှင်သီရိ (Some mysterious happenings from Peta world by Tetkatho Shin Thiri)

- အမေကိုပြစ်မှား၍ မြေမြိုခံရသူများ။ မောင်ခိုင်ခန့်
  (Those who were swallowed by earth for committing sins to their mothers by Maung Khine Khant)
- မဟော်သဓာဇာတ်တော်ကြီး။ အဋ္ဌမတန်း မြန်မာဖတ်စာ (Mahaw Thahtar Jataka/ Grade Eight Myanmar Textbook)
- အခြေခံပညာဦးစီးဌာနမှ မြန်မာစာဖတ်စာ စာအုပ်များ
  (State School Myanmar Text Books by Ministry of Education)
- သူရဇ္ဇ နှင့် ဂမ္ဘီရမဂ္ဂဇင်းများ
  (Thuritza and Gambira Monthly Magazines)
- ပန်းဆယ်မျိုး။ ဒဂုန်နတ်ရှင်
  (Ten Flower Arts and Craft by Dagon Nat Shin)
- ၅၅၀ ဇာတ်ဝတ္ထုများ။ မင်းယုဝေ (550 Nipattaw by Min Yu Wai)
- အိပ်မက်တစ်ထောင် (One Thousand Dreams)
- အိပ်မက်နိမိတ်၊ အသားလှုပ်နိမိတ်၊ လောကီရေးရာအဖြာဖြာ (Interpretation of Dreams, Flesh Shaking and Worldly Knowledge)
- Astrologer Saya U Thein Tun from Pathein St., SanchaungTsp
- Real stories from my grandma, parents, relatives and some local people
- ပဋိစ္စသမုပ္ပါဒ် အရသာ။ အဂ္ဂမဟာပဏ္ဍိတဦးအရိယမထေရ် (ညောင်လေးပင်မြို့၊ တောရတိုက်ကြီး၏ မဟာနာယက)
  [Paticca Samuppad Ayathar/ Aggamaha Pandita U Ariya Mahtei (Abbot of Nyaunglaybinmyo Tawya Monastery)]
- မြန်မာဆယ့်နှစ်လအကြောင်း။ မောင်ထင်
  (Twelve Months of Myanmar by Maung Htin)
- လူမှုဘာသာဗေဒသဘောတရားနှင့် လူမှုဘာသာဗေဒမိတ်ဆက်။ ဒေါက်တာအောင်မြင့်ဦး
  (An Introduction to Sociolinguistics by Dr. AungMyintOo)
- မြန်မာ့ရုပ်မြင်သံကြား (၄) မှ တင်ဆက်သော နွယ်မြက်သစ်ပင် ဆေးဖက်ဝင်ကဏ္ဍ
  (Medicinal Plants programmes by MRTV 4)
- နက္ခတ္တရောင်ခြည်လစဉ်မဂ္ဂဇင်းများ
  (Netkhatta Yaungchi' Monthly Magazines)
- သားလိမ္မာပြန်လာပြီနှင့် အခြားဝတ္ထုတိုများ။ ဉ္ဂါစံ
  (Home coming of a good son and other stories by Oak Gar San)
- Books from the Book stalls along Shwedagon Pagoda and Kabaraye Pagoda